ACCESSORIZING THE BODY

Accessorizing

CRISTINA GIORCELLI AND

PAULA RABINOWITZ *editors*

HABITS OF BEING I

THE BODY

UNIVERSITY OF MINNESOTA PRESS

MINNEAPOLIS • LONDON

The publication of this book was supported by an Imagine Fund grant for the Arts, Design, and Humanities, an annual award from the University of Minnesota Provost's Office.

"The Virgin," "Auspice of Jewels," and "Because of Clothes" are from *The Poems of Laura Riding,* by Laura (Riding) Jackson; copyright 1938, 1980. Reprinted by permission of Persea Books, New York; Carcanet Press, Manchester; and the Laura (Riding) Jackson Board of Literary Management. In conformity with the wishes of the late Laura (Riding) Jackson, her Board of Literary Management asks us to record that, in 1941, Laura (Riding) Jackson renounced, on the grounds of linguistic principle, the writing of poetry: she had come to hold that "poetry obstructs general attainment to something better in our linguistic way-of-life than we have."

Chapter 10 was previously published as "Terra Divisa/Terra Divina," in *These Debatable Lands,* vol. 2, ed. Iain Biggs (Bristol, England: Wild Conversations Press, 2009); reprinted with permission of Iain Biggs.

Published by the University of Minnesota Press
111 Third Avenue South, Suite 290
Minneapolis, MN 55401-2520
http://www.upress.umn.edu

Library of Congress Cataloging-in-Publication Data
    Accessorizing the body : habits of being i / Cristina Giorcelli and Paula Rabinowitz, editors.
        p. cm.
    Includes bibliographical references.
    ISBN 978-0-8166-7578-4 (hc : alk. paper) — ISBN 978-0-8166-7579-1 (pb : alk. paper)
    1. Dress accessories—History. 2. Fashion design—History. 3. Fashion designers—History. I. Giorcelli, Cristina. II. Rabinowitz, Paula.
    TT560.A19 2011
    746.9'2—dc22

                                                        2010036990

Printed in the United States of America on acid-free paper

The University of Minnesota is an equal-opportunity educator and employer.

18 17 16 15 14 13 12 11   10 9 8 7 6 5 4 3 2 1

Contents

Preface and Acknowledgments

The four-volume English-language series *Habits of Being* extracts more than forty of the best essays from the ongoing editions of *Abito e Identità: Ricerche di storia letteraria e culturale,* edited by Cristina Giorcelli and published since 1995 by Edizioni Associate (volumes 1–3) and Ila Palma Press (volumes 4–10) of Rome, Italy, augmenting these Italian essays with a few newly commissioned pieces and with examples of work by contemporary artists who explore the interface between text and textile. The result of fifteen years of research by international teams of scholars from Algeria, France, Hungary, Italy, and the United States, the series focuses on the multiple forms and meanings attached to various articles of clothing in literature, film, performance, art, and other cultural arenas as well as on the social, economic, and semiotic connotations of clothing. Bringing together literary and film critics, art and fashion historians, semioticians, sociologists, historians, and ethnographers, as well as psychoanalysts and fashion designers, these volumes offer an English-speaking audience a rare glimpse of the important work now published in Italy, that most modish of nations.

Moving among thematic, chronological, and aesthetic concerns, this series tracks clothing (and especially accessories) around four cardinal points—top, bottom, inside, outside—to allude to the complex implications of power, meaning, and sensibility associated with, for example, the head (of state as much as of body) or the foot, interiority and exposure. Each book addresses a complex of ideas encased within a set of terms that at times appears contradictory. The first volume, *Accessorizing the Body*, reconsiders the cliché that clothes represent a "second skin" by showing how the body became an accessory within various political and artistic movements of the twentieth century. The second volume will focus on transnational circulation and exchange across time and space to consider how depictions of clothing in classic texts (for instance, Homer's epics) might migrate into understandings of how items of clothing actually mutate within the secondary economy of used-clothing stores. Volume three is more traditional, organized by period (the nineteenth century) and place (Europe and the United States) to explore a crucial era within the consolidation and spread of Western culture, when dress signified class and other distinctions through excess and detail, even as mass production turned clothing into a commodity. The fourth and final volume in the series will interrogate connections between ornamentation and the quotidian, considering how aspects of apparel decorate everyday lives as men daily don sunglasses and women exchange handbags.

Each book addresses social and economic processes involving dress as well as psychic and ontological aspects of identity. For instance, "circulation" references global exchange of commodities or a pair of shoes walking the streets; "movement" stresses the fluidity of meaning—political, sexual, historical—attached to articles of clothing when worn in various contexts; "detail" focuses on accessorizing the body and the role of clothing in the construction of social formations; "intimacies" exposes how what appears outside is a complex of social meanings extending deep inside to the interior of the body and its psychic formations; and "value" addresses economic disparities coded within dress as well as examining how replication and individuation differentiate affect. Obviously these fluid categories leak one into another, because any attention to clothing and its representation necessitates awareness of what is seen and what is remembered for and by whom for what purpose activating which desires.

As an ongoing research project, the subjects covered in these books range from boarding-school attire to Futurist vestments, from lesbian pulp to Henry James, from used-clothing stores to analysts' couches, from Spanish Fascist promotion of appropriate dress to Hungarian Jewish tailors embroidering the yellow star. The mix of essays provides a compelling argument for the inherent interdisciplinarity of fashion studies. Looking at how dress is represented in a work of fiction necessarily opens into a discussion of class, of social procedures, of psychic dimensions, of the very texture of language itself: after all, text is the root of textile. Considering materials—literally, the stuff out of which stuff is made—requires a discourse that brushes economics up against aesthetics. That so many scholars (experts in the history of Italian education, in the history of East European socialism, in the ethnography of Algerian wedding practices, to name a few) can unite through attention to items of clothing speaks to the transhistorical and cross-cultural ubiquity of clothing. It is a basic human need. Yet the vast differences and arcane meanings attached to any particular fashion trend or item of dress vary and change across classes, genders, time, and space. These embellishments appear utterly unnecessary. Such is the contradiction we all face daily.

Fashion studies extends from the ethnographic approach of Joanne Eicher to the art historical readings of Anne Hollander, from literary critic Marjorie Garber's inventive readings of transvestism to Germano Celant's exhibition of Giorgio Armani's couture at the Guggenheim Museum in 2000. This fluidity has attracted many distinguished scholars to our project. Most considered clothing for the first time in their careers. Yet, once analyzed, the subject captivated them so deeply that they willingly extended their research to create many original meditations on the materials covering bodies both real and imagined. By no means exhaustive, these essays offer a range of styles, from rigorously archival to deeply textual, on objects and the affects they induce in their wearers and in those who observe them, desire them, and perhaps also shop for them.

As literary critics, much of our attention is on the ways in which literature relies on and participates in the construction of bodily presence through narrative or lyrical obsession with dress and habit. Because dress is at once tactile and visual—and often aural, as the crinkly sound of a crinoline or the swish of satin attests—the art of creating literary effects of touch and sight (and sound), especially when they are so intimately associated with character, offers tour de force examples of a writer's skill in conveying affect through description. More obviously, film, photography, and visual culture present opportunities to foreground clothing, tracking its changing sensations over time. Film, especially from Hollywood's Golden Era, worked hand in glove with the fashion industry, displaying the latest styles or costuming actresses in period clothing again and again to convey a world of opulence and ease seemingly accessible to all. Dress codes, whether in the form of school uniforms or corporate and government protocols, enforce, by contrast, a sense of clothing as a restrictive binding, controlling one's ability to express individuality. Clothing both opens up and clamps down the body and its myriad identities. Even the same article of clothing can be at once freeing and restrictive—an empty sign full of meaning.

The essays in these collections are concerned with how subjectivity and identity, intimately tied to processes of incorporation, projection, and desire, are evoked by an item of dress. Thus, before scholars engage the subject, each volume commences with an essay by a woman psychoanalyst. Given the complexity of the problematic of clothes, it seemed essential to open each book with a reflection that ponders over its meaning in relation to identity from the point of view of her school—Freudian, Lacanian, Jungian. In every case, her evocative, even innovative, elaboration on the sparse shreds that the various masters have incidentally jotted down in their works calls for new ways of thinking about the habits of being. For instance, Freud noted Dora's *schmuckasten* but could never fathom what she meant when she asserted her right to own, and show off, such a fashionable item—sometimes a cigar is just a cigar, but a purse is never just a purse. In every volume we also include a conversation with or a statement by a noted fashion designer before extending the arena to scholars, and each book features women artists who appropriate traditional Western assumptions that weaving and sewing are aspects of women's work, creating stunning visual links between text and textile. Like careful shoppers, we have been very selective in our choices. They remind us that all clothing is at once conceptual (someone designed each piece) and material (someone made it). Made for use yet extravagant, quotidian yet unique—what else is culture?

Attention to the mechanisms by which clothing and its representations affect psychic and social structures underlies most of these essays, no matter how diverse their approaches. Representations of clothing, like the items themselves, can take on a fetishistic quality. Identity is perhaps little more than a matter of habit, of what is put on every day to construct one's being. A habit of being. Clothed in the world and in the imagination.

This book is the result of deep commitments by our many contributors; we are grateful for their collaboration, enthusiasm, and insights. We thank our indefatigable research assistant, Sara Cohen, for taking care of the finishing touches on this volume. Support for the project has come from the Dipartimento di Studi Euro-Americani of Università degli Studi di Roma Tre and the Department of English and the Samuel Russell Chair in the Humanities of the College of Liberal Arts of the University of Minnesota. Our editor at the University of Minnesota Press, Douglas Armato, has been devoted to this effort from the beginning, and his assistant Danielle Kasprzak, as well as Nancy Sauro and Laura Westlund, helped guide us and trusted us to follow them throughout the process of turning an Italian series into an American one. Caroline Evans, Cynthia Kuhn, and an anonymous reader gave us cogent and encouraging suggestions that made this a stronger work.

Giuliana Di Febo's essay originally appeared in Italian in volume 2 of *Abito e Identità: Ricerche di storia letteraria e culturale*. Volume 4 of *Abito e Identità* first published the essays by Franca Zoccoli (in Italian) and Paula Rabinowitz; the latter also appeared in the Catalan journal *Lectora: Revista di dones i textualitat* 7 and in *Black & White and Noir: America's Pulp Modernism* (Columbia University Press). Essays by Zsófia Bán, Manuela Fraire, and Vito Zagarrio, and the conversation with Micol Fontana were first published (the latter three in Italian) in volume 5 of *Abito e Identità*. Essays by Martha Banta and Jeffrey C. Stewart first appeared in volume 6 of *Abito e Identità*. Vittoria C. Caratozzolo's essay originally appeared in Italian along with Paola Colaiacomo's essay in volume 7 of *Abito e Identità*. Cristina Giorcelli's essay on Sonia Delaunay was published in Italian in volume 9 of *Abito e Identità*. We thank Edizioni Associate and Editrice Ila Palma for permission to publish these essays in English in this volume.

Clothing, Dress, Fashion: An Arcade

The woman shall not wear that which pertaineth unto a man,
neither shall a man put on a woman's garment:
for all that do so are abominable unto the LORD thy God.

DEUTERONOMY 22:5

You must needs have dresses embroidered with gold;
you like to do your perfumed hair in countless different ways;
you must have sparkling rings upon your fingers.
You adorn your necks with pearls brought from the East,
pearls so big that your ears can scarcely bear the weight of them.

OVID, *The Art of Beauty*

A complete description of people's costumes is apt to be tedious, but as in stories
the first thing that is said about the characters is invariably *what they wore,* I shall
once in a way attempt such a description.

LADY MURASAKI, *The Tale of Genji*

Man was an animal compounded of two dresses, the natural and the celestial suit, which were the body and the soul; that the soul was the outward, and the body the inward clothing.... By all which it is manifest that the outward dress must needs be the soul.

JONATHAN SWIFT, "A Tale of a Tub"

The first spiritual want of a barbarous man is Decoration.

THOMAS CARLYLE, *Sartor Resartus*

It was dressed entirely in black, and of the very finest cloth;
it had patent leather boots, and a hat that could be folded together,
so that it was bare crown and brim; not to speak
of what we already know it had—seals, gold neck-chain, and diamond rings;
yes, the shadow was well-dressed, and it was just that which made it quite a man.

HANS CHRISTIAN ANDERSEN, "The Shadow"

What shall we call our "self"? where does it begin? where does it end? It overflows into everything that belongs to us—and then it flows back again. I know a large part of myself is in the clothes I choose to wear. I've a great respect for *things!* ... these things are all expressive.

HENRY JAMES, *Portrait of a Lady*

Fashion includes a peculiar attraction of limitation, the attraction of a simultaneous beginning and end, the charm of novelty coupled to that of transitoriness.

GEORG SIMMEL, "The Philosophy of Fashion"

The clothes are the background, the frame, if you like: they don't make success, but they are part of it.

EDITH WHARTON, *The House of Mirth*

The human animal shows in its clothing as conspicuously as in many other ways, the peculiar power of extraphysical expression.

    CHARLOTTE PERKINS GILMAN, *The Dress of Women*

A blue coat is guided away, guided and
guided away, that is the particular color that is used
for that length and not any width not even more
than a shadow.

    GERTRUDE STEIN, "A Blue Coat"

Let there be fashion, down with art.

    MAX ERNST, *Let There Be Fashion, Down with Art*

There is much to support the view that it is clothes that wear us and not we them.

    VIRGINIA WOOLF, *Orlando*

The eternal is in any case far more the ruffle on a dress than some idea.

    WALTER BENJAMIN, *The Arcades Project*

Fashion is art's permanent confession that it is not what it claims to be.

    THEODOR ADORNO, *Aesthetic Theory*

"Nuncle, you're looking wonderful this evening. Black suits you perfectly. But what are you looking at? Are you courting death?"

    GIUSEPPE TOMASI DI LAMPEDUSA, *The Leopard*

If there's one thing I know, it's how to wear the proper clothing.

    GRACE KELLY to **JIMMY STEWART** in *Rear Window*

The male subject, like the female subject, has no visual status apart from dress and/or adornment.

KAJA SILVERMAN, "Fragments of a Discourse on Fashion"

Dress is a sculpture in movement.

VIVIANE AUBRY, *Costumes II*

As a playful and gratuitous representation and a factitious sign, fashionable dress has broken all ties with the past; it draws the essence of its prestige from the ephemeral, scintillating, fascinating present.

GILLES LIPOVETSKY, *The Empire of Fashion*

A contemporary metropolis is that social site where individuals present and represent themselves first of all through the form and style of appearances.

ROBERTO GRANDI, "Fashion and the Ambiguous Representation of the Other"

The real opposition is not between soul and body, but between life and garment.

MARIO PERNIOLA, *The Sex Appeal of the Inorganic*

I enter the garment. It is as if I were going into the water. I enter the dress as I enter the water, which envelops me and, without effacing me, hides me transparently.

HÉLÈNE CIXOUS, "Sonia Rykiel in Translation"

Clothes like lovers, or, better, instead of lovers.

SEAN BLAZER, *Merchants of Fashion*

To write on clothing implies trying to consider garments no longer . . . as secondary elements, as accessories, but as primary, founding elements that determine individual behaviors as well as social structures.

FRÉDÉRIC MONNEYRON, *The Essential Frivolity: On Clothing and Fashion*

Fashion is the foundation of dress. Style is imparted to it by the wearer, and the accessories are its expression.

CARRIE A. HALL, *From Hoopskirts to Nudity*

Marie Antoinette sold her soul, and eventually the crown of her husband's realm, to her milliner, Rose Bertin.

COLIN MCDOWELL, *Hats, Status, and Glamour*

For clothing, its style is its essence.

ANNE HOLLANDER, *Seeing through Clothes*

Among primates, only humans regularly use adornment.

VALERIE STEELE, "Appearance and Identity"

Adornment *is* the woman, she exists veiled; only thus can she represent lack, be what is wanted.

STEPHEN HEATH, "Joan Riviere and the Masquerade"

Dress is the way in which individuals learn to live in their bodies and feel at home in them.

JOANNE ENTWISTLE, *The Fashioned Body*

Perfume . . . is our own shadow. It is a luxurious mirage, our transparency, a majestic choreography, a kind of inner palace, an architecture of exquisite crystal.

SERGE LUTENS, "My Perfumes"

Clothes are inevitable. They are nothing less than the furniture of the mind made visible.

JAMES LAVER, *Style in Costume*

I think my clothes allow someone to be truly an individual.

VIVIENNE WESTWOOD, in "A Conversation with Vivienne Westwood," by Tara Sutton

ACCESSORIZING THE MODERN(IST) BODY

Cristina Giorcelli

In the words of St. Anselm, "the habit does not make the monk," and ever since, the old adage of not being able to judge a book by its cover has provided consolation for those whose *appearance* did not fully represent their *being*.[1] Or else this adage has been used as a deterrent for those who considered creating a different *being* by changing their *appearance*. Indeed, the saying also became a standard warning used by well-intentioned parents, by all-knowing teachers, and by authorities fearful of being duped by those subject to their rule. It was used, that is, by those who saw themselves as upholders of normative behavior, proclaiming the primacy of *being* over *appearing*, of truth over falsehood.

Literature, history, and folklore, however, all provide examples of how the attire-identity analogue has been so well established that any metamorphosis in dress (as well as in behavior, attitude, or style) may also end up encroaching on the very essence of self. There are various reasons for making such alterations in one's dress: for necessity (to save one's life), as a joke (to make a fool of somebody), to overcome bans and barriers or the limitations of social class and gender.

In modern times, a general sense not only of the indeterminate nature of identity but also of the restrictive nature of roles (*habitus*, from *habeo*, has as much to do with dress as with a way of being) has created an open dialectic between the two terms: clothing and identity. Hence our series title: habits of being, which plays on this dual sense. More than a century ago, George Sand caused a scandal by her ostentatious male apparel (and in so doing addressed herself to the gender that was dominant in society and recognized in the artistic community). More recently, David Bowie won acclaim for his manifest androgyny (where the *coniunctio oppositorum* supposedly charges the "feminine" imagination and continuity with "masculine" power).

Dress (understood not only as clothing but also as mental and behavioral attitudes and rhetorical and linguistic modes) can be used as a mask to deceive others as well as a way to protect one's inner freedom. In fact, identity is perceived as so ambiguous, or so complex, that it defies any kind of external pressure, including pressure regarding costume (as attire, as gesture, as tradition, as demeanor). But, if dress is the *appearance* (or outer layer) that masks an *essence* (or inner content), then it can also be viewed as an epiphenomenon of a lack of essence, of a lack of being. The dialectic embedded within habits of being, between clothing and identity, therefore touches on categories of the metaphysical. As clothing is a means of communication, such communication produces information that, by definition, must partake in the general condition of illusion, allusion, and simulation: the self dresses and disguises itself on the great stage of the world, a fiction reflecting other (and perhaps more disquieting) fictions. If, as Luigi Pirandello so concisely put it, the self is "one, no one, and one hundred thousand,"[2] and modes of dress are likewise, then the self-evident, apodictic meaning of St. Anselm's adage becomes lost in multifaceted relativism.

The subject of this book is modern accessories, especially those accessories hugging the body, close clothes, those that come into direct contact with skin (necklaces, tiaras, hats, shoes, sandals) or cling nearby (vests, gowns, slinky dresses) and their decorations. But accessories are described by the *Oxford English Dictionary* as "contributing in a subordinate degree to a general result or effect; an adjunct, or accompaniment. *spec.* (in *pl.*): the smaller articles of (esp. a woman's) dress, as shoes, gloves, etc.; minor fittings or attachments." Accessories are thus those articles whose function is "secondary . . . adding to the beauty, convenience, and effectiveness" of that to which it is attached (including the body itself), according to *Merriam-Webster,* and are rather difficult to define because they have their own intrinsic but unpredictable rules. One need only consider how women's shoes have traditionally been considered accessories—perhaps because for many years their shape, material, and color were "dependent on bags" (which can truly be considered accessories). Or perhaps also because according to more recent fashion rules—which nowadays are often just as easily broken—shoes are supposed to coordinate with clothes (although parameters of taste are never free from unambiguous codification). From a sociological point of view, accessories were once more or less the preserve of those who had the economic means to purchase them (becoming, from a Marxist viewpoint, "fetishes" within the capitalist system). Now, however, the creative use of plastic, or some other overtly humble material, and the globalized economy have made many of them affordable for and/or obtainable by almost everyone because of their cheap price and indestructibility. In effect, anyone can accessorize, creating a style that appears unique; according to Georg Simmel, however, the infinite number of variations also increases the individual's sense of fragmentation and disorientation.[3]

Therefore, accessories, which are so numerous and so diverse (from fans, vests, hats, and gloves to jewelry, eyeglass frames, ties, shawls, leggings, and umbrellas) should be considered superfluous compared to the other things we are expected to consider essential. But essential in relation to what? Even clothes, although certainly fulfilling an apotropaic role of protection, of hygiene, and of safeguarding modesty, could be considered superfluous compared to the essentiality of the body itself (as naturists assert). Writers and artists tend to disagree with this view, as do many scholars of fashion from the most diverse fields. Indeed, if anything that goes beyond primary needs is superfluous, then what is the rationale for something being "extra"?

In the *Critique of Judgement,* Kant discusses picture frames, the columns of buildings, and the clothes of Greek statues: all *parerga,* whose primary meaning pertains to decoration, ornament, embellishment, and supplement. On this subject, Derrida's view is of particular interest:

A parergon comes against, beside, and in addition to the ergon, the work done *(fait),* the fact *(le fait),* the work, but it does not fall to one side, it touches and cooperates within the operation, from a certain outside. Neither simply outside nor simply inside. Like an accessory that one is obliged to welcome on the border, on board *(au bord, à bord)* it is first of all the on (the) bo(a)rd(er). . . . The *parergon* inscribes something which comes as an extra, *exterior* to the proper field . . . but whose transcendent exteriority comes to play, abut onto, brush against, rub, press against the limit itself and intervene in the inside only to the extent that it is lacking *from itself.*[4]

In other words, although an accessory, the *parergon* influences the *ergon*. What is more, for the *parergon* to exist, the *ergon* must lack something. Neither inside nor outside, neither superfluous nor necessary, the accessory is thus almost indispensable, particularly to any investigation into identity through dress.

An oxymoron by definition, therefore, the accessory has always been the object of inventiveness to a bizarre and even outlandish extent. Women's accessories seem to have been largely created, and to have been lovingly tolerated, under the aegis of what, according to the parameters of the prevailing tastes, is deemed eye-catching—perhaps beautiful, perhaps whimsical, perhaps akin to the misogynist's definition of woman. As to the male equivalent, the more men's clothing inclined toward uniform bankers' gray (as in the nineteenth-century suit or 1950s *Man in the Gray Flannel Suit*), the more men sought a hint of individual character (found in the nineteenth-century popularity of snuffboxes, walking sticks, waistcoats, gloves, pocket watches, and hats of different materials and disparate shapes, and more recently, ties for proper dress, do-rags and b-ball shoes for the street).

Therefore, whether the accessory is an absolute sine qua non (like shoes) or a nonessential item (like a brooch), it has ended up becoming the quintessence of fashion and of market forces. This decentered centrality of the accessory is borne out by its capacity to crown an outfit (for example, a hat), to indicate social class (for example, jewelry), to signal status (for example, a wedding ring), to protect from the weather (for example, a muff), to signal a religion or an ethnic group (for example, a veil), to indicate elegant informality (for example, a foulard) or a youthful sense of adventure (for example, a bandanna), to contain objects that are useful for oneself and for others (for example, a bag), or to be emblematic of seduction (for example, the Chanel No. 5 that the naked Marilyn Monroe wore to bed each night). They can also be markers, imposed by those in power and meant to degrade and control people (such as the yellow star). This volume, and subsequent ones, considers both the exuberant and oppressive forms of these and other seemingly "secondary" clothing items.

When fashion catalyzes public taste, it becomes part of the custom of a place and its time. The way one dresses is, not by chance, one of the components of social life that underlines cultural identity and distinguishes an age. Quite correctly, fashion has been defined as a "ripple of the socio-cultural system."[5] Its function and its symbolic role regulate "the market and tastes, the passion for consumption and ethical scruples."[6]

These studies are meant as illustrative samples in that they are clearly not intended as anything more than preliminary spotlights into a subject that warrants research across a greater number of cultures and contributions from many disciplines and methodologies. The aim of the essays in this collection is not to argue any preestablished theory. In fact, something as mutable as attire and a process as fluid as identity cannot easily be defined a priori in abstract terms because such a critical gesture would result in oversimplification. This volume, therefore, can be viewed as a collection of specific, yet significant, instances—of the modern(ist) habits of being.

NOTES

1. From Latin, "Non habitus monachum redit."

2. Luigi Pirandello, *One, No One, and One Hundred Thousand,* trans. William Weaver (New York: Marsilio, 1990).

3. For discussion of how fashion affects the ego, see Georg Simmel, "Fashion," in *On Individuality and Social Forms,* ed. Donald N. Levine (Chicago: University of Chicago Press, 1971), 316–17; Georg Simmel, "Philosophie der Mode," in *Gesamtausgabe* (Frankfurt am Main: Suhrkamp, 1995), 10:30–31.

4. Jacques Derrida, "Parergon," in *The Truth in Painting,* trans. Geoff Bennington and Ian McLeod (Chicago: University of Chicago Press, 1987), 53–56. "Un *parergon* vient contre, à côté et en plus de l'*ergon,* du travail fait, du fait, de l'œuvre mais il ne tombe pas à côté, il touche et coopère, depuis un certain dehors, au-dedans de l'opération. Ni simplement dehors ni simplement dedans. Comme un accessoire qu'on est obligé d'accueillir au bord, à bord. Il est d'abord l'abord. . . . Le *par-ergon* inscrit quelque chose qui vient en plus, *extérieur* au champ propre . . . mais dont l'extériorité transcendante ne vient jouer, jouxter, frôler, frotter, presser la limite elle même et intervenir dans le dedans que dans la mesure où le dedans manque." Jacques Derrida, "Parergon," in *La verité en peinture* (Paris: Flammarion, 1986), 63–65.

5. Nello Barile, *Manuale di comunicazione, sociologia e cultura della moda* (Rome: Meltemi, 2003), 61, my translation.

6. Patrizia Calefato, *Lusso* (Rome: Meltemi, 2003), 21, my translation.

1

NO FRILLS, NO-BODY, NOBODY

Manuela Fraire

The antinaturalistic origin of clothing (which is not a second skin, because it can be put on and taken off) makes it one of the most significant features of the "symbolic treatment" necessary for the humanization of the living body. Once reduced to an essentiality that places it in competition with the skin covering the body, often considered the "first clothing" provided by nature, dress runs the risk of betraying its own vocation from the outset. If deprived of accessories, clothing is actually comparable to the human skin but only to that of the newborn baby not yet "humanized" by the maternal gaze and care—a skin that has not yet undergone the symbolic treatment that designates the existence, the vesture of a subject, a subject in which to "in-vest."

"In his *Last Judgment,* Michelangelo portrayed himself as Saint Bartholomew (the patron saint of tailors), carrying his own skin on the arm," writes Eugénie Lemoine-Luccioni, hinting that the skin is exactly what is at stake in the attempt to give the body a symbolic meaning.[1] Clothing, therefore, is a second skin only insofar as, like natural skin, it needs to be treated (by language) in order to be rescued from bareness. "It is enough for me to know that the condition of a naked man appears precisely neither very human nor very enviable" (31). Lemoine-Luccioni goes on to comment that Claude Lévi-Strauss sees clothing as instrumental in the establishment of a social hierarchy because "naked" people do not constitute societies. Without clan colors or other signs of membership in any kind of group, the naked body lacks meaning: it can only acquire meaning, and become human, once it is veiled and/or unveiled (32).

The naked man or woman is therefore s/he whose "I" is still not able to wear the markings of his/her own sex, the first radical difference among human beings. In fact, reduced to a bare anatomical feature, the sexual organ is not constituted as a sexual object. This gap is salient to transvestites, as they play on the insufficiency of their anatomical sex to the point of contradicting it through their dress. Through this synthetic gesture, they represent the blankness of the body itself in its anatomical "bareness." Thus the endless work of accessorizing the bare body turns it from a meager transient thing into a subject and object of desire "created" by the laws of culture and language and quite unlike any other thing "created" by humans. Like culture and language, the body is realized through the never-ending act of adding and subtracting something to/from its bar-(r)e(n)ness.

IDENTIFICATION AND DISMANTLEMENT

In many respects, the act of clothing ourselves, and especially the choice of accessories, resembles the endless quest for identity that enables our "I" to engage in its work of self-construction, its search for an ideal image and for a legible identity that can actually be recognized by the Other.[2] The accessory, because of its function in the construction and recognition of identity, is the signature/mark of a subject doomed to incompleteness, but never quite resigned to it.

We inherit this inconsolable state from the very condition of helplessness in which our "I" was born, always searching and always subject to the check imposed on it by the experience of mirroring itself in the Other: an act of juxtaposition and, at the same time, of surrender. The quest for a satisfactory image of the self, which fuels fashion trends, never ceases to undress the body's bareness and redress it with the desire the "I" searches for in the gaze of the Other. It is the gaze of the mother that provides the stuff of our desire and also enables the basis for our many identifications with an ideal image of ourselves to which, in the course of our lives, we try to add or subtract that particular feature that is supposed to make a *(the)* difference. This feature is the precursor of the accessory.

In this perspective, clothing ourselves finds its place among the basic experiences presided over by the processes of identification linking the subject to the Other. "Who am I? Who am I supposed to become?" are questions that our "I" incessantly tries to answer. It does so by means of two different psychical movements: identification and disidentification.

If identification, the primary way we appropriate the Other's image, corresponds to the desire to "be like," to resemble, disidentification corresponds to the equally basic experience of the *dismantlement of the self*: the deconstruction of the identification processes through which the self was constituted, the differentiation from/of the earliest models of identification represented by the parental imagos. To differentiate oneself means overcoming the fear that the change inevitably undergone by one's body (because of biological as well as historical time) does not meet the Other's expectations and/or desires. The dismantlement of the self is itself linked to the accessory, in the sense that all changes, even the most radical, start from the smallest things, those that tend to pass unnoticed; this process constitutes the slow, indispensable erosion of the power exerted by the Other over the self. In short, it is the way in which one learns to walk in her/his own shoes.

"Mantle"—which derives from the Latin *mantellus,* veil—is a word endowed with many meanings. Among them, the *Dizionario Etimologico della Lingua Italiana* gives preeminence to the definition referring to clothing. Here "mantle" is the "whole that wraps, covers or can be uniformly spread out." Dismantling, or removing the mantle, then, means to reveal/unveil the "diversity" hidden and smoothed over by the mantle. The mantle was worn over the suit (in French, the overcoat is still called *robe-manteau*) as the last of many layers covering the bare body and, as a consequence, "dismantling" becomes the process through which the body is bared, layer by layer. The term "mantle" is thus employed as an ambivalent metaphor of shutting out the world and protecting oneself from it or, vice versa, of opening and revealing oneself to it.

In a metaphorical sense, dismantling corresponds to the demolition of fortified military bases, to the destruction of crumbling buildings or ships in disuse, etc. In reference to the operations of the self, it is the procedure through which the groundlessness of an argument or an allegiance is demonstrated. "Dismantlement" stands, therefore, at the base of any deconstruction of structures/constructions that the "I" perceives as alien.

UNITARY TRAIT

Finally, when used to differentiate the sexes, that which makes sexual difference visible, "dismantlement" corresponds to the erosion of costume and fashion, which nearly always begins and ends with accessories. As an example, consider Calvin Klein's perfume *One;* a large share of its success is due to a name highlighting that it does not differentiate the sexes: it evokes the omnipotence of a singularity that doesn't need the Other because it already contains it. The accessory, therefore, presents itself as an epistemological knot, tying the essential and the inessential in a necessary relationship, while at the same time it underpins how inadequate each is on its own. It is the accessory that defines the social-cultural stance of the subject—"the real gentleman is revealed by the details," as an old Italian saying goes; or in English (revealingly, with a sulfurous connotation): "the devil is in the details."

Beyond its face value, this saying has a latent meaning, as all commonplaces do. Let us consider as an example an accessory famous in the 1960s and now enjoying a revival—the Kelly bag—which owes its name to the woman who made it famous, Grace Kelly. This bag has become the symbol of a style, a social class, even an "epoch," and ever since, this simple personal object has become an accessory that can travel among very different people and across very different styles. As a symbol, it still possesses the power to signal a style anonymously: in fact, it is carried by young women who may not know who Grace Kelly was and what she represented—Philadelphia girl turned princess—but who still want "the Kelly."

Sigmund Freud underscores how, among all possible identifications, there is *one* characterized by the fact that it stands for the beloved and/or the chosen object.[3] Its function is to represent its absence. This process of identification limits itself to *borrowing only one of the object's features,* the one that connotes its essential difference. Perhaps it is no coincidence that so many males are at the top of the field of fashion: it is essentially men who strive to find the element that clearly inscribes their mark on the female body, almost a late appropriation of the maternal body.

TETA VELETA

In one of his most touching pages, the poet and film director Pier Paolo Pasolini describes a part of the body that, in his own erotic education, acquired the function of naming and representing pure desire:

> It was in Belluno. I was just over three years old. Watching the boys playing . . . I was mostly struck by the legs, especially by the convex, internal part of the knee where the nerves contract in the elegant and violent act of running. . . . I know it was an acutely sensual feeling. It was the sense of the unreachable, of the carnal—a sense for which a name is still to be invented. I invented one back then, and it was *"teta veleta,"* something like a tickle, a seduction, a humiliation.[4]

Jacques Lacan calls "unitary trait" that which connotes pure difference and does not stand for the unifying whole, but rather for the element of a series considered in its inaugural state.[5] For all their diversity, both Pasolini and Lacan had the skill to give a shape to that unique experience that drives us to search for our own *teta veleta* in a gesture or a defect—a crooked tooth that gives a sensual shape to the lip, for instance, or a peculiar detail in a haircut—that is, that feature, that accessory to the whole, that brings desire back to the object that first surprised us by activating it.

In the beautiful catalogue with which the Guggenheim Museum in New York celebrated Giorgio Armani and his "style," we find a few pictures taken from his family album.[6] Two of these cannot escape our attention. Both portray Armani as a five-year-old, with his mother and elder brother, at the seaside. Mrs. Armani wears a simple, dark bathing suit, made especially elegant by a couple of white buttons placed where the shoulder straps join the body of the suit. Obviously, the buttons are only decorative. In one picture, the one where she sits on the sand, she wears a brooch pinned at the center of the neckline of the bathing suit. This feature is even more striking inasmuch as the whole suit is absolutely simple: the accessory is the mark of a personality endowed with a contained but firm ambition. In a later picture, this woman, his mother, is shown wearing the same bathing suit, together with an equally plain, long, dark skirt, whose uniformity is broken only by its geometric pockets. This time—although the pose is definitely more formal than in the earlier picture—the brooch is missing, but beside her we see a thoughtful Giorgio.

Skimming the catalogue, we can see that the mother, who was not a rich woman, has been a model of elegance for Armani and a constant inspiration to him. We can see this in the details that are specific to his style—a collar, a button or its unexpected absence— a style, or rather an idiom, that constitutes the designer's *teta veleta*, that distinctive detail that remained so impressed on the Maestro's retina that he appears to have invented it. In a way, he did invent it, because the accessory is not merely an object added to a self-sufficient whole; rather it is a mark—always inevitably personal—a target of attraction for the gaze, at once marginalizing the general picture and making it possible through the introduction of an element, the accessory, that is there to attract and distract at the same time. What, then, makes the monk: the habit or the accessory? Lacan answers with a pun: "the habit loves the monk, since this way they are one."[7]

At times, the anatomy and physiology of the human body hint at modalities of function-ing that parallel the psyche's structure. In the eye, for instance, the macula is a small part at the center of the retina in which the stimulus does not elicit any visual sensation and that corresponds to the point of origin of the optic nerve. If we consider this anatomi-cal-physiological detail as a metaphor, we are driven to the uncomfortable conclusion that centrality and periphery, the essential and the superfluous, as well as the fundamen-tal and the accessory, revolve around the Thing; they are constituted as devices that define the topography of desire.

An accessory modeled on female genitalia characterizes one of Freud's most re-nowned cases, that of Dora. Freud's own words still best express the importance of what we call the accessory:

> On that day she wore at her waist—a thing she never did on any other occasion before or after—a small reticule [or drawstring purse] of a shape which had just come into fashion; and, as she lay on the sofa and talked, she kept playing with it—opening it, putting a finger into it, shutting it again, and so on. . . . Dora found no difficulty in pro-ducing a motive: "Why should I not wear a reticule like this, as it is now the fashion to do?" . . . Dora's reticule, which came apart at the top in the usual way, was nothing but a representation of the genitals, and her playing with it, her opening it and putting her finger in it, was an entirely unembarrassed yet unmistakable pantomimic announce-ment of what she would like to do with them—namely, to masturbate.[8]

For our purpose, what matters is not Freud's interpretation but rather the phrase "an en-tirely unembarrassed . . . announcement." Given the shape of the accessory under scrutiny, this sentence tells us more about the nature of the Thing—in this case (and, possibly, in every case) the incestuous sexual drive—and about its nature that is unrep-resentable except by something that common sense has already identified as marginal, superfluous, and accessory, and that, as such, protects the real nature of the desire from being unveiled: "Why should I not wear a reticule like this, as it is now the fashion to do?" Freudian doctrine teaches us the necessity of dealing with the unresolved tensions between what is assigned to the domain of instinct and what is considered to be the effort to reach the drive, specifically the sexual drive, which leads the animal-man into the symbolic universe of desire.

Krizia (Mariuccia Mandelli) has written, "I can understand a lot more about people by looking at their shoes or their watch, than the clothes they wear or the words they say."[9] These words contain a truth that is especially important for the psychoanalyst: they highlight how clothing, like language, is not only part of style but also the main part of what has been defined as *idiom,* pointing at that *something* that allows us to recognize individual subjectivities within a shared language. Clothing is part of one's personal idiom; thus it performs the function of self-narration that through sonic accessories—like voice inflections, standard formulas, and accents in language—makes the body expressive. Had there been no blank to fill (for the skin in and of itself does not indicate the human person), there would probably not be that *system open to the Other* constituted by clothing and accessories, a prosaic version of the essential tension between the basic and the superfluous, between centrality and marginality.

BASIC-ALL-PURPOSE-DURABLE

I still remember with vague uneasiness a teddy bear I saw in a shop window in New York. It was made out of bare, printed material, and it bore the words "no-frills bear" printed on its chest. Under it, in much smaller print, one could read the phrase "basic-all-purpose-durable." The illusion of reaching the essential (basic) and the durable through the elimination of frills gave it a tender and sad look, like some newborns who, still not "clothed" with desire by their mother's gaze, look grotesque and scared. When Lemoine-Luccioni says of clothing that it is the treatment of the nothing that we are, she underscores the basic function of clothing: it does not cover the body but "creates" it. We are obviously talking not about the literal suit made of material but about that first suit constituted by the Gestalt provided by the maternal gaze that invests the image of the child with her own desire. In Maori facial painting, the decoration creates the face, giving it human dignity and social and spiritual value and power. The accessory, decoration, and, in general, the ornament are, then, the *griffe* of a lack, of an impossible completeness often misunderstood as a lost original authenticity. According to the Islamic mystical tradition of Sufism, Satan, oppressed by regret and nostalgia for the past, wants to rescue the world from its transitoriness and to allow it to survive its fatal corruption.[10] He is condemned to this (impossible) loyalty to things that pass, and these he mourns inconsolably. The spirit of the accessory is like the ear of the Islamic tradition that avoids endless mourning by accepting the transitoriness and the caducity of worldly life.

NOTES

1. Eugénie Lemoine-Luccioni, *Psicanalisi della moda* (Milan: Paravia, 2002), 117. (*La Robe: essai psychoanalytique sur le vêtement* [Paris: Éditions du Seuil, 1983].) Henceforth page numbers will be given in parentheses in the text.

2. Alain De Mijolla-Mellor and Sophie De Mijolla-Mellor, "Io (Je) e il progetto identificatorio in Piera Aulagnier," in *Psicoanalisi* (Rome: Borla, 1998), 412–15.

3. Sigmund Freud, "Civilization and Its Discontents," in *Standard Edition of the Complete Psychological Works of Sigmund Freud*, ed. and trans. James Strachey (London: Hogarth, 1959), 21:103.

4. Pier Paolo Pasolini, "Atti impuri," in *Amado mio* (Milano: Garzanti, 1982), 72.

5. Jacques Lacan et al., "Il clivaggio del soggetto e la sua identificazione," in *Scilicet I/4*, ed. Armando Verdiglione (Milano: Feltrinelli, 1977), 197–98.

6. Germano Celant and Harold Koda, *Giorgio Armani* (New York: Guggenheim Museum Publications, 2000), 4–5.

7. Jacques Lacan, *The Seminar of Jacques Lacan, Book XX, On Feminine Sexuality: The Limits of Love and Knowledge, 1972–1973*, ed. Jacques-Alain Miller, trans. Bruce Fink (New York: W. W. Norton, 1998), 6.

8. Sigmund Freud, "Fragment of an Analysis of a Case of Hysteria," in *Standard Edition*, ed. and trans. Strachey, 7:76–77.

9. Mariuccia Mandelli, "Krizia e gli accessory," in *Abito e Identità: Ricerche di storia letteraria e culturale*, ed. Cristina Giorcelli (Rome: Ila Palma, 2001), 4:33. Reprinted in translation in *Circulation and Exchange*, Habits of Being 2 (Minneapolis: University of Minnesota Press, 2012).

10. Massimo Carboni, "Silenzio e verità dell'ornamento," *Il Manifesto*, March 10, 2003.

2

THE CULT OF FEMININITY

Micol Fontana

(IN CONVERSATION WITH CRISTINA GIORCELLI)

I had the good luck and pleasure to speak with Micol Fontana: my good luck because, at the age of ninety-four, she is still vivacious, energetic, and a volcano of initiatives—all feasible; a pleasure because through her words, colorful and immediate, she relives a human world and a city, Rome, in all its fabulous contours, those of the mythical 1950s and 1960s, when, after the horror and devastation of the war, the Eternal City blossomed again and, thanks to the contributions of ingenious creators undertaking enterprises of extraordinary quality (such as the Fontana Sisters atelier) it became the privileged destination of beautiful people, from princesses in exile to Hollywood actresses, from high-society ladies to artists. In those years, Italian high fashion rapidly developed, and for many reasons and a combination of motives, Rome was its capital. As Micol writes, after 1948 "in the Italy that was ready to live its second rebirth, the cult of femininity exploded and immediately made converts. Not the cult of beauty . . . but of femininity, precisely, the new way of being a woman, joyful and carefree."[1] She continues: "The golden, frenetic, sleepless, curious Rome, the Rome of nightclubs, of nights drawn out till dawn, it was all there" (96). This was the Rome that served as backdrop for the fashion shows of the three sisters.

Today Micol Fontana directs the foundation that carries her name, located on the first floor of the building that, since 1957, has housed her famous atelier on Via San Sebastianello, near the Piazza di Spagna. She remembers all of her clients/friends warmly, with admiration, with humor, and a few with deep affection. I converse with her in her study, surrounded by gowns on exhibition and by photographs on the walls of models (even famous ones) who wear afternoon outfits and evening gowns from that golden epoch: in reality, they are timeless works of art. On a mannequin, next to me, there is a short evening dress made of black silk velvet with a low-necked fitted bodice and wide fuchsia and maroon double-satin bands (but the shadings of the colors, boast of the atelier, are, in fact, indescribable) that, above the straight skirt, fall from the waist. It would be a privilege to wear it even today! After having admired its harmony, I examine it closely and am enchanted by the extraordinary finishing: more than seams, what I see are chiselings made by high craftsmen. The style from which the fortunes of the Fontana sisters began derived "from their taste for the past (the remote past, not the dramatic past we had just come out of) with some indulgence to the Renaissance. *Women liked it;* the colors seemed chosen by an artist" (149).

Micol lets herself remember: from Rita Hayworth to Joan Collins, from Colette Rosselli to Renata Tebaldi, from Margaret Truman to Jackie Kennedy, from Marella Agnelli Caracciolo to the enfante of Spain, from Linda Christian to Kelly Le Brock, from Soraya of Persia to Maria Pia of Savoy—to cite only a few—she describes their beauty, their elegance, in some cases, sadly, their adverse destiny, but also their complete faith in her taste and in that of her beloved and inventive sisters, Zoe and Giovanna, who knew how to find the right shape for every body and for every occasion. Micol speaks to me also of her travels around the world and of some of the many invitations and numerous prizes that the sisters received as testimonials and tributes to the refinement of their craftsmanship. She dwells on their Italian artistry and how, even today, illustrious personalities remember them and stay in contact with her (Giovanna and Zoe died several years ago).

Having arrived in Rome from the province of Reggio-Emilia (from Traversetolo, near Parma) in 1936 literally in search of fortune, the young and comely Fontana sisters, descendants of three generations of seamstresses, found what they were looking for. After having worked as helpers in various seamstress workshops, they were able, in a few years—and despite the serious slowdown in productivity due to the war—not only to found their first atelier, integrating themselves perfectly into the big city, but also to become a reference point for the many foreigners who were staying in Rome. Hard workers, gifted with a strong practical sense, rich in imagination, in talent, in audacity and taste for the new, the three sisters had, through the years, found the right materials and up-to-date inspiration for their dresses: one has but to think of the evening "lunar" gowns (created in 1969 after American astronauts set foot on the moon), created by the Fontana Sisters with wonderfully constructed plastic materials.

The Fontana Sisters were among the first to invent, early in their career, the figure of the *mannequin de societé,* the high-society model; that is, they furnished well-off women with their gowns, which would give the sisters' creations publicity when worn at important receptions in Italy and abroad. They were also among the first, at least in Italy, to marry fashion to art: they invented the Fontana Sisters Prize for paintings, won by Anna Salvatore, Renzo Vespignani, Giovanni Omiccioli, Sante Monachesi, Domenico Purificato, among others, that were exhibited in their atelier with fashion models as sponsors.

I hesitate to interrupt Micol because the images evoked are suggestive and her affability is contagious, but I had come to ask her a specific question. I postpone it because I am under the spell of the images that I see on a wall: of a full-length overcoat in velvet with a mink collar, worn by an enchanting Audrey Hepburn (who even off a movie set would wear outfits made by the great Italian couturiers) and of a black dress in lightweight wool with a pointed collar lined in satin that swaddles a stupendous Ava Gardner. (Wasn't her beauty enough to render her unique? Oh, one knows, it always rains when it is wet and, so, women who are already perfect must have fashion designers who exalt their perfection!) Finally, I find the way to ask her what place accessories had in the Fontana Sisters collections, and what, for them, were the most distinctive ones.

Micol is moved and, at first, remembers that she and her sisters had an accessory from which they never parted: when they came of age, their mother gave each one of them, through great personal sacrifice, a three-strand pearl necklace. All their photographs show them with those strings of pearls that, for them, were no longer an accessory, but a part of themselves—also because, as she stresses, with their brightness and brilliancy, pearls "grace the face."

Leaving aside the personal note, Micol Fontana emphasizes that for her "the accessory comes *with* the dress, not *before* the dress." And then she answers, without hesitations, blurting out: buttons and buckles because "they establish the focal point of the dress." She shows me, among the photos and models exhibited, the belt buckles and the buttons specifically designed for some of their dresses. They are very fanciful, of high-quality materials, but not necessarily extravagant (of tortoise shell, of semiprecious stones, of silver) and always very decorative (they "garnish" the dress). Yet as in any construction that is worthwhile (and dress is architecture), they must be functional. In many cases, it is easy to understand how buckles and buttons constituted the magic touch that made the difference (over and above the impeccable cut of the garments). Micol shows me the photograph of a jacket completely covered by buttons of different sizes, shapes, and colors: both amusing and elegant, as she underlines, it was created by her sister Giovanna.

After reminding me that in the years of their celebrity some accessories—such as gloves—were considered indispensable ("One went even to the market wearing gloves") and, as a subtle interpreter of the explicit or implicit clothing function, after observing that gloves have a broad meaning because they "sweeten movements," Micol speaks of the importance of shoes and purses to their collections. She shows me some photographs of shoes: in satin (worked or embroidered like the dress with which they were to be worn), in leather, in suede. They are perfectly matched to the dresses for which they constitute a kind of "seal." I try to comment that, even in the conception of this specific accessory, today's fashion has drawn away from that of forty or fifty years ago, because today shoes match dresses more by evocation than by precision. But Micol sticks with her firm opinion that for true elegance, shoes "must" directly recall the garment. I understand her point and, to judge from the numerous photographs she shows me in which

FIGURE 2.1 Ava Gardner poses with dress and accessories from Sorelle Fontana. Courtesy of the private collection of Micol Fontana.

FIGURE 2.2 Model in jacket with buttons on Sorelle Fontana fashion show runway. Courtesy of the private collection of Micol Fontana.

there is no stylistic discrepancy between any of the accessories and the rest of the apparel, I cannot but agree. They recall an epoch whose many manifestations were much less fragmented and heterogeneous than today's.

About purses or similar accessories, Micol remembers with particular pride the magnificent bouquet in white satin, miniature orchids (sent by the bride's father), and

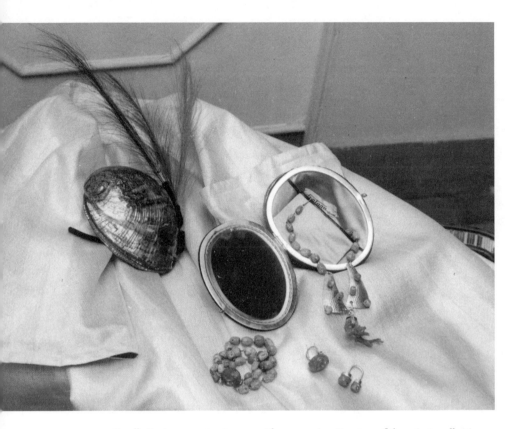

FIGURE 2.3 Sorelle Fontana evening *trousse*, with accessories. Courtesy of the private collection of Micol Fontana.

pearls that was made up in a single day in their atelier for Linda Christian's wedding dress when she married Tyrone Power in Rome. The sisters later became close friends of both actors (indeed, Micol enjoys underlining the fact that the presentation of their first collection in the United States took place in Beverly Hills in 1951 precisely through the good offices of the couple). Along with the splendid dress of satin, lace, and pearls, that bouquet was a touch of great class.

Micol shows me, in the end, an adorable handbag made from two large Pacific abalone shells—mounted in silver with a beautiful fastener of the same metal, the inside of one shell covered in silk and in the other half a small inlaid mirror—to wear to an evening gala. I observe that, while it seems to be an accessory created today, this *trousse* could have been worn even by women in ages far off and belonging to civilizations far different from ours. As with every work of art, Micol Fontana adds. And she is right.

Finally, I linger over head coverings for evening wear or important afternoons, constructed often only of satin or velvet decorations in the form of essential curlicues that embrace the shape of the head. They are a sophisticated touch that adds fantasy and prestige to the rest of the apparel. Leaving her, I wish Micol Fontana the very best for her foundation (that every year, together with the Fulbright Commission, assigns a fellowship to a young designer to specialize in the United States), with its notable archive of drawings, photographs, samples of embroidery, and, above all, splendid gowns so rich in timeless history. She hopes that Fondazione Fontana can be granted a worthy permanent exposition space within the city of Rome and become (or be part of) a Museum of Fashion. In 2005, the city of Rome and the Capitoline Museums staged a major two-month exhibition titled *The Fontana Sisters: Gowns That Have Entered History. From Craftsmanship to Art* and awarded scholarships to young emerging fashion designers.[2]

The Fontana Sisters deserve this attention for their part in the Eternal City.

1. Micol Fontana, *Specchio a tre luci*, ed. Dino Cimagalli (Rome: Nuova Eri, 1991), 48. My translation; further references in text.

2. The exhibition was sponsored by the Lazio Region, the Municipality of Rome, the Municipality of Traversetolo, the Germozzi Foundation, and several artisan committees.

3

FASHION'S MODEL BODIES
A GENEALOGY

Paola Colaiacomo

At first there were dolls. A wooden mannequin—perhaps the most ancient in history—was found in Tutankhamen's tomb. France's Queen Marie Antoinette used to send her mother and sisters back in Austria puppets wearing the latest Paris fashions. In the nineteenth century, fashion dolls traveled as far as India so that colonial officers' wives might have a three-dimensional preview of the dresses they would be ordering from their London dressmakers.

On its decamping from the theater of fashion, the wooden or rag doll left behind nothing but a name. "Mannequin" goes back to the ancient fiction of the homunculus, or mannequin, a creature inhabiting a borderland between the animate and the inanimate. Well into the 1950s, the word "mannequin" was used in Italy side by side with its near synonym *indossatrice,* from the verb *indossare,* to wear, to put on, to don. By the end of the 1960s, *modella* had replaced these terms. "Model" and "modeling" take us closer to the living being, evoking the familiar type of the painter's model, both male and female, and the nude classes in academies of art.

Live fashion modeling started during the mid-nineteenth century, an era of revolutionary changes for painting and the visual arts. The Pre-Raphaelites' interest in fashion design is well known: William Morris included the reform of dress, and especially of fe-

FIGURE 3.1 Madeleine Vionnet and her mannequin. Photograph by Therese Bonney. Copyright 1923–26. Printed by permission of the Bancroft Library, University of California, Berkeley.

male dress, in his program for the improvement of everyday life, as a vehicle to develop a greater sense of happiness for both men and women.[1] His muse, model, and wife-to-be Jane Burden was an archetypal mannequin figure. And the same can be said of her colleague Lizzie Siddal, who modeled for John Everett Millais's *Mariana*, a painting where the mannequin-like pose of the body seems to enhance the velvety substance of the dress. In a famous photographic portrait by Dante Gabriel Rossetti, Jane Burden wears a very sober "reformed" dress, the folds of which are said to have been carefully arranged for that pose by the Maestro himself. The dress was expected to be no less expressive than the face.

An Englishman transplanted to Paris, Charles Frederick Worth (1826–95) is credited with the invention of haute couture. He was active at the same time as Morris (1834–96), and he too asked his wife, Madame Marie Worth, to model his major creations. Worth's pupil Paul Poiret launched the celebrated theme parties where fashion was presented as light dramatic action and the most risqué among his creations were invariably modeled by his wife Denise. In a truly thespian mood, Poiret also started the vogue of taking his models on the road, as far as Russia and North America.

In the heyday of the Ballets Russes, posing for artists and fashion modeling shared a brief moment of contiguity.[2] At the beginning of the nineteenth century, the presence of "modern" dress in painting had been much debated. Was it acceptable? Or was it more respectable for painters to stick to the convention of historical costume? Among the supporters of contemporary dress was Théophile Gautier, who, in a short book titled *De la mode,* cited Jean Auguste Dominque Ingres's portraits as examples.[3] A fine line of thought can be scanned here, one that joins the name of Gautier with those of Charles Baudelaire, Stéphane Mallarmé, Aubrey Beardsley, Oscar Wilde, Max Beerbohm, and many others who defined the trajectory of emancipation of modern dress. All of them, in one way or another, posed the question of its suitability within a work of art, and thus modern dress finally carved a visual space of its own.

For centuries, dress had been perceived as one and the same as the body it covered. Renaissance and Baroque court dresses exacted an idol-like immobility from their wearers: when a niece of Francis I of France was married, at the age of twelve, she had to be carried to church in the arms of an assistant, so great was the weight of the gold and silver cloth of her bridal gown.[4] By contrast, modern, or liberated, dress opens a dialogue with the body underneath. A dialogue always implies a distance, in some cases even a difference. This genealogy can be traced back to the French Revolution and the end of the ancien régime. The Roman and Greek fashions characterizing the Empire style of the beginning of the nineteenth century were at once an experiment in vintage and an immediately popular "new look." Then, during the second half of the century, the debate about the artistic dignity of modern dress already signaled a world where body and dress play separate roles. Precisely at this juncture, fashion's model bodies make their professional appearance.

We recapture an echo of the radical change in self-perception produced by the presence of the mediating body of the model on the scene of fashion in Oscar Wilde's lecture "The Relation of Dress to Art," delivered in 1885 as a rejoinder to a previous talk by James Whistler on the use of color in portraiture. Of course Wilde, in *The Picture of Dorian Gray,* was shortly to interpret the immanent cleavage between character and figure as tragedy. But in his lecture, the exploration is limited to the everyday bland paraphernalia that contrast body and personality through clothes. It would have been banal, on Wilde's part, to enter the by then superannuated quarrel on the uses of modern dress in painting by simply siding with the moderns. He prefers instead to cut what looked like a Gordian knot by drawing a bright line between a supposedly "old" type of models and modeling and a "new" one. In his view, the professional model of the old type was "ruining painting and reducing it to a condition of mere pose and *pastiche*."[5]

Are we not all weary, he asked his bewildered audience, of this "venerable impostor fresh from the steps of the Piazza di Spagna"—because this model is of course Italian and male—"who, in the leisure moments that he can spare from his customary organ, makes the round of the studios and is waited for in Holland Park?" (70). What was wrong with that old type of model was the expectation that he would wear a costume. Be he the patriarch of Canaan or a brigand from the Abruzzi, he would pose in the dress required for the occasion. In the finished paintings, only the costume would be different while the face would remain the same. The irreverent, though logical, conclusion Wilde reaches here is that "All costumes are caricatures." For reality, they will always substitute a series of stereotypes. This is why the model will always remain, at bottom, a "poor peripatetic professor of posing"; however popular, his image must be interpreted as "the sign of the decadence, the symbol of decay" (70).

It is almost impossible, at this point, not to mention Henry James's 1893 short story "The Real Thing." We all know the paradoxical situation around which its plot revolves: a rather vulgar, commonplace, and down-at-heels working-class young girl provides the book illustrator for whom she poses with inspiration, while the couple of fashionable impersonators, graced by impeccable physiques and always attired in the right dress, clamorously fail. Eight years after Wilde's lecture, the severance of the figure from the character already assumes, under James's treatment, the pointedness of a witty epigram. But of course that notorious personage, Dorian Gray, had by then been around for a few years.

A second and more modern type of the model body is offered, Wilde says, by the "exquisite English girls"—presumably endowed with an English, not an Italian face— "strolling by an opal sea in the fantastic dresses of Japan." These girls have already been the excitement of all Chelsea: "has not Tite Street been thrilled with the tidings that the models of Chelsea were posing to the master, in peplums, for pastels?" (69). Here, the feminine firmly occupies the center of the scene, a scene set in the open air. It is certainly very tempting, at this point, to observe that an exotic vein was shortly to run deep in the fashion design of the period. One has only to think of Poiret and Madame Grès just a few years later. With them Hellenism would cohabit with Orientalism.

Wilde as archetypal coolhunter then? It may well be. But it would be disingenuous to respond to the interrogation he puts to us by simply referring to the day's revival of ancient or exotic styles. Much more rewarding to meditate on the subtle ways in which a change in art and life revolves for him on the pinhead of dress and its uses. Let them wear peplums or kimonos, the important thing here is that these ur-Chelsea girls— great-great-grandmothers of Andy Warhol's 1960s ones as they unwittingly are—have succeeded in extracting modern life painting from dead and buried genre painting by the simple act of wearing their peplums, or kimonos, in the right way: not as costumes, that is, but as real dresses in real life, to be worn along the streets of Chelsea or by the shores of an English sea. On this point, Wilde is wholly unambiguous: "the arts are made for life, and not life for the arts" (69). Modern dress, be it *à la grecque* or *à la turque,* can be instrumental to the realization of art as the natural heritage of mankind, for the simple reason that dress belongs to life. Through the mediation of the Chelsea girls, the living quality of dress is made apparent. How could they be denied the status of fashion models?

Once started, the dialogue between dress and body continues without interruption on the streets of the great cities, where we witness it everyday. And the streets, as Wilde never tired of repeating, are "the real schools" (71). If not the exclusive Tite Street, where both Whistler and he himself were privileged to live, then even Piccadilly might do, "in the glaring vulgarity of the noonday" (69). In the streets, dress becomes what it was meant to be from the beginning: "the expression of the loveliness that it shields and of the swiftness and motion that it does not impede ... the natural expression of life's beauty" (70). The expression, that is, of the living body and its beauty. We certainly won't miss the delicious profanity with which, by his reference to the swiftness of movement of the passersby, Wilde here makes use of Baudelaire's poem "A une passante."

If I am drawing from literature so heavily, it is because the literature of the first fin de siècle offers an extraordinary prognosis of our time. The natural link between fashion and art—today such a popular subject for talks and exhibitions—emerges in Wilde's and the other masters' pages, Walter Pater and Henry James above all, as an entirely new approach to the study of the body.[6] Let us take the case of the portrait as the most obvious example of what I am trying to say. Due to a cross-fertilization between art and fashion theories, we now recognize the legitimacy of at least two ways of looking at, say, a court dress in a Renaissance portrait: as the representation of something that "belongs" to that great container—the "period"—or as a designed artifact constructing all the complexities of life, even the act of its painting. In the first case, our *régime* of discourse will be description, and the implied relationship between culture and image will be an imitative one. In the second case, our discourse will be less linear and more energetic, but unavoidably also more tentative. Vision will no longer figure as the inevitable "after" of an obscure "before." Instead we shall have to look at the dress in the painting as at an artifact designed for a living body. A complex knot of pleasure and pain, of desire and anxiety, of imagination and memory, will be there for us to illuminate, according to our capacity of vision. The intersection of art and fashion thus becomes palpable.

We owe it to the new fashion studies if we see dress as a powerful instrument toward self-fashioning, an instrument loaded with the strong potential for individual expression it constantly absorbs from the body: a living, painted, or photographed body.

We all know how the material and cut of a dress can dictate the very movements and postures of the body: nothing like the now fashionable vintage garments shows the impossibility of reproducing the supposedly "original" look. Studying old or castoff clothes reveals changes in its internalized image that our body has undergone, even in the short *durée*. Since her inception in the nineteenth century, the specific task of the fashion model has been to impress the agon between body and dress with the recognizable shape of its times. At the end of the millennium, Jennifer Craik inscribed the fashion model as the "technical body of western consumer culture."[7] This definition was rendered possible by the relationship postulated between the body and the dress that covered—or uncovered—that body: a much more dynamic relationship, by then, than the one implied in the past by the culture of fashion as mere representation.

Implicit in the agon between body and dress is the dissociation of sensibility that would become the staple of fashion advertising. The task of the fashion model is to act and rehearse that dissociation for the benefit of our eyes. Already in the aftermath of World War II, Marshall McLuhan was drawing attention to the "brittle, self-conscious pose of the mannequin, who walks and behaves like a being who *sees* herself as a slick object, rather than is aware of herself as a person." Of course McLuhan was far from complaining about this state of things. Quite the contrary: the commercially sponsored glamor of the mannequin interested him exactly *because* of its "heavy narcissistic quality," which translated as "competitive display," rather than, as might be expected, "spontaneous sensuality."[8] *The Mechanical Bride* was published in 1951. Roland Barthes's studies on fashion, which were to culminate in the *Système de la Mode,* also began in the 1950s. Barthes too speaks of the cover girl's body as mere structure, as nobody's body, its task being that of sending the viewer's gaze back to the garment: annihilating its own bodily substance, as it were.

To *see* oneself as an object. As a "sleek" object. To be two and one at the same time. This, according to McLuhan, was the specific ability of the model exploited by commercial advertising: surely an ability we can trace back to that severance of character from figure that the literary experimentation of that earlier fin de siècle so actively pursued. The rise to prominence of the live fashion model coincides chronologically with that dawning of modernism. She—because it's a "she" we are talking about, at this stage— appears simultaneously with the new optical and visual technologies that shaped the lives of our parents and grandparents: chronophotography, photography, and, later, the cinema. The modernist desire for movement and speed is, if anything, only too literally fulfilled by the fashion show. The opportunity to see dresses in motion, on a live body, in a theatrical or performative setting as a background, was increasingly sought after during the century, by urban audiences in Paris, London, Milan, and New York. There is therefore no denying that fashion's model bodies are to be counted among the forces that shaped the world Susan Sontag so aptly called the "image world." Our world.

And the more so because the visual aesthetics that ruled this novel form of entertainment unequivocally seemed to push the human body—a physically present body and not a shadow, as on film—toward an uncanny proximity to the machine.[9] The mannequin on duty was taught early on to freeze motion, as if in a magical suspension from life: to gaze at a distant point beyond the horizon, sporting an abstract, detached expression. Her movements were to be jerky, almost robotic. She—the heir of the wooden mannequin, after all—had to quote the mechanics of the mannequin during her tireless treading of the runway, up and down, to the rhythm of syncopated music. Her sudden immobilization of face and body—to be executed at fixed intervals, and therefore perfectly predictable—evoked the cinematic freeze-frame effect.

FIGURE 3.2

Model in Vionnet dress. Les Arts Décoratifs, Paris.

We seem thus to have come full circle. From the wooden mannequin of ancient Egypt to the living model body conceived as nobody's body. And if I have somewhat lingered on the first fin de siècle, it is only because I think that Wilde's caveat that "the arts are made for life, and not life for the arts" still has much to say to fashion scholars.

NOTES

1. William Morris, "The Lesser Arts of Life," in *The Collected Works of William Morris,* 24 vols. (London: Routledge / Thoemmes Press, 1910–14), 22:238.

2. Nancy J. Troy, *Couture Culture: A Study in Modern Art and Fashion* (Cambridge, Mass.: MIT Press, 2003), 200–1.

3. Théophile Gautier, *De la mode* (Paris: Poulet-Malassis et De Broise, 1858), 13–14.

4. Mario Praz, *Mnemosyne: The Parallel between Literature and the Visual Arts* (Princeton, N.J.: Princeton University Press, 1970), 230.

5. Oscar Wilde, "The Relation of Dress to Art," in *Miscellanies* (London: Methuen, 1908), 70. All further references appear in the text.

6. This type of thinking about the body will come to prominence with the rise of media and film studies and more recently still with fashion studies. At this crossing, aesthetics, literary theory, art-historical disciplines, and now fashion theory talk to and cross-fertilize each other.

7. Jennifer Craik, *The Face of Fashion: Cultural Studies in Fashion* (London: Routledge, 1994), 70.

8. Marshall McLuhan, *The Mechanical Bride: Folklore of Industrial Man* (New York: Vanguard, 1951), 94.

9. Caroline Evans, "Multiple, Movement, Model, Mode: The Mannequin Parade, 1900–1929," in *Fashion and Modernity,* ed. Christopher Breward and Caroline Evans (Oxford: Berg, 2005), 125–45.

4

WEARING THE BODY OVER THE DRESS
SONIA DELAUNAY'S FASHIONABLE CLOTHES

Cristina Giorcelli

THE CLOTHED BODY

In Genesis, Adam's and Eve's bodies epitomize innocence and truth. According to the biblical narrative, after God created them "they were both naked, the man and his wife, and were not ashamed" (2:25). The statement seems both paradoxical and anachronistic: while it employs the logic of *hysteron proteron*, in which the effect replaces the cause, it also projects a sentiment (shame) that under the circumstances they could not then know.[1] Later, after Adam and Eve ate the forbidden fruit, Genesis tells us that "the eyes of them both were opened, and they knew that they *were* naked" (3:7). Interestingly, while Hebrew makes a subtle distinction between these two moments of nakedness by using two slightly different, nuanced adjectives, the distinction is lost in the authorized (King James) version of the Bible.[2] In the first occurrence, a more accurate translation might have been: both the man and his wife "were nude." "Nude" is applied to the human body in its absolute perfection, in its ideal form: a state that, at this point, the Bible cannot but advocate.[3] But this distinction in Hebrew seems to have disappeared in the English available in the sixteenth and early seventeenth centuries.[4] In the second occurrence, "naked" is appropriate, because, referring to a body that has no garment, no decoration, and no tattoo, it implies some sort of embarrassment.

In this primeval scene, moreover, it is only after the act of looking at each other, now with an awareness of sin, that Adam and Eve felt they needed some sort of covering. They "sewed fig leaves together" (3:7) and made and wore the first clothes.[5] In addition, because, according to the Hebrew Bible's commentator Rashi de Troyes, Adam and Eve used the leaves of the very tree from which they had eaten, they tied transgression and remedy into an indissoluble knot, into an *ouroboros* in which—as entailed in the meaning of this symbol—the death wish pulses.[6]

Born of seeing, clothes thus require that they be seen and, if possible, become visions. Linked to appearances, to impermanent *phenomena,* as opposed to essences, *noumena,* clothes create looks, mental images, and project auras. Contrived by ingenuity and by art, clothes are *arti*ficial. Concealing parts of the body, they fragment it, directing the gaze to each part; but to avoid perversity or fetishism, clothes do so only in a way that maintains a balanced image of the whole. In addition, clothes make one aware of "contrasts between covered and exposed, between left and right, between inside and outside. Without clothing, there is no division, only mass."[7] Consequently, if clothes parcel out the body, at the same time they allow a more detailed assessment of it.

In the Bible, while clothes may be taken as the first manifestation of human consciousness, they also carry the scourge of disobedience and can, consequently, be associated with what followed the Fall: work, childbirth, and death, that is, fatigue, pain, and transience. Revealingly, in English a garment is "worn" both in the sense of being put on a body and in the sense of being used up by a body. Like bodies, garments are ephemeral because their textile decays and because their fashion, like nature, is fleeting. But if clothes are devices concocted to preserve modesty, they also protect the body from harsh atmospheric elements, ornament it, ward off bad luck, and modify its appearance. Clothes can, in fact, shape anatomy (i.e., women's corsets) and, therefore, oppose the divine project by modeling new forms. In the Judeo-Christian tradition, the origin of clothes, prompted by the snake's wiles, keeps manifesting itself. At a subtler level, clothes constantly change the body "by structuring in signs—that is, in culture—what nature still possesses only as a potentiality, as an inclination to become a signifier."[8]

It is also true, however, that "clothing is our triumph over shame. If it abandons us, there is no escaping the humiliation, the aphasia."[9] One classic recurrent nightmare is of finding oneself naked and incapable of covering up. Terroristic, dictatorial powers divest bodies of clothing in an effort to mortify and subjugate: in such a condition people become bare, dejected, "no longer able to make a proposition."[10] Clothes are thus a kind of syntax that allows the body to take up and communicate meaning. This is because as language, as the articulation of the body, clothing is "bound to one's own inner being. There is no inner self without clothing. . . . Grammatically speaking, there is no first person without clothing. The 'I' is formulated and proven in its clothing. . . . A group of naked people . . . become anonymous and speechless."[11] "A person is a unity of textiles and body," it has been argued, because "clothing is not some extraneous addition way out on the periphery, but an essential redefinition. . . . Clothing allows us to appear because it gives us a density, stratification, a depth by which we are not only visible in the way that everything else in the universe is visible, but where we take on meaning, a significance that only we can disperse."[12] Even tattoos, by covering the body (or parts of it), turn it into an aesthetic, social, and spiritual entity to which a role, a mission, has been assigned, as Claude Lévi-Strauss has demonstrated.[13] Dressed is the covered body and dressed is the edible salad: both are ready to be consumed (metaphorically or actually) by and in society.

"Clothes are to the body what context is to text. . . . Clothes and the body, like fiction and fact, context and text, are alluringly different terms for a reality that is both unified and multiple, systematic and chaotic, but necessarily double."[14] In effect, clothes can be seen as the shape of the clad body not differently from language that is the shape of the clad thought. (Both Thomas Carlyle in *Sartor Resartus* and Ralph Waldo Emerson in "Nature" dwell on this comparison.)[15] Clothes talk, revealing one's identity or what one would like one's identity to be. They bespeak economic status (haute couture), social rank (police uniforms, nurses' smocks, judges' robes), ethnic origin and religious beliefs (the kippa, the chador, the turban), class affiliations (Todd shoes, Hogan bags, Lacoste shirts). Such affiliations are made even more striking when, with logos emblazoned on them, garments become inscriptions that metonymically brand the wearing body. The clothed body is, as Patrizia Calefato comments, the "physico-cultural territory in which the visible, perceivable performance of our outward identity takes place" and in which opportunities are provided for "the manifestation of individual and social traits that draw on such elements as gender, taste, ethnicity, sexuality, sense of belonging to a social group, or, conversely, transgression."[16]

Clothes may also disguise the body, making it appear to belong to a different gender, as in transvestism. Yet all clothes can disguise the body in everyday life because they draw attention more to themselves than to what lies beneath them. The epitome of this revolution is the model, the mannequin, the "cover girl": a girl that makes the covers of journals and a girl to be covered by clothes. Her function today is, as Roland Barthes noted, that of signifying not the body ("the cover girl's body is no one's body"), but the dress she is wearing—a dress meant to be more important than she is herself.[17] With her distant, inexpressive face, often covered by heavy maquillage like a Kabuki mask, with eyes that look at no one and nowhere, she catwalks if she were a marionette, a wooden object, one on which clothes are hung. Her almost anorexic body, whose bosom, belly, hips, buttocks must disappear in order for her to become an impersonal, androgynous form, avows its status as a hanger. In 1951, Marshall McLuhan drew attention to the "brittle, self-conscious pose of the mannequin," who "walks and behaves like a being who *sees* herself as a slick object" and is not "aware of herself as a person."[18] According to Walter Benjamin—who sees fashion as "the appearance of the new . . . reflected like one mirror in another in the appearance of the always-the-same" and thus as characterized by a "hellish repetition"—fashion represents the triumph of the commodity form in which the body has become a "gaily decked-out corpse" (thus showing "the sex appeal of the inorganic"). As he phrases it, fashion is "the provocation of death through the woman."[19] Having displayed the charm of a devitalized, estranged nature, the body becomes a cadaver-like support for clothing. Before Benjamin, in 1913, Guillaume Apollinaire had already depicted "the fashionable" as "the mask of death."[20] There is an exchange between the body and its dresses, between the organic and the inorganic.

In Christian Lacroix's words, if clothes cover and shape the body, they are also sculptures that support the body more than the body can support them.[21] In the case of Jean Paul Gaultier's bra aggressively exhibited by Madonna, for instance, it is hard to determine whether it is her body that supports and gives meaning to that piece of "undergarment" or vice versa. In an age of body culture in which fitness, wellness, diets, even surgical interventions are common and pursued at great cost for aesthetic and psychological as well as medical reasons, clothes are at times bodies and bodies clothes, as Charles Baudelaire had maintained.[22]

Such outcomes are evident in the case of a well-known contemporary fashion designer, Martin Margiela, who, while concealing subtle techniques of tailoring and dressmaking, deconstructs garments, accessories, and even fabrics to point out how clothes are made. In so doing, he deconstructs the body as well. He reveals linings and seams and uses buttons and zippers only to exhibit "the secret strategy of fashion by exposing the fetishized female body in the process of construction; he literally takes its slick perfection apart."[23] Margiela seems to echo, in reverse, Barthes's musings when he wrote that, in a profane manner, the garment reflects the ancient mystical dream of seamlessness.[24] If fashion designers used to hide the tricks of their art, Margiela, on the contrary, discloses them in order to emphasize how "the unified ideal body is artificially—and artistically—produced. . . . [He] gives us dresses . . . that bring the hidden inorganic nexus of fashion into the open by reversing the process: the lifeless model as living persona, the living human being as puppet."[25] To reduce the bodies of his models to the status of a hanger, Margiela may cover their faces with foulards, turning them into metaphysical puppets, not unlike Giorgio de Chirico's dummies. Significantly, in his 1998 collection, he replaced models with life-sized puppets, each controlled by a puppeteer. In such extreme, spectacular, iconoclastic cases, the mannequin's body is meant to lose its very life and approach the status of art. Not only are Maison Margiela assemblages often exhibited in museums, but in the 2006–7 winter collection he had his models catwalk with picture frames around their necks.[26] If the frames were used as a sort of necklace, they also outlined the function of models as living paintings.

Commenting on nineteenth-century fashion exhibitions, Gilles Lipovetsky maintains that "governed by the logic of theatricality, the fashion system was inseparable from excess, disproportion, outrageousness." And remarking on today's fashion shows, he notes that "like messages in consumer society, fashion and seduction . . . function largely by way of humour, pleasure, and playful spectacles."[27] If fashion is thus to be taken as a spectacle, clothes should be donned with a sense of amusement.

SONIA DELAUNAY

According to G. W. F. Hegel, Friedrich Schelling, and Thomas De Quincey, clothes empower the body as they magnify its movements.[28] And it is precisely over clothes conceived and realized by an artist who wanted to grant the body freedom of movement that I will linger. Sonia Delaunay (1885–1979) was the famous painter and fashion and costume designer who dressed such movie stars and celebrities as Gloria Swanson, Nancy Cunard, and Alma Gropius. Struck by the 1909 costumes designed by Léon Bakst for Diaghilev and the Ballets Russes, and by those drawn by the Fauves (especially Raoul Dufy), and reacting against Art Nouveau's excessive reliance on flowers and plants for every type of decoration, Delaunay transported modernist aesthetics onto the body through a very modern medium: fashion. At the beginning of the century, she saw clothes as ways of articulating bodies in space. With dresses that had a straight neckline, little complicated seaming, and no waistline, she gave enormous importance to color, which, in her opinion, determined the rhythms of the geometrically patterned textiles that she designed. Her garments' "purity of style, the severity of their geometric arrangement, their vigorous and vivid color were far in advance of the Art Deco fashion," but their taut angularity was also imbued with a look of luxury.[29] Taking her inspiration from popular culture as well as from her native Ukrainian folklore, she was encouraged in her under-

FIGURE 4.1 Plate from portfolio. From *Sonia Delaunay: Ses peintures, ses objets, ses tissues simultanés, ses modes* (Paris: Librairie des Arts Décoratifs Publications, 1925).

takings by Marc Chagall, who, from a similar ethnic and cultural background, was working in Paris in those years and had become a close friend of Delaunay's husband, Robert.

Delaunay was among the earliest fashion designers, if not *the* first, who came close to approaching the prêt-à-porter system of production, thanks to the *pochoir* (stencil) technique.[30] Had she pursued it, this technique would have allowed mass production of her designs without loss of tonal integrity. To celebrate clothing's freedom from and primacy over tailoring, as with Indian saris or Japanese kimonos, she also planned her textiles and garments as if they were growing from inside each other like fruits from flowers. To achieve this, Delaunay invented the so-called *tissus patrons* or the paper-pattern fabric, in which patterns germinated from designed fabrics: she printed concurrently both the cutting outline and the design of the textile to sell them in a package with the length of fabric needed to produce the garment. In this way, she facilitated the trend toward the standardization of garments. Patented by Robert, the idea insured the artistic unity of both the outline and the design. Significantly, Delaunay is imitated nowadays by Issey Miyake, for instance, in the ingenious line he launched in 1999 and named A-POC (the acronym of A Piece of Cloth). This line of clothing is based on the cut-from-one-piece principle. Characterized by a democratic universal clothing size, independent of sex and age, these garments can be cut from one piece of fabric or directly from a roll in which patterns are inserted. With the A-POC concept, a knitting machine generates a piece of cloth in which the garment has already been woven, ready to go. This process makes it possible for customers themselves to cut pieces of clothing from the roll to sew. Although this seems quite different from the Western tradition in which the shape of the body dominates, fabrics are pleated in such a way that garments yield to the wearer's shape.

As if all these novelties were not enough, Delaunay went further in her experimentation. Diana Vreeland—former consultant to the Costume Institute of the Metropolitan Museum of Art in New York and for many years editor-in-chief of *Vogue*—remarked that Delaunay's dresses were "wrapped around the body like a second skin or a mad tattoo."[31] The image of the tattoo is relevant because it also picks up Delaunay's idea that dressing was similar to writing on or painting the body. In 1921, she invented the *robe-poem,* a garment stenciled with poetic verses, following the tradition of Apollinaire's *Calligrammes.* This project indicates her desire to conceive fashion as a means of making the female body speak. She wanted to push the inner self, the personality of the wearer, to the surface to make it visible, readable, as it interacted with colors and words. "Words were thus draped across the body, setting poetry into visual motion, imbuing it with the sensuality of the female form."[32] Tristan Tzara, Louis Aragon, Philippe Soupault, and Andre Breton, among others, wrote poems and statements (some of them obscene) with which she decorated women's clothes—but also men's (mostly vests).[33] While Delaunay stopped making clothes at the outbreak of the Great Depression, in 1937 Elsa Schiaparelli picked up Delaunay's innovation: she sewed with beads a "poem" by Jean Cocteau on an evening gown.

Delaunay's dresses were thus living paintings or, better, were architectural creations on live forms. Like many artists of her time, she attempted to transcend genres and reach for a kind of synesthesia of the arts: she did not wish to distinguish between higher and lower ones (the so-called applied arts) and conceived of all her creations in textile, embroideries, bookbindings, screens, lampshades, and cushions as works of art. In effect, playing on the idea of the sister arts, Delaunay thought of her activity in fashion design as parallel to and a consequence of her achievements as a painter. Because she aimed, through her dresses, at imaginatively linking the wearer's body to its surroundings, she often had her dresses worn by mannequins photographed or filmed against a background of contemporary sculptures, buildings, cars, or against the decor of the upholstery, lampshades, or other objects of interior decoration that she created, or against her husband's paintings. Such settings were meant to emphasize and echo both the fundamentally similar lines and the points of strength in the diverse media as they intersected with one another. Fragmented into visual planes, Delaunay's clad bodies appear broken up in space but in perfect tune with their environments: indeed, in the 1920s her dresses enacted the experience of fast-paced, industrialized, metropolitan life in a staccato rhythm.

Like her husband who had invented the Simultaneity Movement and like her sister-modernist artist Virginia Woolf, who in *Mrs. Dalloway* (1925) succeeded in simultaneously presenting the past and the present of her protagonist, Delaunay's purpose in her painting and garments was that of representing the throb, bluster, and brashness of modern life.[34] As she wrote, "Our era is above all mechanical, dynamic, and visual. . . . The mechanical and the dynamic are the essential elements of the practical dimension of our time. The visual element is the spiritual characteristic of it."[35] One of her motifs was the zigzag, "suggesting a lightning flash, an electrical circuit, or a shiver," thus transmitting the idea of the "fugitive present passing by."[36] Women clad by her—with their bobbed hair, shorter skirts, and especially the meandering motifs on their dresses—became "cinematic."[37] As one critic has maintained, Delaunay "was both celebrating modernity and

FIGURE 4.2 Models in front of Citroën B12 decorated by Sonia Delaunay, Paris, 1928.

immersing the body in its surface effects."[38] She conceived dresses in a radically new way because "hers was no preoccupation with the chic, the look, the glamour of the world of fashion. She did not innovate a shape. . . . What she did was to conceive of fabric as a modus of the modern sensibility."[39]

Like her husband's paintings, Delaunay's designs used strong, even boisterous, contrasts of color and spectacular dislocations of forms to create an abstract language of form and space, or, rather, of form *in* space. In the "simultaneous dress" she devised, each color and form gains its identity through contrast with another.[40] Indeed, her dress's "simultaneity" means both that it is endowed with several characteristics at once and that it offers the possibility of appreciating its many aspects. Specifically, her garments "swirled with a set of interlocking arcs of colour across the body, with a set of triangles and rectangles cut to a point at the bottom edge, also in contrasting colours, across the skirt."[41] It is as if she cut space with colors rather than with scissors.

Delaunay believed that the perception of color values is determined by the contrast of juxtaposed tones; she was convinced that their rhythm is based on number because color can be measured in number of vibrations. As she declared, "colour is the hue of number."[42] In her mind, only colors, through their organization, dimension, and relationships on a surface, determined the rhythms of forms. Moreover, for her, form and color were one and the same.[43] If colors are the constituent components of light, light "is given volume by colour," while "the illusion of light movement . . . is adumbrated by colour."[44] Light clarifies our understanding of reality because "the activity of colours in combination transforms them from separate entities . . . into pulsating unities whose structure disallows separation in either time or space. The experience of this activity, which is visual energy, could actually reveal the concept of simultaneity."[45] As Vreeland wrote, "Colour and geometric forms each have a secret order and integrity: colour is indivisible, a primary element; geometry expresses mathematics' inviolate rules. Delaunay grasped these fundamentals and celebrated their discreet purity."[46]

Delaunay thought of her range of colors (purple, green, antique rose, yellow-orange, Nattier blue, scarlet—the colors listed by Apollinaire in a famous 1914 essay) as if they "were musical scales and took inspiration from people drinking and mixing in popular dance halls."[47] Not by chance, she loved jazz. In her mind, music and dance (the latest popular ones were the fox-trot and the tango) were "analogues of painting, founded as they are upon a concept of rhythm and interval, which in painting is entailed by the complementarity and dissonance of colour."[48] Shapes, colors, and textures (such as taffeta, tulle, wool, flannelette, watered silk, raffia, and fur) were in both complementary and dissonant relationships in her creations so as to impart them a kind of depth and visual rhythm. Her dresses were "a way of producing extended temporal relationships between visual and aural patterns—rhythms—that were symptomatic of modernity," of a style cognizant of, for instance, airplanes.[49] In effect, her imagery and abstract forms often derived from aviation.

Delaunay interpreted pictorial depth as an illusion produced by the contiguity of contrasting surfaces without creating a hierarchy of value between them. For her, depth was a function of surface design, that is, of the dynamics of the surface. Banishing color's gradations in her textiles, she often employed shapes of round, unmodulated discs of pure color (with no chiaroscuro effect) to suggest its natural interaction with light. But there are also figural references in her geometric forms: for instance, discs can also represent parts of the female body—breasts, belly, buttocks—just as shapes like "L" or "E" can recall the bend of an arm or a hand's fingers.

Delaunay began fashioning her garments in 1913; it is probably no accident that the following year connoisseur and devotee of the arts Gertrude Stein, living in Paris, published a poem titled "A Long Dress" in the "Objects" section of *Tender Buttons*. In it, Stein captures the electric element in contemporary garments and colors (like Delaunay's), anticipating in many ways Elsa Schiaparelli and her surrealist creations:

> What is the current that makes machinery, that
> makes it crackle, what is the current that presents a
> long line and a necessary waist. What is this current.
> What is the wind, what is it.
> Where is the serene length, it is there and a dark
> place is not a dark place, only a white and red are
> black, only a yellow and green are blue, a pink is
> scarlet, a bow is every color. A line distinguishes it.
> A line just distinguishes it.[50]

By associating electricity and fashion as both a "current" and a "wind" and by evoking "waste" in "waist," puns are inescapable. While emphasizing the dynamic aspect as well as the rapid decay of fashion, Stein underlines the surprising—because apparently contradictory ("a white and red are / black") or exaggerated ("a pink is / scarlet") or mixed in reverse ("a yellow and green are blue")—clashes of (possibly) Delaunay's dresses' sharp colors.[51] Stein also exalts the "length," the "line," that is, the structural style of such a "distinguish[ed]" dress: a dress that is both in vogue and refined.

Delaunay's colors often dance outside of figuration; her mostly abstract patterns tend to create a patchwork effect. But the patchwork, as has been claimed, suggests that "each element put into play . . . exists as a kind of citation, a fragment drawn from a larger fabric. . . . Although the elements may appear to form a whole . . . they are nevertheless scraps of pre-existing . . . fabrics stitched together into an assemblage." The concourse of apparently different pieces is thus the result of strategically coupled visual discontinuities, along modernist tenets. Moreover, the cutting and reassembling of pieces of fabric implies a shock and a violence: the same shock and violence that is entailed in recutting and reimagining the woman's body (as shown today by Margiela) "according to the superimposed contours of artifice."[52] In Delaunay's dresses, the body is fragmented in space in a way similar to the modernist world that fragments every aspect of life, even when its discrete, juxtaposed units tend toward amalgamation. As Chris Townsend surmises, her "surrender of consciousness in favour of sensation, her enslavement to the superficial, unifying effects of rhythm, mimes modernity's subordination of individual reflectivity, whether personal or historical."[53]

Delaunay thus represented the modernist body both as moving in space and time and as a surface. She proclaimed that a dress does not follow the body's lines; rather, it puts them at a distance and models them by reconstructing them. For her, the woman's body does not signify if it is not incarnated in fabric, if the contours of her body, rather than being accessorized by surfaces of contrasting colors, are not replaced by them. Or, better, do not enter into an integrated symbiosis with them. René Crevel wrote, "S[onia] creates, but what she creates is less a dress or a scarf than a new person."[54] Her dresses reshaped the body "not only through [their] abstract patterns but also through the images these patterns evoke."[55] If the movements of the body imparted a rhythm to the colored patterns of the dress, such patterns, in turn and simultaneously, sent the mind back to the living, moving body. Mobility was Delaunay's primary concern; she was intent upon showing "the body's freedom of movement beneath clothing and the aesthetic effects of fabric in motion." As has been pointed out, "Delaunay transferred the locus of aesthetic-erotic interest from the veiled, but imagined, body beneath to the mobile surface of her fabrics. Rather than suggesting an eroticized but still body within, her clothing invented itself as kinetic three-dimensional painting that suggests—indeed, makes patently visible—the energy and movement within."[56] A dialectic relationship was thus established between the two-dimensional, abstract geometry of her designs that enhanced the natural movement of body parts and the three-dimensional, mobile body that supported such designs. And every accessory in the dress, foremost its buttons (another detail that Schiaparelli and the Fontana Sisters would later exploit), by echoing, on a smaller scale, the same geometrical motifs of the dress, created an optical vortex on the body in movement.

The Swiss-born poet Blaise Cendrars shared Delaunay's devotion to color.[57] In his view, "Colour is a sensuous element. The senses are reality. That is why the world is coloured. The senses build. Then intelligence arises. Colours sing. . . . [Colour is] that sensuous, irrational, absurd, lyrical element which brings a painting to life surrealistically."[58] His famous 1913 poem, dedicated to Delaunay's dresses, is titled "Sur la robe elle a un corps" ("On the Dress, She has a Body"). Intensifying this disconcerting concept, he chants:

A woman's body is as modelled as my skull

Glorious

If you are incarnated with spirit . . .

My eyes are kilos that weigh the sensuality of women . . .

Colors undress . . .

The belly a moving disk

The double hull of breasts passing under the bridge of rainbows

Belly

Disk

Sun

The perpendicular cries of the colors fall on thighs.[59]

Cendrars's poem may be seen as the verbal equivalent of Delaunay's style; through his customary juxtaposition of jarred images and disjointed language, it stresses the round and curved figures in her fabrics as well as her technique of rhythm breaking. Cendrars also celebrates the simultaneity she was looking for: dress and body exist one for the other, one over the other. If the dress is studied for the body, it is the body that acts on color and design, while color and design find in the body their content. Bodies are thus not *under* dresses, they are not *beneath* their power, but enter a dialogue with them by lending them their shape (as in Miyake's clothes).[60]

While disclosing—or, better, while bringing out—the body underneath the dress, however, Cendrars also sees through the ontology implicit in Delaunay's practice, that is, "her tendency to destabilize the hierarchical relation between truth and appearance, eternal form and ephemeral ornamentation." If the textile evokes the woman's sensuality—her "glory" ("Glorieuse"), embodied in the dress—desire "is stimulated by the contrast between artificial and organic shapes," while her curves "are rivaled as a three-dimensional construct by the depth and volume created by the colors *on* the dress." In effect, Cendrars's understanding of Delaunay's garments (and his translation of their effect into poetry) makes him shift "the location of meaning from the physical body to the surfaces that adorn it, from anatomy to the body's spectacular performance."[61]

Delaunay's dresses used colors and different materials as Futurists like Giacomo Balla, Fortunato Depero, and Francesco Lo Jacono did with their vests, hats, shawls, ties, and fans.[62] She may have been influenced by them and, in turn, have influenced them, especially Gino Severini who, like her, was interested in the spinning movements glimpsed in dance halls. Yet Delaunay differed significantly from the Futurists in that she was not an elitist and did not keep everyday life at a distance from art. Her designs refer to such movements as "the gesturing shop windows, racing automobiles, the serpentine smoke of cigarettes, and the serpentine movements of women in the street."[63] She also differed from the Futurists because if they too made "clothing that was suitable for the body, whether for rhythmic dancing or the rhythmic play of light and sound on the body in the mechanized milieu of the nightclub," they used shapes and colors for more muscular and masculine purposes: "for the demands made upon the body in another equally modern environment that sublimates individuality—that of mechanised conflict," that of World War I.[64]

Beyond aesthetics there is a social, utopian project in Delaunay's concept of fashion. The results of both craft and art, her dresses were conceived as parts of a whole, of a "space" that it was the task and the responsibility of the artist to create. She meant her dresses to abolish superimposed boundaries and weave all artistic activities together, tied as they were, in her mind, by a common denominator: the dynamic principle of color. To do so she needed to bestow them upon a body that lent them its life. The risk in such a plan was that of diminishing the individual's subjectivity by emphasizing the body "en masse," as Walt Whitman had called it (though with different purposes and intentions). By sponsoring, on the one hand, "a reflexive, autonomous subjectivity threatened by the historical conditions of modernity" and, on the other, "the subsumed subject of industrial modernity," she implicitly and unwittingly risked celebrating "a loss of . . . identity within larger visual . . . environments."[65] Indeed, she risked promoting the social conditions that she implicitly criticized.

Delaunay's garments bring to mind Oscar Wilde's tongue-in-cheek definition of dress as "the *natural* expression of life's beauty."[66] Delaunay's utopian vision and Wilde's aesthetic remark, while both seeing clothes as ways of enhancing the body's charm, restore us to the biblical Eden after the Fall, when Adam and Eve, aware of their body, covered its sinful "beauty" with a "*natural*" (but also *artificial*) garb.

NOTES

1. Paola Colaiacomo, "Nudo," in *Enciclopedia della Moda* (Rome: Treccani, 2005), 411.

2. In Hebrew the two adjectives come from the same root, but whereas in Genesis 2:25 the word is pronounced "arumim," in Genesis 3:7 it is pronounced "erumim." I gratefully owe this specification to Elèna Mortara and Gianfranco Di Segni.

3. Kenneth Clark, *The Nude: A Study in Ideal Form* (New York: Pantheon, 1956), 3.

4. See "naked" and "nude" in the *OED*.

5. Although God only told Adam and Eve not to eat of the "tree of the knowledge of good and evil" (Genesis 2:17), without specifying which species of tree it was, Rashi de Troyes maintains that

they ate of the fig tree because, since God did not want any of his creations to be humiliated, the same tree that condemned them afterward helped them. *Rashi's Torah Commentary*, trans. Pinchas Doron (Northvale, N.J.: Aronson, 2000), 14.

6. Jean Chevalier and Alain Gheerbrant, *Dictionnaire des symbols* (Paris: Laffont, 1982), 716.

7. Dirk Lauwaert, "Clothing and the Inner Being," in *The Power of Fashion: About Design and Meaning*, ed. Jan Brand and José Teunissen, with Anne van der Zwaag (Arnhem: ArtEZ Press, 2006), 173.

8. Patrizia Calefato, *Moda, corpo, mito: Storia, mitologia e ossessione del corpo vestito* (Rome: Castelvecchi, 1999), 6, my translation.

9. Lauwaert, "Clothing and the Inner Being," 173.

10. Dick Lauwaert, "Morality and Fashion," in Brand and Teunissen, *Power of Fashion*, 21.

11. Lauwaert, "Clothing and the Inner Being," 173.

12. Ibid., 181.

13. Tattoos "confer human dignity on the individual; they ensure the transition from nature to culture . . . they express differences in status within a complex society" (Claude Lévi-Strauss, *Tristes Tropiques*, trans. John Weightman and Doreen Weightman [New York: Modern Library, 1997], 219).

14. Vicki Mahaffey, *Reauthorizing Joyce* (Cambridge: Cambridge University Press, 1988), 158.

15. See Giuseppe Nori, "*Sartor* in *Natura:* La filosofia dei vestiti in Carlyle e Emerson," in *Abito e Identità: Ricerche di storia letteraria e culturale*, ed. Cristina Giorcelli (Rome: Ila Palma, 2008), 8:81–122.

16. Patrizia Calefato, "Fashion as Sign System," in Brand and Teunissen, *Power of Fashion*, 132.

17. "Le corps de la *cover-girl* n'est le corps de personne" (Roland Barthes, *Système de la mode* [Paris: Seuil, 1981], 261). English translation in *The Fashion System*, trans. Matthew Ward and Richard Howard (Berkeley: University of California Press, 1990), 258–59. As the model Moncur once said of her profession, "It's an addiction, because you exist only through others' eyes. When they stop looking at you, there's nothing left" (quoted in Jennifer Craik, *The Face of Fashion: Cultural Studies in Fashion* [London: Routledge, 1994], 91).

18. Marshall McLuhan, "The Mechanical Bride," in *Essential McLuhan*, ed. Eric McLuhan and Frank Zingrone (New York: Basic Books, 1995), 25.

19. Susan Buck-Morss, *The Dialectics of Seeing: Walter Benjamin and the Arcades Project* (Cambridge, Mass.: MIT Press, 1989), 17, 108, 195, 101.

20. Guillaume Apollinaire, *The Cubist Painters: Aesthetic Meditations*, trans. Lionel Abel (New York: G. Wittenborn, 1949), 11.

21. Christian Lacroix, *On Fashion* (London: Thames and Hudson, 2007), 139. On the same page he also states, "What we notice about a distant silhouette is its volume, the outline that a skirt draws in space, the width of the sleeves."

22. "The woman and her dress—an indivisible unity" (Charles Baudelaire, *The Painter of Modern Life and Other Essays*, trans. Jonathan Mayne [New York: Phaidon, 1964], 31). "The Painter of Modern Life" was published in 1863.

23. Barbara Vinken, "Eternity: A Frill on the Dress," in Brand and Teunissen, *Power of Fashion*, 36.

24. Barthes, *Fashion System*, 137. "Le vêtement reflète à sa manière profane le vieux rêve mystique du 'sans couture'" (Barthes, *Système de la mode*, 44).

25. Vinken, "Eternity: A Frill on the Dress," 36.

26. With different purposes Yinka Shonibare also uses headless mannequins for his installations. See Paola Colaiacomo, "Lagos-Londra-Roma: I corpi senza testa di Yinka Shonibare," in *Il vestito dell'altro*, ed. Giovanna Franci and Maria Giuseppina Muzzarelli (Milano: Lupetti, 2005), 179–95.

27. Gilles Lipovetzky, *The Empire of Fashion: Dressing Modern Democracy*, trans. Catherine Porter (Princeton, N.J.: Princeton University Press, 1994), 27, 113.

28. See G. W. F. Hegel's *Aesthetics: Lectures on Fine Arts*, trans. T. M. Knox, 2 vols. (Oxford: Clarendon Press, 1975); F. W. J. Schelling's *The Philosophy of Art*, trans. P. Heath (Charlottesville: University of Virginia Press, 1978); and Thomas De Quincey's "Lessing," in *The Works of Thomas De Quincey*, ed. David Groves and Grevel Lindop (London: Pickering and Chatto, 2000), 6:26–72.

29. Arthur A. Cohen, *Sonia Delaunay* (New York: Abrams, 1975), 77.

30. In 1913, Delaunay began using the *pochoir* technique for bookbindings and collages, preferring it to etching, lithography, or woodcut. *Pochoir* allowed the reproduction of gouaches or watercolors without loss of pigment depth, texture, and chromatic energy (Burr Wallen, "Sonia Delaunay and Pochoir," *Arts Magazine* 1, no. 54 [1979]: 96–101).

31. Diana Vreeland, "Foreword," in Elizabeth Morano, *Sonia Delaunay: Art into Fashion* (New York: G. Braziller, 1986), 9. Before becoming fashion editor of *Vogue* in 1962, Vreeland (1903–89) had held the same position at *Harper's Bazaar*.

32. *Sonia Delaunay: A Retrospective* (Buffalo, N.Y.: Albright-Knox Art Gallery, 1980), 57–58.

33. Monique Schneider Maunoury, "Sonia Delaunay: The Clothing of Modernity," *Art/Fashion* 6, no. 1 (1997): 56–70.

34. "Simultaneity" was based on the concept of light as the unifying force among contrasts. It also "referred to the preoccupation of artists and writers with manifestations of modernity . . . and in particular to the impact of such innovations on the experience of time and space, such as the 'multiple awareness' of events in different parts of the world" (quoted in Tag Gronberg, "Sonia Delaunay: Fashioning the Modern Woman," *Women: A Cultural Review* 13, no. 3 [2002]: 284). Apollinaire—who wrote his poem "Fenêtres" after seeing Robert Delaunay's painting by the same title—defined Delaunay's movement as "Orphisme" (Béatrice Waggaman, "Art Abstrait Pictural et Poétique dans 'Les Fenêtres' de Delaunay et d'Apollinaire," *Revue de Littérature Comparée* 69, no. 3 [July–Sept. 1969]: 287–95). See also Virginia Spate, *Orphism: The Evolution of Non-Figurative Painting in Paris 1910–1914* (Oxford: Clarendon Press, 1979). The Delaunays, however, preferred the term "Simultanéism" to characterize their experimentation with dynamic color contrasts.

35. Quoted in Juli Highfill, "An Aesthetics of Transience: Fashion in the Spanish Avant-Garde," in *Agitese Bien! A New Look at the Hispanic Avant-Gardes*, ed. Maria T. Pao and Rafael Hernández-Rodríguez (Newark, N.J.: Juan de la Cuesta, 2002), 259.

36. Ibid., 258.

37. Gronberg, "Sonia Delaunay," 273. On several occasions Delaunay created costumes for films and ballets.

38. Chris Townsend, "Slave to the Rhythm: Sonia Delaunay's Fashion Project and the Fragmentary, Mobile Modernist Body," in Brand and Teunissen, *Power of Fashion*, 374.

39. Cohen, *Sonia Delaunay*, 81.

40. The expression "couleur simultané" refers to Michel-Eugène Chevreul's 1839 treatise titled *De la loi du contraste simultané des couleurs* in which the author theorized the dynamic counterpoint of dissonant colors when observed in complementarity. According to Cohen, "the Simultaneous meant . . . nothing less than the modern . . . it was intended to obliterate succession in time and placement in space" (Cohen, *Sonia Delaunay*, 29).

41. Townsend, "Slave to the Rhythm," 367.

42. Cohen, *Sonia Delaunay*, 68. Delaunay exerted a strong influence on the Italian shoemaker Salvatore Ferragamo, who used bold colors in geometrically patterned uppers with optical effects

long before op art. Gianni Versace, for his spring collection of 1991, declared that he had been inspired by Delaunay. In a different medium, Delaunay's poster projects for neon lighting anticipate the op art movement of the 1960s.

43. See Guy Weelen, "Robes simultanées," *L'Oeil* 60 (Dec. 1959): 78–85.

44. Cohen, *Sonia Delaunay,* 87.

45. Sherry A. Buckberrough, "An Art of Unexpected Contrasts," in *Sonia Delaunay: A Retrospect,* 104.

46. Vreeland, "Foreword," 8.

47. Townsend, "Slave to the Rhythm," 368.

48. Cohen, *Sonia Delaunay,* 68.

49. Townsend, "Slave to the Rhythm," 367, 369.

50. Gertrude Stein, *Tender Buttons* (New York: Haskell House, 1970), 17.

51. Delaunay's shocking pink would later be prominent in Elsa Schiaparelli's clothes.

52. Carrie Noland, *Poetry at Stake: Lyric Aesthetics and the Challenge of Technology* (Princeton, N.J.: Princeton University Press, 1999), 128–29.

53. Townsend, "Slave to the Rhythm," 379.

54. Quoted in Jacques Damase, *Sonia Delaunay: Rhythms and Colour* (London: Thames and Hudson, 1972), 134.

55. Noland, *Poetry at Stake,* 123.

56. Highfill, "An Aesthetics of Transience," 259, 260–61.

57. Blaise Cendrars was the pseudonym of Frédéric Sauser Hall (1887–1961). Significantly, such a pseudonym derives from the French *braises* (embers) and *cendres* (ashes). He was much inspired by advertising, especially in New York, which he visited in 1911–12. Neon signs, billboards, lights, garish colors represented for him powerful forms of visual art. "It was the visual and sensual simultaneous contrasts and, most important, the sensation of *movement* evoked by Delaunay's art that Cendrars aimed to create with words . . . his language is a kaleidoscope" (Amanda Leamon, "Simultaneity and Gender in the Premier Livre Simultané," *Symposium* 51, no. 3 [fall 1997]: 160).

58. Quoted in Cohen, *Sonia Delaunay,* 66.

59. Quoted in Noland, *Poetry at Stake,* 121–23. The poem was finally published in 1916. The last lines make one think of Delaunay's costumes for *Cléopâtre,* the ballet staged by Diaghilev in London in 1918. The original poem is as follows:

Le corps de la femme est aussi bosselé que mon crâne

Glorieuse

Si tu t'incarnes avec esprit . . .

Mes yeux sont des kilos qui pèsent la sensualité des femmes . . .

Les couleurs déshabillent . . .

Le ventre un disque qui bouge

La double conque des seins passe sous le pont des arcs-en-ciel

Ventre

Disque

Soleil

Les cris perpendiculaires des couleurs tombent sur les cuisses.

60. One might recall the later surrealistic painting *Hommage à Mack Sennet* (1934) by René Magritte.

61. Noland, *Poetry at Stake,* 120, 124, 125.

62. See Franca Zoccoli, "Gli accessori futuristi," in *Abito e Identità: Ricerche di storia letteraria e culturale,* ed. Cristina Giorcelli (Rome: Ila Palma, 2001), 4:91–127. Translated as chapter 5 of this volume.

63. Highfill, "An Aesthetics of Transience," 258.

64. Townsend, "Slave to the Rhythm," 376.

65. Ibid., 364, 362. These are the horns of the dilemma identified by Theodor Adorno as fashion's dangerous hinge. Theodor Adorno, *Aesthetic Theory,* trans. Robert Hullot-Kentor (Minneapolis: University of Minnesota Press, 1997), 316–17.

66. Oscar Wilde, "The Relation of Dress to Art," in *Miscellanies* (London: Methuen, 1908), 70 (my emphasis).

5

FUTURIST ACCESSORIES

Franca Zoccoli

"The Futurist hat shall be asymmetrical and in aggressive, festive colours. Futurist shoes shall be dynamic, each of a different shape and colour."[1] "The Futurist tie, an anti-tie of hard-wearing, shiny, lightweight metal, . . . fully reflects the sun and the blue skies that enrich us as Italians, banishing the melancholy pessimistic look from the breasts of our menfolk."[2] In various manifestos, the Futurists proclaimed a revolution in accessories, which complemented, or rather, was integral to, their revolution in clothing. Many of the artists in the movement put theory into practice. For instance, Giacomo Balla, but also Enrico Prampolini, Tullio Crali, Tato (Gugliemo Sansoni), Gerardo Dottori, Thayaht (Ernesto Michahelles), and Mino Delle Site, to name but a few, created scarves and shawls, buckles and buttons, bags and umbrellas, necklaces and bracelets. This did not cause, however, a shift in fashion trends that immediately influenced what was seen on the street—nor was it meant to. The Futurists never really aimed to place their products on the market or make them part of a process of mass production; the objects they created were handcrafted and often one-offs. These items always held a high ideological quotient because their ultimate purpose was to challenge bourgeois convention. Art historian Enrico Crispolti, who more than any other has studied the phenomenon of Futurism and fashion, argues that "every component, every clothing accessory . . . becomes . . . the direct and ideologically auto-representative sign of a provocative presence of the 'new' in everyday life."[3] Items of clothing can communicate, and their wordless, clear, immediate language has attracted the attention of sociologists and semioticians. "Fashion," writes Roland Barthes, "exists as a system of signifiers."[4]

The invention of striking and dynamic clothing accessories is true to the spirit of the *Ricostruzione futurista dell'universo*[5] *(The Futurist Reconstruction of the Universe)* that was meant to spread to every sphere of human activity and influence all aspects of life, making it joyful and charged with imagination. The first Futurist accessory was the tie that Balla designed in 1912, with its brightly colored, forceful lines.[6] It is also a work of some importance in the history of art, given that those years witnessed the beginning of abstract painting, the birth of which is traditionally taken to be 1910, the year of Wassily Kandinsky's first nonobjective watercolor. It is significant that the Futurists' joyous revolution of the wardrobe started with this particular item of male clothing, this bourgeois fetish, the tie for all seasons that has proven so resilient. After the first tie, Balla produced others in rapid succession. Later, he published *Il manifesto futurista del vestito da uomo (The Futurist Manifesto of Men's Clothing)*, first as a leaflet in French (May 20, 1914),[7] and then in Italian (September 11, 1914) under a new title *Il vestito antineutrale (The Antineutral Suit)*, undoubtedly renamed on F. T. Marinetti's insistence. By then, the Great War had begun and the leader of Futurism was an interventionist.[8] His influence can also be detected in the choice of publication date, the fateful 11th, eleven being a particularly auspicious number for Marinetti. Such details, however, are merely circumstantial and of limited interest; what is important is the content of the manifesto, an out-and-out attack on the dour seriousness and conservative, *passatist* nature of men's clothing. From the very first edition, various design models were illustrated in the manifesto, the most audacious being the "red, one-piece suit of the Futurist painter Carrà" (Carrà referring to the artist who was to wear the suit, rather than its designer). In the sketch we see two intersecting triangles from which head, hands, and feet emerge; where the two triangles meet we see the genitals, represented as two balls and an arrow pointing upward.

Although it was announced as forthcoming, a manifesto on women's clothing did not

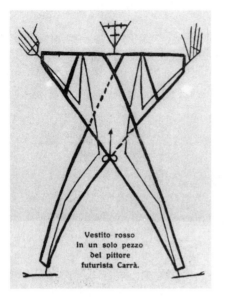

Vestito rosso
in un solo pezzo
del pittore
futurista Carrà.

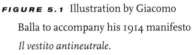

FIGURE 5.1 Illustration by Giacomo Balla to accompany his 1914 manifesto *Il vestito antineutrale.*

immediately follow. Of all possible accessories, the one that the Futurists focused on with such insistence was the tie, that symbolic accompaniment to any suit. In this field, Balla was not just the first but also the most prolific and most imaginative designer. Indeed, he worked on a vast number of ties, often brightly colored and always unconventional and provocative. Apart from those of Balla's own artistic experimentation (from his iridescent interpenetrations to dynamic patterns and lines), there are many others that deserve mention: a noise-making tie, a tie made of celluloid "quivering like jelly," and another that was box shaped with a colored light bulb inside.[9] "At electrifying points in his speech," Anton Giulio Bragaglia wrote in his diary, "he pressed a button and the tie lit up; these were his high notes."[10] The shape also changed; ties could become wider or as narrow as a piece of tape and sometimes they were tied loosely, like a scarf, rather than in the traditional fashion. Occasionally the tie became a pure triangular shape or it even took on the appearance of an airplane propeller.

Mino Delle Site came up with other ideas: in 1932, he designed ties that were asymmetrical and metallic, minuscule ties, and ties in the form of a bandage, without a knot, comprising geometric metal plates.[11] The following year a metal anti-tie was invented by painter and sculptor Renato Di Bosso and writer and poet Ignazio Scurto who organized uproarious evening events to launch their tin accessories. In clear imitation of Marinetti, who had just published a manifesto for the new Italian hat (attacking traditional, *passatist* headgear), the two men wrote a *Manifesto futurista sulla cravatta italiana* (Futurist manifesto of the Italian tie).

The painter and sculptor RENATO DI BOSSO and the poet IGNAZIO SCURTO, assisted by courageous young Futurists from the Veneto region, declare an unrelenting, aggressive and ferocious crusade against the noose-like knots of black, gray, and colored ties....

Italians! Abolish knots, bow-ties and all anti-speed, anti-hygienic and anti-optimistic frippery!...

A man's character is shown by the tie that he wears. Today, in this divine, dynamic, simultaneist motoring age, the character of a man must not be shown by a knot and a piece of material, but by the shine and the purity of metal.

Thus we invite all Italian men to boycott the ordinary tie and wear the Futurist tie, which we launched on March 27th 1933 in Verona.

The Futurist tie, an **ANTI-TIE OF HARD-WEARING SHINY LIGHTWEIGHT METAL**, is a sign that the wearer possesses flexibility, strength, intelligence, sobriety, solid ideas and an innovative Italian spirit....

The metals used should be between one and two fifths of a millimeter thick and thus be of corresponding minimum weight, while the knot must be completely abolished. It should be a few centimeters in length....

The anti-tie, held in place by a light elastic collar, fully reflects the sun and the blue skies that enrich us as Italians, banishing the melancholy pessimistic look from the breasts of our menfolk.

How ridiculous are those young men and boys who wear ties like diplomats or gloomy notaries. Mothers! Give your sons a bright shiny anti-tie which will inspire them with optimistic original ideas and dreams of light and flight.

Indeed, with the anti-tie, every man, every youth and every one of our boys will possess that aviator's look of which all Italians are worthy.

It is better to be adorned with the sunlit wing of an airplane than with a ridiculous rag. . . .

Futurists! Boycott noose-like knots!

Italians! Dress like virile men and not like those about to be hanged!

On the one hand, it is interesting to note the insistent references to the traditional tie as a noose-like knot—and therefore something that constricts and asphyxiates (an idea that had, however, already been expressed in many popular sayings); on the other hand, there is an emphatic glorification of flight. This becomes the leitmotif of the whole manifesto with recurrent references to airplanes, to the sun, to the blue sky, and to light. These were the years in which *aeropittura* triumphed throughout Italy and every creative sphere took on the prefix "aero," from *aeropoesia* to *aerodanza*.[12] True to the spirit of the times, Ignazio Scurto later married a Futurist daredevil pilot, drawing on their romance for the 1938 novel *L'aeroporto* (The airport) with a painting by his wife Barbara on the book's cover.

If Futurism was a revolution (albeit a middle-class one) against the bourgeoisie, it is not surprising that as far as clothes were concerned, criticism was particularly directed at male attire—conventional, monotonous, sad, and synonymous with conservatism—and more specifically at its symbol, the tie. The way men dressed had become established at the start of the nineteenth century, changing little since then. This had never been the case before. In the seventeenth and eighteenth centuries, during the Renaissance and even in the late Middle Ages, European men had displayed their wealth and power by wearing clothes of brightly colored velvets and silks, with sumptuous adornments, plumed hats, and lace collars and cuffs. The extreme austerity of subsequent male dress had its roots in Puritanism and was linked to the rise of capitalism. In the nineteenth century, the new hero was the successful industrialist, sworn to a religion of work of which he was the devoted officiate. The outward sign of this achieved wealth were the clothes of these men's wives and daughters. Yet there was no alternative to the industrialists' priestly garb for the paterfamilias himself.

The Futurists rose up against the unchanging, gloomy nature of this drab uniform, and their call to arms was a joyous one, particularly regarding accessories. However, they did not succeed in vanquishing the suit and tie that survived, practically intact, for the entire twentieth century. The reason for the tie's survival can also be attributed to its early development as a strong marker of sexual identity; because it is a strictly male item and also because of its traditional shape—long and pendulous—it is perceived, if only at a subliminal level, as vaguely phallic. This is why its disappearance has been fiercely resisted. Wearing ties, a hegemony threatened only by the contestation of the 1960s, consolidated power. Only in recent years have signs of its decline been seen. In an age when the middle class is collapsing in on itself, perhaps we can begin a requiem for the tie. On the eve of its supposed disappearance, however, this piece of clothing can boast an extraordinary longevity: two whole centuries.

Another item of clothing the Futurists were drawn to was the vest. Always eccentric and often brightly colored, waistcoats were to be worn even under an ordinary suit and were particularly adept at undermining the austerity of male clothing. To tell the truth, the idea of transforming this traditional item was not completely new; indeed, there was already a precedent as Robert Delaunay had created "simultaneous" vests in 1913, some ten years earlier.[13] The Futurists, however, gave to their creations a markedly subversive function and a highly ideological bias.

As with the tie, Balla made an important contribution. Beginning in the 1920s, he created vests at his own domestic studio, where his wife and daughters worked, in particular his elder daughter Luce, born in 1904. One vest displayed an abstract pattern embroidered onto canvas. It is based on the interplay of letters that spell BALLA, a motif also found on a foulard from more or less the same period.[14] In both cases, the artist works the letters into geometric abstractions to such an extent that they are indecipherable to anyone who has not been alerted to them. There are also vests decorated with "analogies of landscapes," asymmetrical designs suggesting natural views, and finally, pieces with more geometric designs whose stark wedge shapes recall the vector lines of some of his paintings, for example, a sketch from about 1930 with an elegant design of sharp triangles, executed in tones of gray and pink. Therefore, as with the ties and shawls, these items parallel the artist's paintings, and as such are marked by dynamism and chromatic inventiveness. "If the lines communicated a sense of movement and expansiveness,"

FIGURE 5.2 Giacomo Balla, "Futurist Embroidered Waistcoat," 1924–25. Courtesy Biagiotti Cigna Foundation.

writes Maurizio Calvesi, "the lively, clear, strong and vibrant colors announced a vital epiphany of light."[15]

Other vests were made in the then flourishing *case d'arte*, including the most famous studio, that of the "wizard" Fortunato Depero in Rovereto, which was in fact presided over by his wife.[16] Much more than an excellent organizer and skilled manager, Rosetta was an artist herself, creating various objects even though she always kept to the sidelines and did not acknowledge her own work. Her extremely refined skills at combining colors (albeit on the advice of her husband) contributed to making Depero's tapestries and cushions more fascinating than his paintings. Like the cushions, the vests are made from a patchwork of materials in bright, but never gaudy, colors in bold chromatic combinations. In particular, the outer face of the vest is covered with vaguely heraldic figures with floral and animal designs. These brilliantly evoke a fairy-tale atmosphere of flaming crowns, sinuous leaves, and stylized dragons of incredible vitality, but with a benevolent air. Another waistcoat, produced in Sicily and designed by Pippo Rizzo, was characterized by a decoration of applications and marked stitching to create an overall serrated, irregular effect. The Palermo workshop was extremely active in the 1930s, often producing highly original pieces.[17]

On February 26, 1933, Marinetti's *Il Manifesto futurista del cappello italiano* (The futurist manifesto of the Italian hat) appeared in the *Gazzetta del Popolo*.[18] Indeed, some members of the movement had been interested in hats from the very beginning and invented pieces soon after the publication of the original manifesto. It could hardly be otherwise: from earliest times, in every place and in every culture, headgear has been the attire that has acquired greater symbolic importance than any other as it represents the highest degree of clothing's semantic value. From a monarch's crown to tribal headdress with horns or plumage, not to mention ordinary feather-adorned hats for men and women, displaying animal or mineral attributes, headgear becomes a sign of appropriation for the wearer: it signals authority and physical strength, imparting added height and aerial grace. Even in modern times, there continues a very strong emblematic factor to hats, despite the disappearance of their more direct references. Therefore, apart from the actual manufacturing of hats—which will be touched on briefly later—there also had to be an official Futurist position on headgear.

Marinetti provided it with his manifesto. It begins with a reference that is also a decisive stance:

> The much-desired and indispensable revolution in Italian men's clothing began on September 11th 1914 with the great Futurist painter Giacomo Balla's famous manifesto, "The Antineutral Suit."

Emphasizing the importance of the fight against the bourgeois suit, and with an approving nod to the Fascist regime, Marinetti comes out strongly against the tendency of going hatless and the resulting "savagery of untidy hair, aggressive to varying degrees." Therefore, affirming the aesthetic need for the hat:

> 1. We condemn the Nordic use of black and neutral colours, which bring a muddy stagnant melancholy to the rainy, snowy and foggy streets of the city making it look as if there are enormous logs, boulders, and turtles being swept along in a brown deluge.
>
> 2. We condemn that traditional, passatist headgear that is so out of touch with the aesthetics, the practicality, and the speed of our great mechanical civilisation. For example, the pretentious top hat that prevents fast movement and attracts funerals.
>
> In August, when the Italian streets are full of blinding light and torrid silence, the black or gray hat of the man in the street drifts above, as dreary as dung.
>
> Colour! Colour is needed to compete with the sun of Italy.
>
> 3. We propose the Futurist functionality of the hat, which until today has been of little or no use to Man, but which from this day forth must illuminate him, mark him, take care of him, defend him, make him faster, and cheer him etc.
>
> We will create the following types of hat . . . :
>
> 1. The velocity hat (for everyday wear); 2. The night hat (for evening wear); 3. The luxury hat (for parades); 4. The aero-sport hat; 5. The sun hat; 6. The rain hat; 7. The mountain hat; 8. The sea hat; 9. The defence hat; 10. The poetic hat; 11. The advertising hat; 12. The simultaneous hat; 13. The plastic hat; 14. The tactile hat; 15. The light

signal hat; 16. The sound hat; 17. The radio-telephone hat; 18. The therapeutic hat (resin, camphor, or menthol with a band moderating cosmic waves); 19. The automatic greeting hat (with a system of infra-red rays); 20. The intelligent-making hat for idiots who criticise this manifesto.

They will be made of felt, velvet, straw, cork, lightweight metals, glass, celluloid, compounds, hide, sponge, fibre, neon tubing, etc. either separately or combined.

The colourful nature of these hats will bring the flavour of huge dishes of fruit and the luxury of huge jewelry shops to the streets. The streets at night will be perfumed and illuminated by melodious currents which will destroy forever the tired-out sentimentality for moonlight.

We must admit that Marinetti had his eye on the future! He predicted many things several decades in advance: a type of Walkman (the sound hat), what amounts to a mobile phone (the radio-telephone hat), and even something very like a device to protect the wearer against electromagnetic radiation (the therapeutic hat with a band to reduce cosmic waves). It is noticeable that, as with the tie, the Futurists argued not for the disappearance of the hat but for its transformation on modern, dynamic grounds. Indeed, the Second World War was eventually responsible for its demise, just as the First World War had been responsible for raising women's hemlines. Apart from the shape of the hat, the materials used in its making were to be innovative (including metals, celluloid, and neon tubes) and the colors lively. The manifesto appeared on March 5, 1933, in *Futurismo* when the Roman weekly magazine also launched a competition for a Futurist hat.[19] The famous Borsalino company took part and, encouraged by the submissions, launched their "aerodynamic hat" the following year.

As with the other accessories, Balla was a pioneer, designing a polygonal hat in 1912. While the shape was revolutionary, the color was still sober. Just two years later, the artist really unleashed his imagination, proposing adventurous color combinations in line with what he had declared in the manifesto *Il vestito antineutrale:* "The Futurist hat shall be asymmetrical and in aggressive, festive colours." From the years of the First World War throughout the 1920s, Balla not only designed headgear for men, but also worked on styles for women, the latter involving knots and woven adornments in dazzling colors. To create the possibility of making hats unique, the artist also designed *modificanti*, variants that he had already invented that, when applied, changed any item of clothing. Often it was in the design of headwear that his sense of provocation and irony was at its most extreme. Writing in 1919, Lucien Coperchot bears witness to this: "Balla also designed hats that figured trails of smoke over a woman's head; or perched on her hair like a circumflex accent, imitating the flight of a martin."[20]

While Balla was undoubtedly the most prolific designer, many other Futurists unleashed their hat fantasies too. From the post–First World War period to the beginning of the 1930s, Thayaht combined practicality with innovation in a number of designs for both sexes.[21] His final contribution was the *Manifesto per la trasformazione dell'abbigliamento maschile* (Manifesto for the transformation of male attire) that he wrote with his brother Ruggero (also known as Ram) in 1932. Among the hats (whose imaginative names often involve a play on words) are *lo spiovo* (winter headgear), *l'asole* (a light summer cloche), and *il radiotelfo* (a light traveling helmet). More or less in the same period— and some delightful sketches have survived—Marcello Nizzoli added fluttering, colorful tufts to his cloche hats, which gave them a particularly dynamic look.[22]

In 1916, Bruno Corra exhorted: "Each one of us should dress . . . in our streets . . . with a certain lively, dynamic look, wearing an eccentric hat, an imaginative tie, a pair of unusual shoes. It is necessary. It is imperative. It is urgent."[23] Hats were also on display at the *Grande esposizione nazionale futurista* (Great national Futurist exhibition) in Milan, Genoa, and Florence in 1919. Later on, Tullio Crali invented various items of headgear, including "the space hat" for women to wear with their afternoon gowns. Some of his studies survive (dated 1931 and 1932), and their elegant essential nature, edging toward abstraction, is of remarkable artistic interest.[24] In these sketches, the women's attire is adorned with imaginative headdresses in different layers, with asymmetric wings or ample brims.

Finally, we should not forget Mino Delle Site, who, a year before the Futurist competition, came up with a type of beret that was decidedly sporty but intended for everyday use. He described it as "an aerodynamic hat made of different colored felts, with a light aluminium visor-support frame and a sunshield adjustable in three positions: 1) pushed back onto the crown when not in use; 2) horizontal, as an antireflective extension to the visor; 3) vertical, like a celluloid parasol, tinted according to one's optical needs. The underside of the visor is lined in soft green cloth. This extremely useful item also allows you to wear graded spectacles." This description is accompanied by a drawing of the beret with the visor in different positions and by a table (like a concrete poem) that explains the ideology behind it. We read "abbasso la tuba e la bombetta" (down with the top hat and the bowler hat), where "down with" is expressed by the inverted letter "w," and "tuba" (top hat) and "bombetta" (bowler hat) are presented as calligrams with the letters arranged in such a way as to form the shape of the two types of hat.[25] The aim here, not just for Delle Site but for all the others, was to finish off the past and indicate a way forward to the future.

But did the Futurists really wear such controversial, outlandish clothes? The answer is not a simple yes or no; it depended on the time and on the individual. It is obvious that none of the artists dressed in Futurist style from dawn till dusk. Broadly speaking, the vests and the ties were worn—for ideological purposes—at their uproarious soirées and on other official occasions. Even this, however, was not always the case. Despite wearing items created by his friends on several occasions, Marinetti, who was well known for his elegance, generally preferred to wear a bowler hat (or a straw hat in summer). He also wore a quintessentially bourgeois dark suit or, in the evening and on ceremonial occasions, dressed in tails, a dinner jacket, or a frock coat. Various documents and photographs of the period bear witness to this.[26] Such apparently stiff conformity was, however, another, more subtle transgression; it defied the cliché of the slightly unkempt bohemian artist with a floppy cravat about his neck. In a similar vein, many other Futurists, from Umberto Boccioni and Balla to Carlo Carrà and Gino Severini, made a point of being elegant, perhaps allowing themselves to wear, as a little touch of originality, the bow tie so favored by Marinetti. In this way, it seems they wanted to assert the status that the movement had acquired; it was an experimental movement of revolt, but with an extremely serious ideological basis, ambitious plans, and a vocation to spread the word. Far from being a tramp, the follower of Futurism looked every inch the gentleman.

Without doubt, starting in 1912 when he designed some clothes for himself, it was Giacomo Balla who wore Futurist clothing more than any other artist. From Düsseldorf, where he went on business twice that year, he wrote various letters to his family describing the success of his extravagant suits, suitably accompanied by an equally original hat, shoes, gloves, and an "art tie," perhaps triangular in shape, like the one seen in a contemporary sketch. In this way, the artist made himself into a real "living plastic complex," to use an appropriate expression that Volt (Vincenzo Fani) was to coin in 1920. Every item of Balla's outfit was made in his home workshop by his wife Elisa, who, as coartist, must have been very pleased to read that "the black suit with the white stripe caused a sensation."[27] Balla continued to wear his designs for decades with the precise intention of proclaiming the new. For example, we know that he arrived in Paris for the *Exposition Internationale* in 1925 wearing a long gabardine cloak painted with dynamic "speed lines" in the colors of the Italian flag, which also appeared on the visor of his beret.[28] When working in Rome, he wore a suit of kaleidoscopic design like the work decorating his house. Both admirers and the plainly curious were allowed to visit this strange place on Sundays; the house, dazzling with the array of Futurist paintings covering the walls, was presided over by the host in his garish clothes.

Among the other artists who expressed their avant-garde credentials by dressing in this fashion were the aeropainter Tullio Crali and the sculptor Thayaht. At the beginning of the 1930s, Crali designed various items characterized by their practicality; he had three of each made and wore them in rotation, as he later claimed, almost every day. Thayaht, with the aim of publicity, often went around dressed in overalls, which he had created in 1918 as a revolutionary "suit for every occasion." He was therefore something of a pioneer in his attempt to launch the trend that has only now become established: "casual sports clothing, once strictly limited to purely informal occasions, has now spread to everyday life."[29] Cool, hygienic, comfortable, economical, and one-piece, the overalls, in line with the plastic forms of his three-dimensional works, enjoyed an extraordinary long-term success (even without industrial production).

Aside from women's headwear, there were numerous other items that the Futurists created for women, particularly shawls, foulards, and scarves, as well as jewelry, belts, and bags. Except for a few items (made 1916–18) these accessories were created later, from the 1920s onward. In general, however, the Futurists tended to be interested in male clothing and accessories. There seem to be two main reasons for this: (1) the need for a complete overhaul of the sad, monotonous, *passatist* male suit; and (2) the male chauvinism that was an unquestionable (though lately reassessed) characteristic of the Futurist avant-garde.

The manifesto of women's clothing that Balla announced he would compose in 1914 never appeared. The Futurists, therefore, hardly registered the greatest revolution to occur in the history of Western clothing since the invention of weaving replaced animal skins for material. In 1924, when Second Futurism was in full swing, women's skirts rose as far as the knee. Despite the ongoing changes in hemlines, which continued to rise or fall according to the whim of fashion, dresses would never again trail along the ground, collecting dust and hampering movement. Although appearing at the Paris fashion shows of that year, this change was largely a spontaneous one; the impetus came from the street. Indeed, for some years, women had already begun to wear less cumbersome, shorter skirts, especially in the United States, where fashions inspired by practicality have generally originated. However, this momentous shift in women's attire had no appreciable countereffect in the way the other half dressed.

In 1920, on the very threshold of this revolution, the *Manifesto della moda femminile futurista* (Manifesto of Futurist women's fashion) was written finally by Volt, an atypical follower of the movement.[30] "Women's fashion has always been more or less Futurist," he claimed, clearly referring to its various tones of color, to the vast array of materials, and to the imaginative and continually evolving patterns.[31] One essential detail, however, was ignored by Volt: practicality. For centuries this had been denied by constricting corsets, imprisoning hoops, long trains, and all the other instruments of torture, which were passed off as adornments. His lack of attention in this respect is emphasized by the fact that, among the other extravagances, he suggests "shoes of different colours and heights." Above all, Volt was interested in the fantastic potential of fashion that, in his opinion, was to be encouraged by "removing any restraints that prevent it from running, from flying dizzyingly high over the sharp peaks of the Absurd." Thus, there might be "the toilette . . . sarcastic, sonorous, noisy, deadly, explosive" and there would be "the machine gun woman," "the aircraft woman," or "the submarine woman." Based on paradox and hyperbole as means of provocation, the manifesto proposed a fashion with "the more aggressive lines and the louder colours of our Futurist paintings."

Fashion, as an "exaggerated art," would obviously remain an abstract proposal with an ideological basis. Indeed, much of the clothing for women the Futurists created was, both in shape and in the material used, fairly traditional, because it was closely tied to its practical function. This is particularly true for the shawls, scarves, and foulards produced in the various studios of the movement. What were experimental, however, were the fabric designs based on dynamic lines and vibrant colors. The square shape of a large handkerchief or the rectangle of the scarf became canvases for Futurist painting: floral syntheses, dynamic landscapes, or geometric motifs of intersecting curved and straight lines. Balla, who designed a large number of these accessories, called some of his sketches "volume forms," "lines of direction," and "currents of transmission." Indeed, the artist also paid particular attention to "scarves that, above all in the 1920s, gave him ample opportunities for decorative solutions (and were often embroidered by his daughters)."[32]

Similarly, Fortunato Depero designed brightly colored backgrounds for his triangular shawls with kaleidoscopic effects or patterns with plant and animal motifs, adopting the fairy tale–like register that characterized much of his production. The Sicilian Futurist Guglielmo Jannelli exuberantly declared in 1925:

> The irresistible impact of these decorative designs is largely due to the very violence of the color, the blinding juxtaposition of strong and bright, or soft, velvety shades; with the vigor of certain explosive forms, they illuminate and they assail, like wild and joyful fireworks, or they become entwined, like the trunk of a wisteria bush, but softer and more obedient than a woman's beautiful hair. Depero possesses a brutality that is clean,

but mighty, dazzling and thunderous . . . ultimately, there is a characteristic ironical in-clination of spirit and imagination that marks his work . . . a definite and clear individ-ual tone . . . coloring it with magic.[33]

The shawls were created by Depero two years before the competition organized by the Ditta Piatti silkworks of Como, the leaders in the field at the time. The organizers fa-vored less forceful works, and Depero was not chosen. Marcello Nizzoli, however, was among the winners. An artist of the Nuove Tendenze group, Nizzoli had a Secessionist background and he drew on these motifs, re-elaborating them creatively into elegant compositions resembling Art Deco. His scarves were innovative, without jarring the sen-sibilities of the time, and they enjoyed enormous success. Nizzoli created scarves as if they were paintings, quite often using embroidery. A fine example of the latter was the so-called *sciarpa oceanica* (ocean scarf) of 1925–26, which boasted a dynamic pattern al-luding to marine flora and fauna. Nicolay Diulgheroff (who came to Futurism from Bauhaus) and Rosita Lo Jacono worked in a similar vein. For his scarves, Diulgheroff, mindful of his East European roots, combined echoes of *Jugendstil* with the decorative, folk motifs of his homeland. In contrast, Lo Jacono used street signs, laid out with ut-most skill, for a "neckerchief."[34] This particularly inventive Sicilian artist, the "designer and maker of carpets, cushions, curtains, and plates, but also of foulards and jewelry that demonstrated her original and skillful use of geometric decoration, exhibited a good sample of her work in 1927" at the Villa Reale in Monza, where in 1923, 1925, and 1927, the most important Italian exhibitions of decorative arts were held.[35] In a category all its own is the interesting shawl-like cloak designed by Dottori in the 1930s as an acces-sory to *un vestito per avantgardista futuristista*.[36] These were the years of the Italian inva-sion and occupation of Ethiopia, and Dottori's design seems a direct expression of the imperialist political climate of the time, being clearly an appropriation of the *shamma* worn by Abyssinians. However, such an item, not painted or decorated in any way, is an absolute exception.

Various accessories were occasionally created for other Futurists. Among the many, we can mention the two shawls designed by Balla as a present for Benedetta, Marinetti's artist wife: "one dazzling in bright Futurist colors, the other more sober, in tulle, representing the natural energies of a landscape (a pond surrounded by trees, perhaps the Giardino del Lago at Villa Borghese)."[37] Benedetta, that fascinating "lady of Futurism," feted by many followers of the movement, also had an extraordinary set of jewels designed for her by Thayaht. These were as light as a breath of wind. The necklace beads resembled metal bolts but, in this case, the innovative feature was the material rather than the form—an extraordinarily light alloy that the artist named *thayahttite*, after himself. With great emphasis on practicality, the custom of adorning a woman with jewels might continue, but she should not be burdened by heavy chains around her neck and wrists or have weights hanging from the lobes of her ears.

In 1930, Thayaht denounced foreign designers for stealing many Futurist ideas: "Do you see those shoes in two colours, fresh, youthful, and sleek? Those are Futurist shoes! They are from America; but the clash of different colors and the grain of the leather, as well as the particular cut, which seems to increase the lightness of stepping forth, that combination we appreciate and which is indeed elegant, that practical combination of tactile values (leather, canvas, rubber) derives from Italian Futurism."[38] Given their dedication to "active-empowering" clothing that did not "reduce walking speed," the Futurists often showed a specific interest in shoes. Closely linked to the idea of movement, shoes were deemed extremely important because "the body, with its force and its energy, emerges" from them.[39] However, the only artist who designed and occasionally even manufactured shoes was, as ever, Giacomo Balla. An inexhaustible experimenter "beyond painting," Balla's attention was attracted by every sector and every item of fashion, particularly accessories. "Futurist shoes shall be dynamic, each of a different shape and colour," he wrote in the *Manifesto del vestito da uomo*. Nevertheless, the element of provocation was attenuated when passing from theory to practice. Each of the pair that Balla made for himself is a different color, but they are of a matched symmetrical design. Moreover, although the women's shoes he created (often for his daughters, particularly in the 1930s) have colored fabric or leather applications or dynamic lines painted on silk, they have a classic low-cut form with a medium heel.

Less of an "artist," Thayaht was more revolutionary and ideological. Interested above all in form, he gave little importance to color. Creator of the overall, in his *Avvertimenti alle "tutiste"* leaflet (Advice to female wearers of overalls), he states that this new item of clothing must be worn without a hat, stressing further that "the woman who has the courage to get rid of high heels, will be a true pioneer in the world of hygiene and art." In Thayaht's sketch (1919), *Studio di tuta da donna* (Study of female overalls), the woman wears a simple, sack-like, calf-length dress, her head uncovered, with her hair to the wind—and comfortable, rigorously flat-heeled shoes. More than ten years later, in his *Manifesto per la trasformazione dell'abbigliamento maschile,* cowritten with his brother, Thayaht confirmed his commitment to the practicality and hygiene of footwear. Here he proposed the deep-sea-diving-style galosh, the so-called *scafa*—"A heavy, shiny, self-fastening shoe that is waterproof in leather or rubber, brass and aluminium"—and the *aeroscarpa:* "A sort of light, elastic shoe, designed to provide the foot with ventilation, in light, matte colours for the summer," that is, a shoe that breathes, predating the present-day Geox brand.

Bags and handbags lend themselves to a greater variety of shapes, given that they are not required to fit any part of the body. Starting in 1916, Balla produced many of them over a fifteen-year period. They were rounded, trapezoidal, or horizontal or vertical rectangles with short handles or shoulder straps. They were occasionally embroidered and usually made from a patchwork of markedly different materials, either soft or rough, and in a great variety of grains and colors. In this way, he created an abstract decoration characterized by a dynamic impact that bore a strong resemblance to his own contemporaneous paintings. In a sketch from 1916, this dynamism includes the shoulder strap, revolutionizing even the shape so that the rounded bag breaks out toward the top into a pointed triangle on one side, while forming an empty fan-shaped semicircle on the other.

Other handbags were created in the highly productive *case d'arte* of Sicily where, among others, Gigia Corona worked, and in Tuscany, where Uberto Bonetti[40] designed an elegant "aerobag," decorated with concentric circles and the sharp nose sections of three converging airplanes touching in the middle. Again, in the South, Mino Delle Site, the "aeropainter" from Puglia, invented a sort of *ante litteram* handbag for men. It borrowed the military term *giberna* (ammunition pouch), though in this case it was designed to carry not ammunition but any object at all. With slight adjustments for male or female versions, this item went with the strictly unisex "thermal suit."

It might be surprising to find two items among Futurist women's accessories that could be defined as belonging to a *passatist* tradition: the parasol and the fan. In 1925, Vittorio Corona designed a parasol for his wife Gigia decorated with motifs of women-butterflies (the butterfly being an insect that was also dear to Balla, as his magical *futur-farfalle*—future-butterflies—testify).[41] In bright colors, Corona's parasol gave a dynamic, Futurist quality to Viennese secession forms. Three years later, Pippo Rizzo, perhaps imitating his colleague, created a parasol for his wife in which he took up the much-favored motif of dancers, so integral to the idea of movement.[42] This was the time when the fashion for suntans had already caused a decline in this once obligatory female accessory. Indeed, the parasol had survived as a mere coquetry, having lost its function of keeping a lady's skin pale. Corona and Rizzo were from Sicily, and they both worked there. This might partly explain their choice, if we give credence to there being some residual southern conservatism even in avant-garde circles. But what can be said of the fan? Its success was not limited to the provinces, but prospered on a large scale and was even popular abroad.

In 1932, Mino Delle Site used an elegant economy of lines to produce what he called a *Bozzetto di Ventaglio futurista: Auto-scafo, aerocorsa* (Sketch for a futurist fan: motorboat, air race). With a touch of apparent contradiction, he described the fan as "an accessory for sporty women, it exalts the speed and the beauty of airplanes, the motorcar, and the motorboat in an exhilarating race."[43] The different means of transport are hardly visible here; the really important features are the trails that they leave in their wake. There is a dynamic sweep across the whole breadth of the fan, and the sense of movement increases when the fan is opened.

Many years earlier, around 1918, Balla had created a masterpiece, revolutionizing the very form of the fan by giving a third dimension to its lines of force. The usual, arc-like outline of the fan is broken up, split into both aggressive irregular points and dynamic

FIGURE 5.3

Giacomo Balla,
"Sketch for a Fan,"
1918. Courtesy
Biagiotti Cigna
Foundation.

curves, while the shaped surface is covered with motifs of vibrantly colored interpenetration. The sketch made in 1923 by the Russian Suprematist Sergei Chekhonin for the magazine *Atelier* is clearly inspired by Balla's fan. The geometric decoration is less projected in this case; the individual elements of the fan, attached to the slats, open up to produce a crisp jagged line both above and below.

In both of these cases, the resulting object, highly distorted, is completely redefined. However, it is still basically a fan, and therefore an accessory that is decidedly nonfuturistic. Perhaps the Futurists' imagination was captured by its dynamic function; indeed, the fan has meaning only when it is in movement. When still, it is closed and hidden, resembling a stick. The rediscovery of the parasol and the fan might be an unconscious expression of the misogyny characterizing Futurism. On the one hand, Futurism was a movement that broke with the past, supported female emancipation, and attracted many women to it—a fact that is not as widely known as it deserves to be.[44] On the other hand, women were often kept out of the limelight and relegated to traditional roles. Above all, this was the case with Balla. Although his theories and his art were advanced and futuristic, he kept his daughters Luce and Elica psychologically cloistered like two nuns in a convent, albeit surrounded by the dazzling decorations and the bright colors of his house/studio—the most famous and spectacular of all the Futurist homes—they themselves had helped to create.[45]

A woman, Alma Fidora, was the first artist in the movement to create a fan, in 1914, the year of the *Nuove Tendenze* exhibition in Milan.[46] A painter and textile designer who was interested in the applied arts, Fidora was undoubtedly encouraged in this by her partner, Ugo Nebbia, the driving force of Tendenze (a moderate branch of Futurism) and, to a certain extent, the precursor of the *Ricostruzione futurista* (Second Futurists). The 1914 fan was the traditional shape—an open semicircle—but with dazzlingly colored abstract patterns entwined dynamically on silk.

Alma Fidora was not the only Futurist who was active in the field of the decorative arts, a field where women, in fact, made a considerable contribution. These women were strongly attracted to them as textiles and design offered an acceptable outlet for their talents, their visual-tactile perception and decorative sense developed over the centuries because women have traditionally been involved in sewing, embroidery, weaving, and pottery.[47] Yet for these very reasons, the applied arts appeared to be overidentified with women and therefore represented the danger of reinforcing the stereotype of woman as housewife—refined, decorative, and diligent. The most important women artists, from Ruzena Zatkova and Benedetta to Rosa Rosà and almost all the aeropainters, avoided the production of these objects. Nevertheless, there were others, above all wives of Futurists, who became the driving forces behind the *case d'arte,* not just as seamstresses or occasionally as inspired managers. Many designed the objects that they went on to produce themselves, although their work generally went unrecognized. Only some women became well known, such as Bruna Somenzi (Brunas)[48] and Gigia Corona and Rosita Lo Jacono.[49]

No woman's name appears among the designers who made belts, buckles, and buttons. Few Futurists were interested in them. Of these, Balla, as usual, was one of the most important. Belts for women, often conceived as independent elements, could also go with non-Futurist clothes; the dynamic patterns and lively colors take up typical Balla motifs, but here with greater recourse to symmetrical effects. A simple cloth belt, worn by his daughter Luce, was part of a dress, and the decoration is limited to the galalite buckle, recalling the abstract pattern and colors—bluish green, black, and beige—of the dress itself.

In 1932, Uberto Bonetti, designer of the aerobag, created innovative and amusing "center-belts" to attach to simple swimming costumes. Seen in his *Studio per accessori* (Study for accessories) in an enlargement of the detail on two buckles—in one an airplane flies through the sky, in the other a propeller rotates with dizzying rapidity—these symbols, these hymns to speed, acquired greater intensity on those agile and sleek bodies of young women poised to dive into a new era. Halfway between buckle and button was the disc that Thayaht suggestively positioned at pubic level in one of his designs, intended to hold the folds of an evening dress (*Une robe de Madeleine Vionnet,* 1922).

The Futurists paid attention to every item of clothing, including buttons. These, in particular, became a casus belli in the controversy surrounding the theft of Futurist ideas at the 1925 *Exposition Internationale des Arts Décoratifs et Industriels Modernes.* Interviewed on that occasion with Balla, Guglielmo Janelli made an impassioned attack, listing the cases of copied designs that could be seen in the various pavilions. According to him, many things had been imitated and rendered banal, naturally without acknowledging the originals, from the colored fur coats, velvet cloaks, and textile designs to the shoes, "an explosion of shapes and colors," and the handbags. As far as buttons were concerned, the Sicilian Janelli claimed that they could be found "produced at the stand of the Parisian Casa Bauer." Balla added, "We have the honour of saying that we have Futurist buttons before us. I have been running around like mad here; I get there *dolcemente* and I find them already made!"[50]

The artist, however, was not too concerned. Entering the fashion market was not among the aims of the Futurists, whose articles were, by their very nature, handcrafted and therefore largely limited to one-off items. The workshop at home, ready to turn inspiration into a reality faithful to the design, was considered more suitable than the factory with its mass production, extended time scale, and need for compromise. Only on some isolated occasions did the Futurists have links with fashion houses. Thayaht worked with the Parisian Maison Vionnet, and (after he had moved away from the movement but was still influenced by it) Marcello Nizzoli designed shawls and pajamas for the Ditta Piatti silkworks in Como. Marinetti's position is telling in this respect. As he claimed in a 1920 manifesto against female luxury, fashion was a flattening dictatorship that deprived a woman of individuality.

The relationship of the Futurists to fashion was therefore quite different from that of artists belonging to various other movements. Enrico Crispolti reflects that "Missing . . . from the Futurists' activity in the world of fashion . . . was that spirit—also a spirit of compromise—regarding real market principles that distinguishes the production of the *Wiener Werkstätte*. In this respect, freedom for the Futurists was absolute."[51] Futurism was clearly different from Bauhaus. They both struggled to break down the barriers between the major and minor arts, shared a keen interest in the relationship between man and the environment, and paid close attention to the material and psychological needs of ordinary people. In contrast to the Italian movement, the German school (which followed the principles of the *Deutsche Werkbund*) favored the creation of prototypes for eventual production on a large scale. Besides, the formal outcomes were also at loggerheads; in one case, there was economy of means, solidity, and rigor and, in the other, overabundance, accumulation, excess, and emotion. By choosing a "warm" approach, which in some ways anticipates postmodernism, the Futurists eschewed rational order for the natural creativity of the irrational.

The rigid uniformity of mass-produced articles clashed with the Futurists' idea of an art centered on the transitory and the ephemeral. In 1911, just after the movement had been founded, Georg Simmel wrote that fashion supplements people's "lack of importance, their inability to individualize their existence purely by their own unaided efforts, by enabling them to join a group characterized and singled out in the public consciousness by fashion alone."[52] Although they asserted a sense of belonging to their own avant-garde movement, the Futurists opposed such uniformity; they attacked the sameness of fashion where "everyone has to make themselves similar to everyone else," and "do as everyone does" so as not to "be noticed."[53]

The Futurists' emphasis on the practicality and hygiene of clothing has often been noted, but even this aspect, while undeniable in some cases, is essentially of marginal importance. The tie in the form of a box with a light bulb that could be switched on and off, shoes of different heights, hats issuing plumes of smoke, and long scarves of embroidered tulle were not exactly emblems of comfort. The Futurists were interested in dress believing that clothes and accessories take on an important role in interpersonal communication. Their aim was to shock the imagination, to amaze continually; their brief was provocation for its own sake, and this would not have been possible if their creations had been produced industrially. They would have been neutralized if they had become part of an industry with its usual trajectory of what is in and what is out of fashion. As with all utopias, there was no room for business.

The gaudy vests, the weird asymmetrical hats, and the metallic or the noise-making ties were meant to be a stroke of lightning that stimulated the imagination, a harmless bomb that exploded in optimism. The Futurist cry of rebellion would have been senseless if it had been mitigated by the reductive effect of mass circulation.

NOTES

1. Giacomo Balla, "Il vestito antineutrale—Manifesto futurista," (leaflet) September 11, 1914.

2. Renato di Bosso and Ignazio Scurto, "Manifesto futurista sulla cravatta italiana," Verona, March 1933.

3. Enrico Crispolti, *Il futurismo e la moda* (Venice: Marsilio Editori, 1986), 7. For information on Futurism and fashion see also Massimo Duranti, ed., *Futurismo: Prodromo del Centenario,* exhibition catalogue (Perugia, Italy: Effe, 2007); and Sofia Gnoli, "La velocità nella moda," in *Il mito della velocità,* ed. Eugenio Martora and Patrizia Pietrogrande, exhibition catalogue (Florence: Giunti, 2008), 40.

4. Roland Barthes, *Il sistema della moda* (Turin: Einaudi, 1970); Barthes, *The Fashion System,* trans. Matthew Ward and Richard Howard (Berkeley: University of California Press, 1990).

5. The manifesto is dated 1915 and its authors are Balla and Depero. This is considered one of

the most important of the many manifestos issued by the Futurists after the first, founding manifesto published by Filippo Tommaso Marinetti on February 20, 1909, in the French daily newspaper *Le Figaro*. An English translation of the Balla and Depero manifesto is available in Umbro Apollonio, ed., *Futurist Manifestos*, trans. Robert Brain et al. (New York: Viking Press, 1973), 197–200.

6. Giacomo Balla, born in Turin in 1871, moved to Rome in 1895. He joined Futurism in 1910 when he signed (with Boccioni, Carrà, Russolo, and Severini) *La Pittura Futurista, Manifesto Tecnico* (The manifesto of the Futurist painters), and he soon became the leading representative of the movement in Rome. From then on he took part in the most important exhibitions of the Futurists in Italy and abroad. In the mid-1930s he moved away from Futurism and abandoned it completely in 1937.

7. The title of the French publication was: "Le vêtement masculin futuriste: Manifeste." An English translation is available in Apollonio, *Futurist Manifestos*, 132–34.

8. For more information on the subject, see Crispolti, *Il futurismo e la moda*.

9. Francesco Cangiullo, "Le serate futuriste," 1930.

10. Crispolti, *Il futurismo e la moda*, 117.

11. Mino Delle Site (Domenico), born in Lecce in 1914, moved to Rome in 1930. The following year he came into contact with the Futurists and became an aeropainter. He was also active in the field of the applied arts.

12. *Il Manifesto dell'aeropittura*, signed by Marinetti, Balla, Benedetta, Depero, Dottori, Fillia, Prampolini, Somenzi, and Tato, appeared in its final version in early 1931, but already in 1929 Marinetti had published an article with the first draft of the manifesto, probably written by Mino Somenzi.

13. The contribution of Orphism to fashion was significant. Besides being painters, Robert and Sonia Delaunay were actual fashion designers. See Cristina Giorcelli, "Wearing the Body over the Dress: Sonia Delaunay's Fashionable Clothes," in this volume.

14. This vest belongs to the collection of Laura Biagiotti and is reproduced in the catalogue of the exhibition: Fabio Bensi, ed., *BALLA: Futurismo tra arte e moda—Opere della Fondazione Biagiotti-Cigna* (Milan: Leonardi Arte, 1996).

15. Maurizio Calvesi, "Da comparsa a leader del futurismo artistico: Giacomo Balla e l'arte applicata," in Bensi, *BALLA: Futurismo tra arte e moda*, 14–15.

16. Fortunato Depero, born near Trento in 1892, devoted himself to painting at an early age.

During a stay in Rome in 1913, he joined Futurism and began to take an interest in the theater (stage settings and costumes). In 1919, he settled in Rovereto (near Trento) where he opened his *casa d'arte*, carrying out wide-ranging activities that also included advertising. The artist spent two years in New York (1928–30) and held many exhibitions in Italy and abroad.

17. See Anna Maria Ruta, ed., *Fughe e ritorni: Presenze futuriste in Sicilia*, exhibition catalogue (Napoli: Electa, 1998).

18. Filippo Tommaso Marinetti, born in Alexandria, Egypt, in 1876, moved to Milan with his family in 1894. Active as a writer and critic, he wrote novels, poems, essays, pamphlets, and articles. In 1909, he created Futurism and from then on, travelling extensively, was a tireless supporter and promoter of his movement.

19. The driving force behind this weekly newspaper was Mino Somenzi who cosigned the manifesto along with Enrico Prampolini and Francesco Monarchi.

20. "Balla fabrique aussi des chapeaux qui doivent figurer des volutes de fumée au-dessus de la tête des femmes, au se poser en accent circonflexe sur leur chevelure, pour imiter le vol d'un martinet" (Lucien Coperchot, *Lettres sur la jeune Italie* [Nancy, France: Berger-Levrault, 1919], 47). Quoted in Crispolti, *Il futurismo e la moda*, 100.

21. Thayaht (Ernesto Michahelles) was born in Florence in 1893 into a family of Anglo-Swiss origin. A complex artist—painter, sculptor, designer, writer, inventor—he spent periods in Paris where he designed clothing for the Maison Vionnet. He also went to the United States where he attended courses at Harvard University. He took part in many important exhibitions including Futurist shows.

22. Marcello Nizzoli, born near Reggio Emilia in 1887, was a painter and a designer. In 1914, he joined the group Nuove Tendenze (considered the moderate wing of Futurism) and exhibited with them in Milan. He was active in the field of the applied arts and particularly interested in the decoration of fabrics.

23. Bruno Corra, "E' bene dipingere subito il mondo," *L'Italia futurista* 1, no. 1 (June 1, 1916). Bruno Corra (Bruno Ginanni Corradini), born in Ravenna in 1892, was a writer. He is the author of Futurist theoretical essays and a novel. In 1915, he published theater syntheses with Marinetti.

24. Tullio Crali, born in Dalmatia in 1910, encountered Futurism in the mid-1920s. He often took part in the Futurist shows of aeropainting. Besides being a painter, he was also active in the fields of stage design, advertising, and fashion.

25. Drawing and text are published by Crispolti, *Il futurismo e la moda*.

26. Much photographic documentation can be found in Geno Pampaloni, *Mario Verdone, I futuristi italiani* (Florence: Le Lettere, 1977). The best-known photograph was taken in Paris, in February 1912, on the occasion of the exhibition *Les peintres futuristes italiens*. We can see Marinetti in the middle, Russolo and Carrà to the left, Boccioni and Severini to the right.

27. Elica Balla, *Conballa* (Milan: Multipla Edizioni, 1986), 279–82.

28. This was the *Exposition Internationale des Arts Décoratifs et Industriels Modernes* from which Art Deco derived its name.

29. Ugo Volli, *Block Modes: Il linguaggio del corpo e della moda* (Milan: Lupetti, 1998), 83.

30. Volt (Vincenzo Fani) was born in Viterbo in 1888. A writer (particularly journalism) and a diplomat, after meeting Marinetti he became interested in Futurism and wrote *tavole parolibere* (free-word compositions).

31. The manifesto was published in *Roma futurista III* 72 (February 29, 1920).

32. Enrico Crispolti, "Balla oltre la pittura: La 'ricostruzione futurista' della moda," in Bensi, *BALLA: Futurismo tra arte e moda*, 22.

33. Guglielmo Jannelli, "I futuristi italiani all'Esposizione Internazionale di Parigi," *Trentino* 7 (July 1925), 135–36.

34. Some works of the artist were exhibited in Palermo in the show *Fughe e ritorni*.

35. Anty Pansera in Ruta, *Fughe e ritorni*, 84.

36. Gerardo Dottori, born in Perugia in 1884, was the most important aeropainter. After meeting Balla toward the end of 1911, he joined Futurism and founded the Futurist group of Perugia. Beginning in 1920, he took part in many important exhibitions, in Italy and abroad. During his stay in Rome (1926–39), he became a leading figure in the movement.

37. Franca Zoccoli, *Benedetta Cappa Marinetti: Queen of Futurism* (New York: Midmarch Arts Press, 2003), 29.

38. Volli, *Block Modes*, 81.

39. Ibid.

40. Inspired by drawings by Depero, Uberto Bonetti designed Burlamacco, the clownish figure that symbolizes the Carnival of Viareggio, the city where the artist was born (1909) and lived.

41. Vittorio Corona, born in Palermo in 1901, was one of the leading artists of the Futurist group in Sicily. A painter, he was also interested in the applied arts. After coming into contact with the

movement in the early 1920s, he exhibited with the Futurists for a decade. In the 1930s, he gradually moved away from Futurism.

42. Pippo Rizzo, born near Palermo in 1897, was a painter and a designer. He met Marinetti and Balla in Rome in 1919, but had already shown his interest in the movement earlier. Back in Palermo in 1922, he opened a *casa d'arte* where he created objects for interior decoration. Renato Guttuso was among his pupils. For about ten years, before he left the movement, Rizzo was the most important representative of Futurism in Sicily.

43. Enrico Crispolti, *Mino Delle Site: Aeropittore e oltre, dal 1930,* exhibition catalogue (Lecce, 1989).

44. See Mirella Bentivoglio and Franca Zoccoli, *Women Artists of Italian Futurism* (New York: Midmarch Arts Press, 1997).

45. See Zoccoli in *Women Artists of Italian Futurism,* 144–45 and 192.

46. Alma Fidora was born in Milan in 1894, where she met the critic Ugo Nebbia and exhibited at the show of the Nuove Tendenze group. Active in the field of the applied arts (mainly textiles but also glass) she was also an aeropainter, but almost all of her pictures were destroyed during the First and Second World Wars. For more information, see Zoccoli in *Women Artists of Italian Futurism,* 93–95 and Franca Zoccoli, *Futuriste delle arti visive* (Rome: De Luca Editori, 2008).

47. For more information about textiles created by women in that period, see Pier Paolo Pancotto, *Artiste a Roma nella prima metà del '900* (Rome: Palombi Editore, 2006).

48. See Anna Maria Ruta, "Farfalle d'acciaio," in *Avanguardie femminili in Italia e in Russia, 1910–1940* (Milan: Mazzotta, 2007), 36.

49. Both Sicilian, Corona and Lo Jacono were rediscovered thanks to research by Anna Maria Ruta. See her works: *Arredi futuristi: Episodi delle Case d'Arte Futuriste* (Palermo: Novecento, 1985) and *Fughe e ritorni.* Gigia Corona was the wife of Vittorio.

50. Pier Luigi Fortunati, "I futuristi italiani all'Esposizione Internazionale d'Arte Decorativa di Parigi: Intervista con Giacomo Balla e Guglielmo Jannelli," *L'Impero* 20 (June 2, 1925).

51. Crispolti, "Balla oltre la pittura," 23.

52. Georg Simmel, "The Philosophy of Fashion," in *The Consumption Reader,* ed. David B. Clarke et al. (London: Routledge, 2003), 241.

53. Edmund Goblot, *La barrière et le niveau* (Paris: Presses Universitaires de France, 1925).

6

COCO, ZELDA, SARA, DAISY, AND NICOLE
ACCESSORIES FOR NEW WAYS OF BEING A WOMAN

Martha Banta

There are certain periods (quite rare, indeed) when the so-called addendum of accessories do more than *reflect* shifts in fashion, when they do more than *define* an era's deepest desires and achievements, when they do an exceptional thing by actually *creating* the social and cultural milieu. This is not a matter of a single item being used to adorn a woman's costume; it involves a highly charged cluster of visible manifestations of inner impulses. When this occurs, credit cannot be given to a single event or individual, but the instances addressed here are clearly marked by overturnings of everything after the First World War and by the catalyst provided by Gabrielle "Coco" Chanel. The story of Chanel's impact on the 1920s is extraordinary, but so too are the chronicles of Gerald and Sara Murphy and their friends F. Scott and Zelda Fitzgerald and the fates of Daisy and Nicole narrated in *The Great Gatsby* and *Tender Is the Night*.

To trace, however briefly, the time line that gives context to Chanel's evolving career, one goes first through the subtle but telling alterations in fashion taking place in France between 1900 and the start of the Great European War; next a glance at the startlingly rapid social shifts of those tumultuous years; finally a plunge into a world experienced as for the first time, variously called the Jazz Age, the Roaring Twenties, and the Flapper

Era. This time line marks the gestation of the New Woman brought into being by Gabrielle Chanel, the iconoclast who rearranged society's sexual categories and realigned traditional gender identities. Like her creator, this new species was forever experimenting with provocative forms of self-expression through the feminization of the masculine, the celebration of youth, and the replacement of the salon with the sporting life. Not that there was not a dark side to these changes: the tendency to self-destructiveness (an unbearable lightness of being that resulted from hurtling oneself too quickly into an unknown future while not caring a damn for happiness) and self-erasure (the danger of becoming a product whose only motive is to possess products).

These major moves command the forefront of this essay through its scrutiny of the accessories to personal existence introduced by Chanel, borne out by the lives shared by the Murphys and the Fitzgeralds and the events imbedded in *The Great Gatsby* and *Tender Is the Night*. What will not be reviewed at any length is the life story of Gabrielle "Coco" Chanel, as fascinating as it may be. The more sensational details of her story (her peasant background and illegitimate birth, the initial irregularity of her social status, and her multitude of lovers, including Igor Stravinsky, the Grand Duke Dimitri Pavlovich, and the Duke of Westminster) are available in a large number of (often gossipy) biographies, three of which will be cited as providing useful information for her career. To follow the example of the famed Chanel look, all is here stripped back to the essential "accessories" that matter most to the essay's argument: the facts that the Chanel style was derived from the ability to negotiate her way in a world run by men; that a woman once dependent on financial support from various lovers had to escape the label of "kept woman"; that the neat little hats, casual slacks, easy-going pullovers, gorgeously fake jewels, and entrancing perfumes were inspired by the life she had had to live as well as the one she chose for herself. Then there are the "accessories" modeled with pride, but often at great emotional cost, by Scott and Zelda Fitzgerald and their friends Gerald and Sara Murphy. First comes "Chanel's World," which outlines the historical and social circumstances that were the "givens" of her generation. Next is "The Chanel Woman," the figure of independence she actively created by means of the styles she introduced into the social scene. "The Chanel Look" follows with its examination of the inner essentials of that woman and the specific external accoutrements Chanel marketed with such élan. This leads inevitably to the conclusion—"Marketing Products/Becoming an Accessory."

CHANEL'S WORLD

The historical scene of 1900 into which Gabrielle Chanel first entered as a village naïf of seventeen was definitely a man's world. If a woman aspired to be more than a decorative object that ornamented the social decor and required masculine backing, she had to learn how to make her way in that world on terms that simultaneously pleased men and satisfied herself. Without question there were brilliant designers in control of the Parisian fashion scene, whose couture models provided both impetus and obstacles to any future Chanel might imagine for herself. By 1908, Paul Poiret had banished the corset, shortened skirts, and bobbed the hair of his models.[1] Notwithstanding Poiret's boldness and great sense of color, he did not, however, initiate a fashion revolution as radical as Chanel's would prove to be. The difference? The fact that within another ten years Chanel had begun to revolutionize the way a woman lived as well as dressed.

Chanel was quite willing to take credit for Poiret's innovations (the shorter skirts, the bobbed hair, the elimination of the corset), but by 1916, she was clearly the agent behind "such decisive changes in fashion that she compelled it to change centuries."[2] Aided by her current lover, Boy Capel, Chanel's first modest moves into fashion began in 1911 with the hats she designed and sold out of the Paris apartment of her former lover Etienne Balsan to his former mistresses. She bought flat-topped straw hats and boaters from the Galerie Lafayette and turned them out stripped of plumes and any elaborate trimmings. These "nervy little Chanel hats" had the charm of "a new form of eccentricity"; they possessed "little airs of defiance that made conversation"; and once the actress Gabrielle Dorziat wore them on stage in the 1912 production of the play based on Guy de Maupassant's *Bel Ami,* they caused the kind of sensation that starts brash young women on successful fashion careers.[3] The shop Chanel set up in Deauville with Capel's backing during the summer of 1913 was the next step in launching her adoption of the British style and textiles snatched from the locker rooms of this famous Normandy racing resort.

Until then, clients of the reigning designers were "silk-packaged, swathed in turbans and aigrettes." A turning point was reached once some of the more daring young women who, "by abandoning the 'style Scheherazade,' had already heralded the decline of both the turban and the house of Poiret."[4] Business success comes to those who know when the moment is right to shake up the rules of the game. Chanel ordered lengths of materials with which she was familiar (not only from her association with Deauville's racing establishment but from her earlier days as the companion to jockeys, grooms, and cavalry officers in Royallieur). Out of appropriated masculine fabrics she created knit pullovers and flannel blazers that were sporty, with a free and easy line that merely suggested the slender body beneath. By featuring clothes that directly opposed the prescribed look of the times, she took a great chance; but it worked, as the response to what her Deauville shop had to offer made clear. Her simply executed boaters of 1911 had made "the belle époque fruit bowls that passed for hats" seem outmoded and did away with Poiret's "orgy of feathers, colors, and dizzying pleats and folds."[5] But it was Chanel's sportswear of 1913 that drove forward in the direction of fashion function and logic. Even though Poiret's "Asiatic princesses" had been brilliantly inspired by the modernist art of Kees van Dogen, Henri Matisse, Andre Derain, Raoul Dufy, and Sergei Diaghilev's Ballets Russes, they proved too exotic as Europe edged closer to the start of World War I. Chanel's instinct for simplicity won out.

Axel Madsen views Chanel as "the fashion spirit" of the years both during and just after the war: "Fashion in clothes and much else was turned upside down as the war changed the way of life, attitudes, society, politics, and people themselves."[6] Public attire and personal mores changed radically, but the mood of the times changed even more. Scott Fitzgerald said it best in the lament voiced by his protagonist, Dick Diver, in *Tender Is the Night* on his visit to one of the French battlefields. Conflicts such as America's Civil War proved what General Ulysses S. Grant meant when he spoke of "mass butchery," but in Diver's romantic view something more terrible took place during the European conflict.

This kind of battle was invented by Lewis Carroll and Jules Verne and whoever wrote Undine, and country deacons bowling and marraines in Marseilles and girls seduced in the back lanes of Wurtenburg and Westphalia. Why, this was a love battle—there was a century of middle-class love spent here. This was the last love battle. . . . All my beautiful lovely safe world blew itself up here with the great gust of high explosive love.[7]

Lacking the resiliency for which Chanel was noted, Fitzgerald's males take things very hard. In Fitzgerald's 1925 novel *The Great Gatsby,* Jay Gatsby's "high explosive love" for Daisy Fay has its start because he (a man from nowhere, who was nothing) gains entrance into the elegant household where his upper-class princess resides because he figures as a handsome, "classless" suitor in his dashing officer's uniform. Fitzgerald intuited that war can alter men's appearance, elevate their social status, and seduce them into placing their faith in love battles; he also sensed that when war ends no simple reversion is possible to what had been before, or during, the war.

Eduoard Jozan, French aviator and briefly the lover of Zelda Fitzgerald, later commented about Fitzgerald that he kept "looking for an explanation of the world which had not yet stabilized itself after the upheaval of World War I."[8] He never found it. Life turned out to be a catastrophe that did far more harm than good both to his art and his love, and to Zelda as well. In contrast, Chanel would state, "The war helped me. Catastrophes show what one really is. In 1919 I woke up famous."[9]

One of the ways that war "helped" Chanel resulted from the alacrity by which women from "outside" of society came "inside" once the boundaries set against them melted away. Gerald and Sara Murphy are good examples of those who cared not a whit for the realignments in social ranking taking place in France. An authentic social status was their possession from birth; they did not need to struggle to claim it in either the States or in Paris or on the Riviera. But Chanel cared, and cared greatly. She had always had to, particularly given the rigid strictures applied to a woman of no background and less means whose sexuality was her only apparent means of support. As Madsen puts it with brutal candor:

The *belle epoch* had a number of euphemisms to designate the categories of the vast underclass of kept women. These ranged from the *grande horizontale* or *croqueuse de diamants* (literally, "diamond scruncher"), who destroyed fortunes and reputations and fascinated the gossip columns, through the *irreguliere*, the near-permanent mistress who for family reasons a gentleman could not marry, down through the *demi-mondaine*, the *cocotte*, the one-hundred franc "little woman," to the bordello inmate and street tart.[10]

Adrift in the early years of the twentieth century, Chanel recognized the relation between the kept woman's position and the clothes she wore. As she described them,

> All those ladies were badly dressed, in their body armour, with their bosoms out, their behinds jutting out too, bound in at the waist until they were almost cut in two. They were dressed to the teeth. Actresses and *cocottes* set the fashions, and the poor society ladies followed, with birds in their hair, false hair everywhere, and dresses that dragged on the ground and gathered mud.[11]

Chanel decided never to dress in the flamboyant, ostentatious "luxury" that declared a woman to be a man's possession. As Edmonde Charles-Roux puts it, "She already believed so strongly in the *costume* that she imagined all she had to do was not wear it to avoid being cast in the *role*."[12] Indeed, by the 1920s, Chanel achieved fame, fortune, and social élan by creating a style (only available from the House of Chanel at great expense) that insisted on a woman's independence from moneyed relations with men.[13] The Chanel look (a "uniform" of the kind that rendered Lieutenant Jay Gatsby acceptable to "good society") affirmed classlessness through the eradication of the sexual categories made overt by belle epoque attire.[14] As we shall see, Chanel also helped alter gender definitions, a quite different thing.

A given of great importance in the world Chanel inherited came from the extraordinary assaults being made on the sensory nerves of the time. Chanel herself was never fully interested in the aesthetic statements emerging in the realms of ballet, painting, and music. Rather, she was fascinated by the excitement prompted by these events and the cachet that came from belonging to the circle surrounding their creators.[15] Consider what the Chanel world looked like, sounded like, and felt like through the impact of the following productions, all of which were witnessed in person by Chanel: in 1910–11, *The Firebird, Petrushka, The Spectre of the Rose;* in 1912, *Parade* with Cubist curtains by Pablo Picasso; in 1913, the notorious opening and major social event of *The Rites of Spring* mounted by Igor Stravinsky, Vaslav Nijinsky, and Léon Bakst; in 1915, further creative eruptions courtesy of the Picasso, Stravinsky, and Jean Cocteau clique; in 1921, *Pulcinella, The Three Cornered Hat,* and the return of *The Rites of Spring;* in 1922, the designing of costumes for Cocteau's *Antigone* with Arthur Honegger's music and Picasso's sets; between 1923 and 1937, Chanel's costumes for Cocteau's *Orphée, Oedipus Roi,* and *Les Chevaliers de la Table Ronde.*

Chanel could hardly have been more involved in the Parisian art world of the 1920s, despite not fully accepting modernist aesthetics or modernism. In contrast, the Murphys were true believers.[16] After all, Gerald had left the family business behind in order to pursue his own studies in painting techniques (a mixture of realism and abstractionism) upon arriving in Paris in 1921. The American couple was deeply committed to the new art forms of Picasso, Fernand Leger, Stravinsky, and Diaghilev whose endless experimentation so excited them. "Everyday was different," they found, as they reveled in productions by Francis Poulenc and Georges Auric and of Stravinsky's *Les Noces,* and one of the highlights of Gerald's life came when he designed the backdrops for *Within the Quota,* a charming little ballet with music by Cole Porter. For the Murphys, Paris was like a "great fair" where everyone was "so young."[17]

This, then, was the world that Chanel "illustrated" and "choreographed" by means of her own notions of stylistic experimentation, creating clothes for those with the belief that being "so young" in the midst of the "great fair" of France was the gift given by the 1920s.[18]

Questions of causes and effects insist on entering into discussions of whom or what led to which consequences. So it continues to be the case as one muses over the aftermath of the Great War of 1914–18 that brought about new modes of massacre and new forms of music, painting, dance, and social behavior. These events are among the givens of history that framed Gabrielle Chanel's drive toward creating her own response to the times.[19] That something, in the broadest sense, was the image of a woman endowed with greater freedom of bodily movement and the release of imagination that gained her own desires. Chanel's chroniclers are apt to be somewhat melodramatic in describing "fragile, precious objects" that existed prior to the war—"chattels" with "fettered" bodies whose "submissiveness" would not "endanger" a man's ownership or allow them to be "part of life among the living."[20] There is no question, however, that the Chanel woman of the 1920s might dance, walk, and ride with a freedom she had not previously experienced. Independence of bodily movement meant imaginative independence as well. She could experiment, resist old rules of behavior, and *be different from* what had been expected by the male world that had previously defined her being. Not that these expectations did not continue to exist; they only came in other forms, as Chanel knew well from personal experience. Or as Scott Fitzgerald presented it in his stunning analysis of the lives of Nicole Diver and her friends in France just after the war, "They were all happy to exist in a man's world—they preserved their individuality through men and not by opposition to them. They would all three have made alternatively good courtesans or good wives not by the accident of birth but through the greater accident of finding their man or not finding him."[21]

Still, the time might come (as it did for Chanel) that a Nicole Diver might win her own love battle by fighting back against her husband's intelligence and charm: "Again she struggled with it, fighting him with her small, fine eyes, with the plush arrogance of a top dog, with her nascent transference to another man.... She fought him with her money ... her health and beauty against his physical deterioration.... And suddenly, in the space of two minutes she achieved her victory and justified herself without lie or sub-terfuge, cut the cord forever."[22]

In the United States the Chanel woman quickly became identified with the Ameri-can flapper—the special type (both "beautiful" and "damned") around which Scott Fitzgerald centered his fictions. The Flapper was the young person whose eulogy Zelda Fitzgerald presented in the essay she wrote in 1922; she was honored and lamented as the one who seized the right to live extravagantly "as a transient, poignant figure who will be dead tomorrow."[23] As Zelda described her (and lived out her life), the Flapper creates herself from both outer adornment and inner qualities in order to win the "love battle" lost during the war:

> the Flapper awoke from her lethargy of sub-deb-ism, bobbed her hair, put on her choice pair of earrings and a great deal of audacity and *rouge* and went into battle. She flirted because it was fun to flirt and wore a one-piece bathing suit because she had a good figure, she covered her face with powder and paint because she didn't need it and she refused to be bored chiefly because she wasn't boring. She was conscious that the things she did were the things she had always wanted to do. . . . She had mostly mascu-line friends, but youth does not need friends—it needs only crowds.

But youth does not last. Flappers "die" long before their bodies do since "they have to live on to any one of many bitter ends." That this would prove the fate of both Zelda Fitzgerald and Gabrielle Chanel was not something Chanel spoke of when she launched her career. She was too practical to allow so mordant a thought to intrude into her mind. She embraced the 1920s when youth and its excitements were an essential part of the atmosphere and there was fame and fortune to be had. "Living well is the best revenge" was the code taken up by the Murphys, just as it was the response to life by which Zelda and Scott Fitzgerald tried to abide until their lives crashed around them, while "Make something out of nothing" was the wisdom that grounded Chanel.[24] That "something" came from her facility at imagining how to create an art of life—in her case, aided by the flair by which she devised the style that defined that imagined life. It was the same with the Murphys: the glorious parties and pleasures they planned, the experimentation in taste they lavished upon the details of their daily doings emulated by their friends, and—above all—the resistance to the realities of what "you couldn't do anything about" (their beloved sons' illnesses and deaths) through having faith in "the invented part of life"—"the unrealistic part." As Scott Fitzgerald fought his own failures as a writer and a husband faced with Zelda's madness, he had to struggle to understand the Murphys' position. "Do you mean you don't accept those things?" Gerald's response: "Of course I accepted them, but that I didn't feel they were the important things really. . . . For me only the invented parts of our life had any real meaning." Later Fitzgerald would agree that "life was something you dominated" and that "one must learn not to take life at its own tragic valuation."[25]

Like the Murphys, Chanel was very good at "dominating" life by means of the creative imagination. Unfortunately, the Fitzgeralds expended their energies on seeking out "happenings" marked by wildly extravagant actions and irrational "dramas" that pulled them down the path of self-destruction. Chanel and the Murphys shrewdly used tactics of preservation, while the Fitzgeralds, who considered personal "conservation" uninteresting, fed imaginations that were unhealthy, not stimulants to growth. Yet *Tender Is the Night* presents a vivid scene that serves as a metaphor for the steady foundations of the House of Chanel and the Murphys' Villa America at Cap d'Antibes set in contrast with the rotting infrastructure (figuratively and literally schizophrenic) that failed to sustain the Fitzgeralds' existence. A group of partygoers in search of "happenings" goes to a house in Paris "hewn from the frame of Cardinal de Retz's palace." Outside, "the masonry, seemed rather to enclose the future so that it was an electric-like shock, a definite nervous experience, perverted as a breakfast of oatmeal and hashish, to cross that threshold, if it could be so called, into the long hall of blue steel, silver-gilt, and the myriad facets of many oddly beveled mirrors."

Two kinds of people crowd into this space with an uncanny likeness to the decor Chanel created for the House of Chanel:

There were the Americans and English who had been dissipating all spring and summer, so that now everything they did had a purely nervous inspiration. They were very quiet and lethargic at certain hours and then they exploded into sudden quarrels and breakdowns and seductions. The other class, who might be called the exploiters, was formed by the sponges, who were sober, serious people by comparison, with a purpose in life and no time for fooling. These kept their balance best in that environment.[26]

Gabrielle Chanel, accomplished exploiter, full of carefully rationalized purpose, and with no tolerance for fooling around, was the perfect person to create the look whose stylistic balance best suited environments newly "hewn" from the past.

THE CHANEL LOOK

Having absorbed the historical, cultural, and social givens of her generation, Gabrielle Chanel moved into action—tentatively at first, then with increasing rapidity and self-confidence. Her inspirations came from the sporty world of thoroughbred horse racing and, soon after, from the beach life that was coming into play along the French coast. Her own physical type aided in the choice she made early on to feminize the masculine, enhancing a slender body that was the stage on which charming tomboyishness consorted with what Jean Cocteau called her sexual virility.[27] Whatever apparent androgynous elements underlay the costuming that Chanel selected for herself and marketed to others were offset by calculated touches that unmistakably signaled female power. The postwar world would have to learn how to interpret this provocative image. Through Chanel's genius at controlling that interpretation, the consuming public came to desire the Chanel look as a valuable product.

In the 1920s, women did not want to be mistaken for boys. Looking young was what they most cared about, even though their future leads toward a tragic ending, as Zelda Fitzgerald foretold in her 1922 essay on the flappers who become "dead" once their youth has vanished.[28] Unisex and cross-dressing might also play a part in their public projections, but "straight people" preferred to confine gender switching to play: as when Chanel organized a mock wedding in which she assumed the role of best man dressed in clothes purchased in the junior boy's department of La Samaritaine, in the company of Boy Capel costumed as the bride's mother; as when Scott Fitzgerald fetchingly dressed as a chorus girl in 1915 for one of Princeton's all-male follies; as when Fitzgerald's lead couple in *Tender Is the Night*—Dick and Nicole Diver, sharers of the code-name "Dicole"—have their hair trimmed short at the same barber shop.[29]

Gabrielle Chanel compiled her hugely successful collection of items that underscored (not undermined) the new woman's provocative femininity. Packaged as a total product, the parts of the whole of the Chanel look were crucial to the accumulative look. Those "nervy" little hats in 1913 were the first of Chanel's marketing coups; another came in 1915 when the shop in Deauville featured slouchy sweaters and casually draped jersey dresses; but the first intimation of the nature of that combination of "things" later marketed as the look came when, at twenty, to satisfy her private pleasure, Chanel took a pair of jodhpurs borrowed from one of the grooms at the Royallieur stables to a local tailor to be copied. Over the next years she added shirts, jackets, and skirts (sporty clothes "to watch sports in"), introduced fabrics seldom used for couture fashions, promoted bathing suits to celebrate summers on the sandy beaches of France and Spain, and insisted that her jewelry and perfume be an integral part of the inventory of precious accessories necessary to create *the* look.

Dressing for the sporting life gained new elegance in Chanel's hands. She wore men's sweaters with jewels or cinched in at the waist with a silk scarf, and brought men's turtleneck pullovers or open-necked shirts off the polo fields into the spectator stands. Menswear fabrics (broadcloth and Scottish tweeds) were supplemented by silk from Lyon and the machine-knit jerseys Chanel procured during the war years when other fabrics were difficult to get. Chanel never ventured into the business of designing men's clothing, but by the 1920s men of consequence were displaying the same elegance of slender cut and fine materials worn by the Chanel woman. After all, if a woman's appearance was still intended to enhance her role as a male trophy, men of style and wealth also became accessories for the women who viewed them as part of their own success.[30]

Gerald Murphy was noted for the beauty of his apparel that made him stand out in his group, perhaps because Sara (a natural beauty) cared little for fashion. Both the

Fitzgeralds were singled out for their élan in public, Scott handsomely tailored, tapping a silver-headed cane on the sidewalk, and Zelda dressed expensively, simply, in brilliant colors. In the words of an acquaintance, "They were so smartly dressed and striking. . . . They were beautiful—the loveliness."[31] It is to be expected therefore that memorable scenes from *The Great Gatsby* and *Tender Is the Night* bear out how important the male look was in the Chanel world—not merely to serve as decor but to furnish the emotional force of people's desires.

Jay Gatsby expresses his aspiration to live up to the beauty he finds in Daisy Buchanan (née Fay) in a wardrobe that includes a "caramel-colored suit" and "a white flannel suit, silver shirt, and gold-colored tie."[32] When Daisy finally comes to Jay's flamboyant house on West Egg (the "wrong" side of Long Island Sound), she falls back under his spell when he throws open "two hulking patent cabinets, which held his massed suits and dressing gowns and ties, and his shirts, piled like bricks in stacks a dozen high"—an array as seductive as any that might be found in the dressing room of the Chanel woman herself. (And certainly so once Karl Lagerfeld took over the House of Chanel.)

> He took out a pile of shirts and began throwing them, one by one, before us, shirts of sheer linen and thick silk and fine flannel, which lost their folds as they fell and covered the table in many-colored disarray. While we admired he brought more and the soft rich heap mounted higher—shirts with stripes and scrolls and plaids in corals and apple-green and lavender and faint orange, with monograms of Indian blue.

How could Daisy resist this display of Gatsby's love? "Suddenly, with a strained sound, Daisy bent her head into the shirts and began to cry stormily. 'They're such beautiful shirts,' she sobbed, her voice muffled in the thick folds. 'It makes me sad because I've never seen such—such beautiful shirts before.'"[33]

Because Fitzgerald wrote tragedies rather than advertisements that celebrate the glories of high fashion, this passage foretells the betrayal of Gatsby by Daisy and his murder. The following scene from *Tender Is the Night* is also used by Fitzgerald to announce "a turning point in Dick Diver's life." "Dignified in his fine clothes, with their fine accessories, he was yet swayed and driven as an animal." Wandering through Paris, on his way to commit adultery, Dick comes to "a melancholy neighborhood" where he sees "a sign: '1000 chemises.' The shirts filled the window, piled, cravated, stuffed, or draped with shoddy grace on the showcase floor: '1000 chemises—count them!'" Nearby is a shop for "'Pompes Funèbres.' Life and death":

> But Dick's necessity of behaving as he did was a projection of some submerged reality; he was compelled to walk there, or stand there, his shirt-sleeve fitting his wrist and his coat sleeve encasing his shirt-sleeve like a sleeve-valve, his collar molded plastically to his neck, his red hair cut exactly, his hand holding his small briefcase like a dandy.

Imprisoned in the elegance of his clothes and his vanity, Dick believes himself unable to follow the life of abstention and the rejection of worldly power chosen by St. Francis of Assisi, who "once found it necessary to stand in front of a church in Ferrara, in sackcloth and ashes."[34] The death of love and hope for Dick is finally sealed as he kneels on the sand by the Mediterranean. "He raised his right hand and with a papal cross he blessed the beach from the high terrace"—an act that follows soon after Nicole "crossed herself reverently with Chanel Sixteen" in acknowledgment of her newly liberated life.[35]

Beach life with its sexual atmosphere of casual pleasures and the clothes to match was not invented by Gabrielle Chanel. Colette had been one of the first to go to the Riviera, followed shortly by the Murphys in 1923, breaking with the tradition that, once summer came to the Mediterranean, people of society escaped from the sun and sea. Before Chanel finally purchased a villa in 1928, the Fitzgeralds and the Picasso entourage were already in place at the Murphys' Villa America, and the chic crowd driving down from Paris had started to fill up the beaches around Cap d'Antibes. The Murphys first set the style of dashing functionality with Gerald's appropriation of the French sailor's striped jersey, working cap, and casual duck pants—which is how the readers of *Tender Is the Night* are introduced to the Divers' world: Dick with a jockey cap and red-striped tights and Nicole whose "bathing suit was pulled off her shoulder and her back, a ruddy, orange brown, set off by a string of creamy pearls shown in the sun."[36]

Jewels were necessary accessories for the Chanel look, intended to be worn casually in the manner practiced by Sara Murphy and replicated in Fitzgerald's portrait of Nicole Diver. Chanel always championed the use of large, obviously fake costume jewelry juxtaposed with real rubies and emeralds. Only then could the Chanel woman make clear she was not like the *cocottes* Chanel remembered from her youth—women who flaunted the extravagant gifts given by their lovers in payment for their services. Perfumes in the manner created by the House of Chanel also became a distinctive element in the total look—perfumes perfect for the 1920s because they departed from the floral fragrances of earlier times; perfumes such as the famous Chanel No. 5 introduced to sophisticates in 1923—synthetic permutations of unfamiliar odors created in league with Ernest Beaux's laboratory in Grasse.

Color was an essential component in creating the full effect. The "little black dress" became synonymous in many minds with what it meant to dress *à la Chanel;* it replaced the wearing of black for occasions of mourning with black as the perfect color for elegant afternoon and evening parties. But whiteness was also very much a Chanel accessory. Not the pristine white once restricted to strictly proper little dresses of white linen worn by innocents at the century's turn but the "free" white of clean, loose dresses, slacks, and pajamas. Once again Scott Fitzgerald serves as a chronicler of similarly staged Chanel tableaux. Daisy Buchanan and Jordan Baker in Long Island as first viewed by readers in the opening chapter of *The Great Gatsby:* "The only completely stationary object in the room was an enormous couch on which two young women were buoyed up as though upon an anchored balloon. They were both in white, and their dresses were rippling and fluttering as if they had just been blown back in after a short flight around the house." Daisy Fay in Louisville during the eager days of her reign as Southern belle: "She dressed in white, and had a little white roadster, and all day long the telephone rang in her house and excited young officers from Camp Taylor demanded the privilege of monopolizing her that night." Daisy as Jay Gatsby's object of desire: "Gatsby was overwhelmingly aware of the youth and mystery that wealth imprisons and preserves of the freshness of many clothes, and of Daisy, gleaming like silver, safe and proud above the hot struggles of the poor."[37]

FIGURE 6.1 Man Ray, *Coco Chanel,* 1935. Printed by permission of the Granger Collection, New York.

The Divers on display on the Riviera in *Tender Is the Night,* their whiteness set off against their tanned skin, that necessary accessory now that a darker hue no longer bore the class stigma of peasants who work the fields, now that women of society no longer have to swath their faces in veiling or carry parasols to protect their delicacy from the sun: "The Divers went out on the beach with her white suit and his white trunks very white against the color of their bodies." Nicole with her "white crook's eyes" appraised admiringly by her lover: "He inspected the oblong white torso joined abruptly to the brown limbs and head, and said, laughing gravely, 'You are all new like a baby.' 'With white eyes.' 'I'll take care of that.' 'It's very hard taking care of white eyes—especially the ones made in Chicago.'"[38]

Women tutored by Chanel and imaged by either Scott or Zelda Fitzgerald can be summed up in part by Jordan Baker from *The Great Gatsby:* "a slender, small-breasted girl, with an erect carriage, which she accentuated by throwing her body backward at the shoulders like a young cadet." This describes Gabrielle Chanel as well, her personality embellished by this further description of Jordan: she is "this clean, hard, limited person, who dealt in universal scepticism," whose world is inhabited by "only the pursued, the pursuing, the busy, and the tired."[39] The key here is that the Gabrielles and the Jordans of the 1920s are highly perfected manifestations of the capitalist system with which Chanel allied herself in order to make her fortune possible. It is, however, the power of Scott Fitzgerald's portrayal of Nicole Diver that forces us to see what it means to be the primary engine of a consumerist system that transforms one into both "the pursued and the pursuing." This is Nicole out shopping along the Riviera:

> Nicole bought from a great list that ran two pages, and bought the things in the windows besides. She bought colored beads, folding beach cushions, artificial flowers, honey, a guest bed, bags, scarfs, love birds, miniatures for a doll's house and three yards of some new cloth the color of prawns. She bought a dozen bathing suits, a rubber alligator, a travelling chess set of gold and ivory, big linen handkerchiefs for Abe, two chamois leather jackets of kingfisher blue and burning bush from Hermes—bought all these things not a bit like a high-class courtesan buying underwear and jewels, which were after all professional equipment and insurance—but with an entirely different point of view.

Fitzgerald makes clear that his American heiress, Nicole Diver, buys all these "things" —by and large, unnecessary products—as the consequence of her own entanglement in the worldwide business of production:

> Nicole was the product of much ingenuity and toil. For her sake trains began their run at Chicago and traversed the round belly of the continent to California; chicle factories

fumed and link belts grew link by link in factories; men mixed toothpicks in vats and drew mouthwash out of copper hogsheads; girls canned tomatoes quickly in August or worked rudely at the Five-and-Ten on Christmas Eve; half-breed Indians toiled on Brazilian coffee plantations and dreamers were muscled out of patent rights in new tractors—these were some of the people who gave a tithe to Nicole, and as the whole system swayed and thundered onward it lent a feverish bloom to such processes of hers as a wholesale buying, like the flush of a fireman's face holding his post before a spreading blaze. She illustrated very simple principles, containing within herself her own doom, but illustrated them so accurately that there was grace in the procedure.[40]

One must never forget that Gabrielle Chanel ran a business, a highly successful one. Born poor, she acquired great wealth through products that enticed women to buy, with or without "grace." It is also imperative to realize that the products of the House of Chanel sold because Chanel had consciously formed herself into a new product fitting the times. Her consummate shrewdness showed her how to sell expensive items that let a woman "look poor" (nonchalantly casual and young) when the society discovered it was chic to disdain the look of a financially comfortable matron who was part of her husband's property or a bought woman who signaled her keeper's wealth.[41] She also knew how to exploit those people who will "buy anything," secure in the faith that "anything" entailed luxury.[42]

Scott Fitzgerald's rendition of the lives of the Divers (cum-Murphys) in *Tender Is the Night* depicts how narrow an edge there is between buying things and creating art—the edge along which the House of Chanel made its way. The "appurtenances" purchased by the Divers to accessorize their beach life at Antibes are unreadable to Rosemary Hoyt, the untutored onlooker: "four large parasols that made a canopy of shade, a portable bath house for dressing, a pneumatic rubber horse, new things that Rosemary had never seen, from the first burst of luxury manufacturing after the War, and probably in the hands of the first purchasers." Yet "in their absolute immobility, complete as that of the morning, she felt a purpose, a working over something, a direction, an act of creation different from any she had known."[43] This "expensive simplicity" left Rosemary unaware of its complexity and its lack of innocence, unaware that it was all a selection of quality rather than quantity from the run of the world's bazaar; and that the simplicity of behavior also, the nursery-like peace and good will, the emphasis on the simpler virtues, was part of a desperate bargain with the gods and had been attained through struggles she could not have guessed at. At that moment the Divers represented externally the exact furthermost evolution of a class.[44]

Gerald and Sara Murphy had left the United States in order to achieve the beautiful life, dedicated to art and the creation of authentic pleasure. This was possible because Gerald's father had made a success of the Mark Cross firm located on New York City's Fifth Avenue. After careful study of the accessories that defined upper-class European life, "the elder Murphy introduced, among other things, Minton china, English cut crystal, Scottish golf clubs, and Sheffield cutlery, as well as the first thermos bottle ever seen in the United States" together with the design and marketing of the first wrist watch.[45]

In the words of Edouard Jozan, Scott Fitzgerald gave himself in all seriousness to the study of "the resources of society: social position, the effectiveness and the force of money, of which, being a good American, he knew both the power and the burden. 'Ford,' he said, 'runs modern society and not the politicians who are only screens or hostages.'"[46] Unfortunately, the Fitzgeralds were themselves hostages to the "Ford" ethos; they became products as well as the extravagant purchasers of products. In 1923, *Hearst's International* ran a two-page photograph of this beautiful couple, with Scott looking all too much like the J. C. Leyendecker ads for Arrow Collars and Shirts, and Zelda wearing what she called her "Elizabeth Arden Face."[47]

Gabrielle Chanel generally managed to skirt the temptations to which the Fitzgeralds were susceptible, largely because she had quickly learned how to package herself for her own profit, not for the profit of others. She saw to it that her reputation as well as her physical image and the clothes she designed remained highly marketable. Keep in mind that she was born in 1883 (although reluctant to admit this freely); that she grew up in the provinces receiving what education she had from a local convent school; that, with a cloudy family history and an indeterminate legitimacy, she spent her life into the early 1910s under the "protection" of men in and around military camps and racing stables; that, in other words, she was a woman whom correct society could not call "proper." Yet by 1915, Chanel was on her way toward being a successful, independent woman, accepted by the people who mattered. She also began the process of redefining what it meant to be a desirable "product" of her times. Although hypothetically the same age as Chanel, Lily Bart, the heroine of Edith Wharton's *House of Mirth,* published in 1905, comes to a tragic end. Lily dressed beautifully and was strikingly attractive, but she was unable to convert her talent for tasteful consumerism into the talent for protecting her value in the American marriage market that demanded sexual purity in its female products. (She even failed when it became crucial that she be as expert a milliner as she had once been in wearing hats.) Lily dies penniless as a virgin because she lived in a society that did not "see" her as a virgin. Unlike Lily, Chanel triumphed because she, no virgin, rejected this fate by creating for herself and other young women the "look" that replaced the cachet of undamaged goods. Unlike Lily Bart, dead a mere two years before the vivacious Zelda Sayre had her "coming out" in Montgomery, Alabama, Zelda was emboldened to resist what was exacted of her sex and her class by the toast (symbolized by a vessel of cold, clear water) offered by one of the male social clubs of the University of Alabama: "To woman, lovely woman of the Southland, as pure and chaste as this sparkling water, as cold as this gleaming ice, we lift this cup, and we pledge our hearts and our lives to the protection of her virtue and chastity."[48]

By the 1920s, Chanel women figured prominently on the cultural scene in France or the United States. Who of the women viewed throughout this essay can claim being one of that estimable group, accessories to their generation? Jordan Baker certainly is, but not Daisy Fay Buchanan. Daisy had the look but not the steely stamina to take what she most desired. Her voice was "full of money—that was the inexhaustible charm that rose and fell in it, the jingle of it, the cymbals' song of it. . . . High in a white palace the king's daughter, the golden girl," but the true Chanel woman does not try to escape the world of buying and selling by staying high in a white palace, the object of another's desire.[49]

Nicole Diver, the capitalist's daughter (and victim of his incestuous desires), manages to emerge from madness with her "white crook's eyes" to dominate her life.[50] Zelda Fitzgerald also possessed the flair of the Chanel woman; she too had "strange eyes, brooding but not sad, severe, almost masculine in their directness ... perfectly level and head-on."[51] Yet Zelda would slip into the madness that Nicole was able to abandon and the realm Chanel never allowed herself to enter. Sara Murphy was *not* the Chanel woman because she did not need to be. She possessed many of her attributes: the hard, clear, direct gaze; authentic beauty; pearls spilling over her tanned shoulders; extraordinary talent for bringing pleasure into the lives of those around her; and incorruptibility. But Sara did not seek to become the complete package Chanel so successfully marketed. Content as wife and mother, she found her completeness there, not elsewhere. However, for many other women of the 1920s, Gabrielle Chanel gave them everything their hearts desired.

NOTES

1. Marcel Haedrich, *Coco Chanel: Her Life, Secrets,* trans. Charles Lam Markmann (Boston: Little Brown, 1971), 91. Haedrich also notes that Paul Poiret was the first dressmaker to market his own perfume, but only under his daughter's name. In *Chanel: A Woman of Her Own* (New York: Holt, 1990), Axel Madsen provides details (58, 66–67, 71) on the earlier influence of Charles Worth, Jacques Doucet, Madeleine Vionnet, Jeanne Paquin, and Jeanne-Marie Lanvin, none of whose establishments were able to survive the changes so perfectly represented by Chanel. Also see Martha Banta, "The Excluded Seven: Practice of Omission, Aesthetics of Refusal," in *Henry James's New York Edition: The Construction of Authorship,* ed. David McWhirter (Stanford, Calif.: Stanford University Press, 1995), in particular the bibliographical references given in 35, 37–39.

2. Chanel claimed for women "the right to be comfortable, to move about freely in their clothes." "Style" replaced "adornment" as the ruling value; expensive materials took second place to "the sudden ennoblement of 'poor' materials," making possible "the rapid growth of fashion within reach of the majority"—a striking breakthrough first seen in "the chemise dress" of knit jersey featured in America's *Harper's Bazaar* during the First World War. See Edmonde Charles-Roux, *Chanel: Her*

Life, Her World—and the Woman behind the Legend She Herself Created, trans. Nancy Amphoux (New York: Knopf, 1975), 156–58.

3. Madsen, *Chanel,* 54, 59.

4. Charles-Roux, *Chanel,* 125.

5. Madsen, *Chanel,* 68–69.

6. Ibid., 75. Poiret's lingering influence ended completely at the 1925 *Exposition Internationale des Arts Décoratifs et Industriels Modernes.* "The grand priest of extravagant assertion and theatrical abandon, of the luxurious and tactile qualities of satin, gold and silver lamé, velvet taffeta, chiffon, faille, and moire totally missed the art deco turn that made *easy* and *practical* the key words of fashion seduction." By 1925, Chanel had introduced "the Chanel suit, which, with its collarless, braid-trimmed cardigan jacket with long, tight-fitting sleeves and its graceful skirt" took over the fashion scene (ibid., 139, 163).

7. F. Scott Fitzgerald, *Tender Is the Night* (New York: Scribner's, 1933), 57.

8. Quoted by Nancy Milford in *Zelda* (New York: Harper and Row, 1970), 141.

9. Haedrich, *Coco Chanel,* 95.

10. Madsen, *Chanel,* 15.

11. Chanel quoted in Haedrich, *Coco Chanel,* 68.

12. Charles-Roux, *Chanel,* 94.

13. Chanel was not kind toward the young women under her employ whom she believed did not share her drive for independence. Notorious for underpaying the models at the House of Chanel, she told the *chef de cabine* it was unthinkable for her to consider increasing their salaries. "They are gorgeous girls, why don't they find lovers. They should have no trouble finding rich men to support them" (Madsen, *Chanel,* 160).

14. The clash between the overt sexuality of belle epoque lavishness and Chanel's tailored chic has not entirely ended. An analogy can be made between today's woman who chooses to wear the tarty extravagances of Donatella Versace and the one who prefers the severe restraint introduced by Jil Sander.

15. Miserly as Chanel was in regard to her own employees, she was enormously generous in giving financial aid to the artists of her acquaintance.

16. Details of the Murphys' embrace of the French art scene are given in Calvin Tomkins, *Living Well Is the Best Revenge* (New York: Viking, 1962). Their close friends, the Fitzgeralds, were

indifferent to the rush toward modernism in art and in literature; interestingly so, as Fitzgerald's writings are an important example of the American move into modern literary techniques and themes.

17. Ibid., 33, 42.

18. The House of Chanel flourished throughout the 1930s. It was also marked by Chanel's bitter rivalry with Elsa Schiaparelli, by her trip to Hollywood to design costumes for a Gloria Swanson film, by her increasing turn toward the right-wing views held by her lover Paul Iribe and the fright she experienced during leftist street demonstrations prior to the start of the Second World War. During the war and the occupation of Paris, her business continued, as did her liaison with Hans von Dincklage, which led to her brief arrest and quick retirement from the fashion scene immediately after the war. Then there was the debacle of her "comeback" show of 1954, followed by her reentry into favor, although more and more seen as outmoded by many. After Chanel's death in 1971, the House of Chanel passed into the hands of Karl Lagerfeld.

19. Valerie Steele, in *Fashion and Eroticism: Ideals of Feminine Beauty from the Victorian Era to the Jazz Age* (New York: Oxford University Press, 1995), dismisses "the Zeitgeist theory" that imposes "a single attitude" upon the fashions of any one period. She argues for the influence of "a multiplicity of competing and often contradictory world views" and believes that changing styles "are related not only to changes in the larger culture, but also reactions to previous fashions" (21–23). Indeed, Chanel had "history" as her inheritance before she took the chance to do something with it.

20. See Charles-Roux, *Chanel*, 96; Haedrich, *Coco Chanel*, 92.

21. Fitzgerald, *Tender Is the Night*, 53.

22. Ibid., 301–2. That Nicole becomes "free" to give herself to another man is assumed, as it was by Chanel.

23. Passages from Zelda Fitzgerald's "Eulogy on the Flapper," published in the June 1922 issue of *Metropolitan Magazine*, are given in Nancy Milford's *Zelda*, 91–92.

24. Charles-Roux, *Chanel*, 109.

25. Tomkins, *Living Well Is the Best Revenge*, 122–23. The next comments about the Fitzgeralds' mishandling of "invented lives" are from 42, 103, 109, 145, 154–55.

26. Fitzgerald, *Tender Is the Night*, 72.

27. Madsen, *Chanel*, 120. Photographs of the young Chanel (who well into middle age appeared to be a decade younger than her actual years) depict a lovely adolescent, both tantalizingly asexual and sensual.

28. Those who encountered Chanel in her seventies either accepted her studied attempts to re-tain a younger woman's appeal or were repelled, and saddened, to find this "national monument" endlessly talking, endlessly smoking, "overly made up, aggressively so, with too-red lips, oversized and over blackened eyebrows, harshly dyed hair" (Haedrich, *Coco Chanel*, 4). The fashion scene of Chanel's adolescent years nurtured the idea of women looking like little girls, fueled by the popu-larity of Colette's enormously popular "Claudine" novels. (See Madsen, *Chanel*, 35–36.) Female Pe-ter Pans take center stage in the 1958 film version of Colette's *Gigi* and the lip-smacking pleasure taken by Maurice Chevalier as he sings "Thank heaven for little girls" while surrounded by romp-ing girls in the Paris park. That no one at the time appeared to associate Colette's Claudine with Nabokov's Lolita of 1955 is itself an interesting cultural fact.

29. Charles-Roux, *Chanel*, 123–24; Fitzgerald, *Tender Is the Night*, 103, 307.

30. "Dick Diver came and brought with him a fine glowing surface on which the three women sprang like monkeys with cries of relief, perching on his shoulders, on the beautiful crown of his hat, or the gold head of his cane" (Fitzgerald, *Tender Is the Night*, 83). What better way for a man to look, who had grown up without wealth but married an heiress? As for Chanel, "What was [the Duke of] Westminster to Coco if not, first and foremost, the dazzling symbol, visible to the ends of the earth, of the success of the House of Chanel?" (Haedrich, *Coco Chanel*, 132).

31. Milford, *Zelda*, 136.

32. F. Scott Fitzgerald, *The Great Gatsby* (New York: Scribner's 1925), 65, 85. The role taken by gorgeous automobiles, necessary accessories to both Jay's and Daisy's lives, lead to death, murder, and the end of love's dream. But who can forget Gatsby's car: "It was of a rich cream color, bright with nickel, swollen here and there in its monstrous length with triumphant hat-boxes and supper-boxes and tool-boxes, and terraced with a labyrinth of wind-shields that mirrored a dozen suns" (64). It seems more like the blatant voluptuousness that courtesans paraded than the more covert eroticism the Chanel look commended.

33. Ibid., 93–94.

34. Fitzgerald, *Tender Is the Night*, 91.

35. Ibid., 314, 291. Chanel declared that no woman can have a future unless she wears perfume; in this scene, Nicole claims a future for herself, cleansed from a past poisoned by incest and mad-ness, damaged further by her unsettled marriage to her caretaker, Dr. Richard Diver. Unfortunately, as Nicole gains strength and a future, Dick declines, losing all chance at a future.

36. Ibid., 6. Shortly after, our attention is again drawn to Nicole, "her brown back hanging from

her pearls" (16). Picasso was fascinated by Sara Murphy's habit of wearing her pearls slung over her shoulder, an image he copied in certain of his "classical paintings" of this period. Nicole is described here as with a "face hard and lovely and pitiless"—the look that, in praise, Fitzgerald saw in Sara Murphy before he applied it both to Zelda and to Nicole.

37. Fitzgerald, *The Great Gatsby,* 11, 75, 150.

38. Fitzgerald, *Tender Is the Night,* 280, 295.

39. Fitzgerald, *The Great Gatsby,* 11, 181. Jordan's clean, hard look comports with the value Chanel gave to cleanliness (she praised the clean smell she associated with the *cocottes* she met in her early years and disdained the dirtiness of the society women with whom she came into contact). See Charles-Roux, *Chanel,* 202; Haedrich, *Coco Chanel,* 68; Madsen, *Chanel,* 198, 205. It is important to note that Scott Fitzgerald so liked the hard look of Sara Murphy's eyes that he endowed both Jordan Baker and Nicole Diver with the same attribute. See Tomkins, *Living Well Is the Best Revenge,* 115; Milford, *Zelda,* 120.

40. Fitzgerald, *Tender Is the Night,* 54–55.

41. "It gave women great delight to play at looking poor without having to be any the less elegant on that account." "Demanding very steep prices for her little cardigans and her daringly austere jersey sheaths, she subjugated the whole world to the snobbery of the poor look." These comments by contemporary fashion experts are quoted in Haedrich, *Coco Chanel,* 118, 172. Chanel wanted it both ways and said she was furious when some spoke of her "soup kitchen style." She said, "Nothing is more idiotic than confusing simplicity and poverty. I wonder how a suit cut out of the finest cloth, very meticulously finished, luxuriously lined, can look poor, especially when it's worn with the accessories I've made fashionable—the chains, the necklaces, the stones, the brooches, all the things that have enriched women so much and so cheaply, since they're imitation. This is just the opposite of the poor girl. Thanks to me they can walk around like millionaires" (ibid., 119).

42. During the war years (both the First and the Second World Wars), Chanel was ready to take advantage of profiteers with loose money on hand; at the same time, she had contempt for "people who insisted on possessing everything they admired." What mattered to her was that the "expensive things" be art (Charles-Roux, *Chanel,* 151, 186). It was only when she became romantically involved with the right-wing satirical cartoonist and journalist Paul Iribe that Chanel lost her balance in regard to the ambiguous qualities of luxury. Even then, Colette praised Chanel for never capitulating fully to "the contagious effluvium of gold, the indiscreet glow exuded by the weak and over-

prosperous" (ibid., 279, 285). In sharp contrast to Chanel's authenticity of self and the originality of her designs is the meretricious career of Tamara De Lempicka, who came to Paris in 1919 by way of Italy, where she reigned as socialite and portrait painter. In the words of a critic appraising her role as an Art Deco icon, Lempicka "was able to shape her career, acting out a role exactly corresponding to the expectations of the cultural moment.... *Haute couture*, expensive motor-cars, and an impeccable arrogance were essential to the formula typified by Lempicka's self-publicizing 'My Portrait,' 1929." In marketing this and like emblems "of masculine forthrightness" that barely concealed "ardent femininity," Lempicka borrowed this "formula" to glamorize the equation "woman equals modern machine" expostulated by Marcel Duchamp and Francis Picabia (comments by Roger Cardinal regarding the exhibition of Lempicka's work at London's Royal Academy of Art: "Beware: Chic at the Wheel," from *Times Literary Supplement*, August 6, 2004, 16–17).

43. Fitzgerald, *Tender Is the Night*, 18–19.

44. Ibid., 21. Fitzgerald brilliantly inserts a scene toward the end of the novel that suggests the decline (physical and moral) of Dick Diver by describing the quite different manner in which he begins to accumulate things that have no relation to the creative life: "the new paraphernalia, the trapezes over the water, the swinging rings, the portable bathhouses, the floating towers, the searchlights from last night's fetes, the modernistic buffet, white with a hackneyed motif of endless handlebars" (281).

45. Tomkins, *Living Well Is the Best Revenge*, 11–12. The younger Murphys were able with care to live as deeply involved expatriates in Paris and the Riviera throughout the 1920s until the parent store went bankrupt in 1931. Then, having lost both sons to illness, they returned to New York, where Gerald (without joy) used his innate taste and imagination to create still new items to sell at the Mark Cross store.

46. Milford, *Zelda*, 141.

47. Ibid., 128.

48. Ibid., 38. In terms of the time and the place (the 1910s in the deep South), these words carried an ominous message not only to lively young Southern belles, but also to Southern blacks, potential victims of contemporary social rituals of lynching.

49. Fitzgerald, *The Great Gatsby*, 120.

50. Fitzgerald, *Tender Is the Night*, 292, 293.

51. Gerald Murphy's description of Zelda in the mid-1920s (quoted in Milford, *Zelda*, 158).

7

PRECIOUS OBJECTS

LAURA RIDING, HER TIARA, AND THE PETRARCHAN MUSE

Becky Peterson

Unlike many women poets who subvert the Petrarchan male poet–woman muse dynamic by writing poems in which the authorial voice is female and the "inspiration" male, American poet Laura Riding collapses the entire poetic subject-object structure by depicting herself as both subject and object, poet and muse. In this way, she rejects the system of domination present in the traditional Petrarchan model. Riding's decision to assume the muse/object role—in her poetry and in her attention to dress and ornament—locates her in the company of several of her modernist contemporaries.[1] Riding's position on subject-object relations extends from a revision of Petrarchan poetics toward a radical view of feminism and a highly individualized expression of her position as a woman artist.

Throughout her career, Riding made significant use of literal and figurative "precious objects." In this essay, I focus on two types of precious objects: the elusive female muse (the inspiring, objectified figure in Western poetic tradition), and the presence of jewelry in Riding's art and life, as represented in her poetry and in a gold tiara she owned and wore.[2] Riding employs these elements to articulate the condition of otherness—by positioning herself as an object, and by paying close, serious attention to trivialized decorative objects, she talks implicitly about marginalization, particularly the marginalization of women artists. Riding theorizes the objectified Other in various forms—poetry, fiction, essay—from a position of negativity and impersonality.

For many Jewish immigrants in the early twentieth century and their children (Riding was one of these children), Jewishness was something imposed from outside.[3] Female poets at this time occupied a similar position—women were defined as muses, not writers. Riding's work asks: How might we talk about otherness from this position of passivity? How can we read in a way that makes room for the "precious object"—including the person treated as a precious object—to speak? Hovering behind my argument that Riding self-consciously positions herself as object/muse/Other is poetry's *übermuse*, the Laura of Francesco Petrarch's *Rime Sparse*. Investigating the figure who haunts Petrarchanism shows how Riding responds to a specific established cultural sense of what it means to be a woman in the world of poetry and publishing: an anomaly, a muse who frustrates by not only inspiring but writing.

Riding, the daughter of secular Jewish socialist garment workers in New York, eventually stated her dislike of the communist movement and established literary alliances with the conservative editors of the journal *Fugitive*. Riding's father, Nathaniel Reichenthal, managed a chain of clothing stores, and Riding was president of Cornell's Socialist Society while an undergraduate there.[4] Her passionate belief in the "truth" of poetry and formalist literary critique echoes the idealism of her father's socialist devotion. Both Riding and her father locate their truths in language and are committed to stripping words of hypocrisy. Jeanne Heuving, pointing to Riding's impact on New Criticism and the practice of close reading, notes that the presence of her Marxist father could reconfigure how we view the intersections of these critical movements. Heuving discusses the two possible ways Riding may have influenced the formation of New Criticism. She mentions Riding's book *A Survey of Modernist Poetry*, cowritten with Robert Graves, and its effect on William Empson. She also describes how Riding's father trained Riding to read newspapers with an eye for capitalist subtext. Of Riding's close reading with her father during childhood, Heuving notes that "if (Riding) Jackson is right [about her influence on New Criticism], a curious footnote to literary history would be the leftist derivation of a practice of reading that enabled the politically conservative New Criticism."[5]

Riding's first book, *The Close Chaplet*, was printed in 1925 by Virginia Woolf's Hogarth Press. Her poems caught the attention of Robert Graves, and she began a long-term literary and personal relationship with him. Their Seizin Press published several writers, including Riding's friend Gertrude Stein. Around 1940 (accounts vary), Riding renounced poetry, married critic Schuyler Jackson, and moved to Florida, where she continued to write prose.

Describing her first meeting with Riding in 1985, biographer Elizabeth Friedmann writes, "[Riding's] hair was pure white, the color of Christmas-tree angel-hair, and framed her face in a luxuriant halo."[6] This reference to a "halo" of hair resonates with the extreme reactions, both critically and biographically, Riding has received throughout her lifetime until the present: she is either angel or devil.[7] It also suggests a laurel-like item of jewelry that Riding owned and wore: a gold tiara, which serves as a touchstone for discussing Riding's struggle to negotiate her roles of poet/muse/critic/woman within Petrarchan, patriarchal poetic tradition. Biographer Deborah Baker mentions that after her suicide attempt in 1929, before she moved to Spain, Riding "seemed more interested in the design of a fillet for her hair (ordered by Robert [Graves] from a London goldsmith) than in her injuries."[8] Friedmann's account supports the existence of this piece of jewelry and also reveals that a poem was engraved on the ornament:

> A friend in London, a jewelry-maker, had given Laura a lovely gold chaplet that she had designed especially to mark the publication of *The Close Chaplet*. On one side was engraved the name "Laura" in Greek letters, and on the other was a short poem, a moral statement connecting Laura with truth and reason. Laura had sometimes worn it to keep her hair back from her face when she was bent over her writing table, but decided it was too elegant for everyday use and put it away to be worn on special occasions.[9]

Riding's decision to separate the tiara from "everyday use" shows how she participated in perpetuating its "precious," removed quality.

Joyce Piell Wexler quotes from T. S. Matthews's description of Riding, whose "dazzling and lightning-like brilliance," Matthews writes, was "frightening": "When she was in full regalia her dignity matched and enhanced her costume, and I can't remember anyone thinking it laughable or even eccentric that on these occasions she was crowned by a tiara of gold wire that spelled LAURA."[10] The tiara acts as crown of laurels for the poet. Matthews's word choice in describing Riding's "lightning-like brilliance" is interesting because, according to a footnote for rime 5 of Petrarch's *Rime Sparse,* "the laurel was supposedly immune from lightning."[11] Laurels have a magical, protective quality. While clothing in general provides "immunity" from the elements and from cultural taboos about undress, decorative objects such as this tiara do not usually have a function other than indicating royal status. However, in these biographical examples Riding's head ornament serves a real-life, protective purpose: it distances her from those surrounding her, maintaining a mode of control and creating for her a "full regalia" that remains unquestioned by others.

Friedmann also notes that Riding reportedly wore a picture of Graves's wife Nancy around her neck while she was romantically involved with Graves, and that she owned a scarf made for her by Len Lye with a design in the shape of the scar she developed after her suicide attempt.[12] The designs of these three ornaments (the tiara, necklace, and scarf) are explicitly—outrageously—autobiographical, a quality that infuses them with emotion and memory. In addition, Riding was a resident of Mallorca from 1929 until 1936, and accounts of her physical appearance during this time indicate that she had developed a particular clothing style that incorporated elements of folkloric Spanish dress, including a bizarre nunlike headdress. These instances serve as visual records of social taboo (suicide, extramarital sex, unconventional adornment) that reinforced Riding's status as outsider.

Focusing on the material object—specifically, the physicality of the gold tiara—opens Riding's poetry to new interpretations that fracture her rejection of biography. Considering Riding's relationship with Petrarchanism through this object and its connotations of power, status, and femininity incorporates cultural contexts alongside in-depth readings of her poetry. She has been viewed by some as disdainful of sartorial issues and dismissive of feminism. She disliked the label "feminist" and resisted poetic "tradition."[13] Locating Riding in a feminist poetic tradition, and looking at her use of materials in her art and life, is certainly not in line with her theory of how literary criticism should oper-

FIGURE 7.1 Laura Riding in traditional Mallorcan dress with the photographer Ward Hutchinson and his wife Dorothy. For a while Riding shared a home with Robert Graves in Mallorca, Spain, and William Graves, his son, remembered that "as kids, my siblings and I used the clothes Laura left in her wardrobe to dress up in for plays." Reprinted by permission of the William Graves Collection.

ate. However, resisting her own desires brings her into contemporary literary and fashion conversations as an equal worthy of rigorous materialist critique.

Riding's interest in the visual construction and perception of women, especially their dress and ornament, locates her in a particularly feminized discourse, one that voices the connections between apparel, appearance, and gender. Susan Schultz provides valuable insight into Riding's relationship with clothing as well as her role in the poet-muse tradition.[14] In her first endnote for "Of Time and Charles Bernstein's Lines: A Poetics of Fashion Statements," Schultz writes that "Laura (Riding) Jackson's dislike of fashion, in clothing and in poetry, can be found throughout her poetry and her polemics, from the beginning to the end of her bifurcated career." In "Laura Riding's Essentialism and the Absent Muse," Schultz examines how Riding's rejection of image and metaphor allows her to reject the publishing establishment as well as the conventional male poet–female muse relationship: "To write poetry that is true to poetry and not to the literary market-place, then, is to go naked and without a muse."[15] Schultz explains that Riding's self-objectification eventually resulted in her renunciation of poetry. Schultz's arguments need reconsideration; specifically, there needs to be a clear distinction between how Riding reads "fashion" in dress as opposed to "fashion" in trends in the business of poetry.

Riding certainly disapproved of the professionalization of poetry—but if we associate "fashion" with dress/clothing/ornament, there is no clear evidence for a "dislike." In addition, I don't think Riding's decision to make herself a muse should necessarily be interpreted as a motion toward self-defeat. Literary and cultural histories have remembered far more female muses than female poets—Riding's self-objectification may have been a move on her part to secure a place for herself in poetic memory. In Riding's life, dress and ornament provided a way to maintain control over how she was perceived. This was a primary concern of Riding's, especially in regard to her writing. Just as her numerous letters and articles disputing responses to her work reveal a refusal to relinquish any control to the literary establishment, her conscious attention to physical ornament allowed Riding a mode of asserting control over her self-representation.[16]

Laura, the major figure in fourteenth-century poet Petrarch's *Rime Sparse*—with her ethereal powers, inaccessible body, and symbolic name—significantly influenced the concept of the literary muse. Reflecting qualities of the mythological muses who preceded her, Laura served as an important source of inspiration for the establishment of the Petrarchan sonnet and the Renaissance lyric form, which in turn influenced twentieth-century modernist poets. For many modernists, early modern poetry itself operated as a kind of muse. For T. S. Eliot, Virginia Woolf, Ezra Pound, H.D., and others, the invocation of the past (both remembered and mythological) and the impact of poetry from the Petrarchan lineage were crucial. Robert Durling points out that, although Pound rejected Petrarch, it is necessary to consider the "affinities between [them]—their fascination with Propertius, Ovid, and the Provençal poets, with the broodings of memory, with the fragmentation of experience and poetic form." Intersecting these poets' similar interests are questions raised by the presence of the female muse.[17]

Obviously Petrarch's Laura shares the same name as Riding. I am reading Riding in part through the lens of her reception in literary history—a history in which Petrarchanism was foundational. Petrarch's muse may not have been a real person, but Petrarch pays close attention to the name "Laura" in his poems, and the act of naming was important for Riding: throughout her lifetime, she changed her last name from Reichenthal to Riding to Riding Gottschalk to (Riding) Jackson.[18] Whether or not she was aware of this connection, Riding comments on the effect and subversion of the Petrarchan tradition centuries after the writing of his poems.[19] Her acute awareness of herself as a poetic "persona" in the literary community—in her copious letters responding to critics and admirers of her work—suggests that she was resisting tradition while at the same time seeking to situate herself in the canon. Representations of dress, both in the *Rime Sparse* and in Riding's poetry, illuminate issues within the poet-muse structure, including parallels drawn between poetic forms and the "form" of the body, the role of clothing and appearance in the portrayal of women, and recurring concerns with power.

In order to talk about Riding's self-positioning as a muse, it is necessary to briefly revisit Robert Graves's ideas about the poet-muse structure, as he was, in real life, the perceived "poet" to Riding's "muse." Riding's involvement with Graves has overshadowed much of her work—with good reason; yet many recent scholars read Riding without referencing Graves. Riding's first book, *The Close Chaplet,* takes its title from an epigraphed Graves poem describing the back of a woman's neck, "where the close chaplet / Of thought is bound."[20] In response to Graves's popular book, *The White Goddess: A Historical Grammar of Poetic Myth,*[21] in which Graves locates the "language of true poetry" in the worship of ancient muse figures, Riding condemns Graves's destructive appropriation of her being, calling the book "a literary machine designed for seizure of the essence of my reality."[22] Investigating how Graves characterizes the literary muse in his book shows how he drew on the elements of Petrarchanism to describe the muse figure to a twentieth-century audience. Graves makes several direct references to early modern lyricists. These instances in his book describe a central aspect of the Petrarchan muse—her fluid, malleable self. Graves writes, "Donne worshipped the White Goddess blindly in the person whom he made his Muse; so far unable to recall her outward appearance that all he could record of her was the image of his own love-possessed eye seen reflected in hers."[23] Of Thomas Wyatt, Graves argues that his concern is with "the Goddess, not the individual woman," and that "it is not *She flees from me,*' but *'They flee from me.*'"[24] Graves's comments suggest some awareness of the self-interest and objectification involved in the act of muse-making. Graves does not mention Riding often in *The White Goddess.* He does at one point, however, make a connection between Riding and the poet's muse. Speaking of the insatiability of the muse figure, he quotes from Riding's poetry and writes that "a poet cannot continue to be a poet if he feels that he has made a permanent conquest of the Muse, that she is always his for the asking."[25]

In this quotation from *The White Goddess,* Graves touches on one of the muse's key qualities—her inability to be "possessed." Possession necessarily implies a divide between active and passive. The muse moves back and forth between activity and passivity. Riding confronts this quality in her poem "The Virgin," from her 1938 publication *Collected Poems.* The eleven-line poem seems in several ways to adopt the muse—and particularly the Petrarchan muse identified by her "unvanquished chastity"—as speaker:[26]

My flesh is at a distance from me.
Yet approach and touch it:
It is as near as anyone can come.

This vestiary stuff
Is a true relic,
Though I have never worn it,
Though I shall never be dead.

And the possession?
The violence will be over,
A forgotten passion,
Before I learn of it.[27]

Like Petrarch, Riding links the crucifixion with sex, but instead of casting her speaker as a spurned, "crucified" lover, she creates a virgin/object who discusses her own body. The last stanza complicates this, depicting the speaker as distant from the "violence" and "passion" of sex, just as, in the New Testament, Jesus's resurrection separates and elevates him from the "violence" and "passion" of the crucifixion (which takes place in the world of "flesh"). In this poem Riding refers directly to the muse's inaccessibility, illustrating in the first stanza how the virgin's skin serves as a sort of wall between her and her audience—touching it is "as near as anyone can come." Calling her skin "vestiary stuff," "a true relic," the speaker of "The Virgin," while apparently scoffing at her physical being, also magnifies its importance, portraying her flesh as a spiritually significant piece of clothing, too delicate to be "worn" casually.[28] In "The Virgin," the speaker "wears" her body like a garment.

The ability to access or not access the body fluctuates throughout Petrarch's poems, creating an always changing balance of power. As an object, the veil functions as a mode of alternation between dress and undress. The absence of clothing is often as—or more —important as its presence. In his discussion of the relationship between the male poet and the matriarchal moon goddess of poetry, Graves notes the superiority of the naked woman, writing, "Truth has been represented by poets as a naked woman: a woman divested of all garments or ornaments that will commit her to any particular position in space and time. . . . The poet is in love with the White Goddess, with Truth: his heart breaks with longing and love for her."[29] In the *Rime Sparse*—and in Graves's account— the male poet's ability to see truth is paralleled with his ability to see the naked woman. The clothed woman maintains a visual barrier between the poet and his object. In Petrarch's poems, the undefined, constantly moving veil is an obstacle preventing the poet from accessing truth, and this frustrated desire inspires his art.

Petrarch's references to the "veil" between Laura and the speaker enact a constant negotiation of power that takes place in the visual realm. Roland Greene describes the power exchange within the erotics of looking in his examination of the relation between colonialism and discourses of love poetry, by looking at a poem by Christopher Columbus:

[In the poem] the veil (*velo*) not only encloses the woman's head from the breeze (*l'aura*) but effectively hides her from all sight . . . [the poem] celebrates the erotic charge of not seeing, of awaiting the undressing, of experiencing love as an auto-erotic circuit that (perhaps) does not engage the woman at all.[30]

In addition to suggesting the inspirational Laura in the word *l'aura,* the veil evokes Laura's influence by measuring the transfer of power between the speaker and his object of interest. Petrarch charts how the veil hides Laura and takes on an authoritative role: he says that "the veil controls me" (rime 11), expresses "fear at a lady's hiding the wisdom of a living man within her trim garment or under a little veil" (rime 182), and speaks of the veil over his eyes that "made me not see what I saw, in order to make my life suddenly more sorrowful" (rime 328). In this constantly moving locus of power, the domination of the subject over the object may be subverted. Heather Dubrow notes the syntactic blurring of the expected power dynamic in lines 7–8 in rime 118: "if Laura is both subject and object in the sentence, thus eliding the two roles, so too do Petrarch and Laura, the figures who are normally interpreted as the antithetical subject and object of love poetry, themselves elide."[31]

Riding's poem "Pride of Head" also blurs subject and object. As in "The Virgin," "Pride of Head" incorporates a narrator who experiences a disconnection between self and body: the head is depicted "rolling in its private exact socket," "nodding and blowing on my neck." The independently moving head is where the narrator "[lives] mostly and most of the time" and is the "gem of the larger, lazy continent just under it."[32] Riding employs colonialist imagery in "Pride of Head," depicting a controlling "I"—"the idol of the head"—that brings "streams of sense" to "the savage, half-awakened land" of the body, "civiliz[ing] it as well as they can." This is a problematic image, one that seems to locate power distinctly in the "civilized" mind.[33] At the same time, however, the differences among "head," "I," and "the rest" suggest that this is not a strict duality but an uncertain movement of control among multiple elements.[34] Riding depicts struggle through images of empire and land exploration—an image that, like her tiara, makes her regal. The narrator is a "gem," an "idol," a "haughty" "autocrat." Echoing the effect of her gold tiara,

Riding's language locates her narrator in a place of conflicted power, the exceptional, cerebral ruler separate from "what's outside of me" and "the challenge of other things."

The particular language of naming in the selected works by Petrarch and Riding intersects with this changing power dynamic and is closely identified with appearance and materiality. Petrarch puns on Laura's name in reference to laurels, the decorative head ornament symbolizing poetic victory—in rime 359, she tells him "the laurel means triumph" (line 49). Riding's gold "Laura" tiara, which not only demonstrates a self-crowning with poetic laurels but provides an opulent display of Riding's first name—the only part of her name to remain unchanged during her life—is a material statement denying her father's and her husbands' names. The "(Riding) Jackson" version of her name maintains the earlier "Riding" by embedding it—like a gem—parenthetically. Visually, parentheses suggest the circular embracing of laurels or the tiara around the poet's head. This type of ornamentation calls attention to the head, separating it from the body as in "Pride of Head," by highlighting its importance with a golden halo. "(Riding) Jackson" preserves her "Riding," distinguishing it and protecting its history, by enclosing it within her first and married names.

In the world of Laura and Petrarch, the poet's muse is characterized, like Elizabeth Friedmann's description of Riding, by the glittery golden light—an "aura"—around her head and neck. In her analysis of rime 185, Mary B. Moore states that the poem "metamorphoses Laura into [a] jeweled object; she becomes gilded feathers, a necklace, a diadem, and a light that illumines the air." Moore adds that the word *l'aurata,* which means "gilded," occurs in the poem as another pun on Laura's name.[35] In rime 366 Petrarch addresses the "beautiful Virgin who, clothed with the sun and crowned with stars, so pleased the highest Sun that in you He hid His light." At the same time as the "jeweled object" is decidedly material, its spiritual connotations infuse it with an immaterial holiness and preciousness.

"Precious" implies not only rarity and personal meaning, but financial significance. Although jewelry is often seen as trivial and frivolous, it is a firm declaration of wealth. Riding's gold tiara evokes the power of money as well as spiritual and feminine powers. In addition to wearing jewelry in her personal life, Riding references jewelry in her poetry. The poems "Jewels and After" and "Auspice of Jewels," also included in the *Collected Poems*, explore the issues of power exchange discussed in reference to the tradition of Petrarchan poetics and point toward Riding's definition of utopian artistic space.[36] Ella Zohar Ophir focuses her interpretation of "Auspice of Jewels" on the second and seventh stanzas, arguing that here Riding is using images of ornament to investigate "the ruses and guises of sexual power," for example in depicting "traditional adornments of women as the condensation and displacement of raw masculine desire" and "elaborate costuming [as] a form of confinement."[37]

Ornamentation, for Riding, is a space of confinement; but it is also a space of freedom. It allows for "eloquent concealment," providing a form that liberates. This poem investigates the speaking ability of "silent given glitter." Throughout "Auspice of Jewels," Riding posits a struggle—between "they" and "us." She establishes the conflict in the first stanza:

> They have connived at those jeweled fascinations
> That to our hands and arms and ears
> And heads and necks and feet
> And all the winding stalk
> Extended the mute spell of the face.[38]

The "we" of the poem are those who are—passively—"endowed" and "studded" with jewels. "We" wear the "jeweled fascinations" that frustrate and cause "they" to "connive." These jewels "extend the mute spell of the face"—the ability of the face and of adornment to simultaneously speak and not speak. The "spell" suggests words infused with magical power, like the spell cast by the word "Laura" on the gold tiara. "Spell" also recalls the word "auspice" in the title, attributing a prophetic quality to jewels. Like the jeweled "forms" referred to in the poem, the poetic language here is "obscure and bright," demonstrating an astonishing sharpness in its pointed, "glittering" vocabulary while at the same time refusing to provide an unobstructed view of the poem's "meaning."

"Jewels and After" portrays ornamentation as both dangerous and reassuring. Riding writes,

On the precious verge of danger
Jewels spring up to show the way,
The bejewelled way of danger,
Beautied with inevitability.[39]

The narrative of the poem hints at a retelling of the Orpheus-Eurydice myth—a story associated with Eurydice's inspirational role in lyric tradition—in its inclusion of "the look-back," which leads to a loss "of danger" and then death. Jewels both lead to danger and are associated with "dangerlessness" in the second stanza. Riding plays with grammatical negativity in this poem, inventing words such as "dangerlessness," "unharshed," and "unprecious." The indecipherability of words such as "unharshed" reveals the inability of language to conform to a dualistic system. Simply adding a negative prefix or suffix does not neatly reverse meaning. In the same way, the imposing of identity definitions (i.e., "Jew," "woman") attempts to create a neat I–Other opposition. By writing from the position of the defined, passive Other, Riding troubles the rationality that would claim, for example, that "woman" is the "opposite" of "man."

Joyce Piell Wexler argues that Riding's views on women are idealist, merely reversing the traditional subject-object dynamic. Wexler states that Riding's "image of an ideal world placed the special qualities traditionally associated with women at the peak of her society's values. Instead of trying to make women more like men, she advocated making women the model men would emulate."[40] I read, in Riding's work, a more dialectical relationship to language, the mind, and the body. This multifaceted (like a jewel) vision of how power works is expressed in Riding's images of utopia. "Jewels and After" ends with the lines, "The unprecious jewels of safety, / As of childhood." "Childhood," like the young girl's dress-up fantasies Riding describes in her short story "Socialist Pleasures," provides a utopian space of safety.[41] Curiously, "unprecious jewels" are as "safe" as "childhood." The word "unprecious" removes associations of rarity while keeping the original word, "precious," on the page, reminding readers of what Riding is trying to counter. This is a vision of a place where jewels are powerful but not isolated from everyday life—a place where, say, Riding could wear her gold tiara all the time instead of putting it away, as she did in real life. A vision, too, of a place where a woman poet could exist as a poet without occupying a rarefied, unequal position.

In her poem "Because of Clothes," Riding suggests that the world of clothing provides a utopian space where the mind/body split is healed:

> The head is one world
> And the body is another—
> The same, but somewhat slower
> And more dazed and earlier,
> The divergence being corrected
> In dress.[42]

Here, the "corrective" abilities of dress show readers the potential for an alternative "world." "Without dressmakers," the speaker imagines in the first line of the poem, "we should be two worlds." "The union of matter with mind" occurs "by the method of raiment." Interestingly, Riding ends the poem by attributing this power to a passive object: "the neutral grace / Of the needle." The "neutral" needle, an object that takes on definition only when it is used by its maker—like a muse—here asserts an active existence.

This description of a struggle between mind and body, and the way a seemingly insignificant material object can articulate that struggle, echoes my biographical account of Riding's gold tiara. Both the needle and the tiara are trivialized, feminized objects—though in different ways. The needle suggests the anonymous women workers of the "needle" trades, while the tiara asserts its (usually female) wearer's separation from labor and namelessness. This difference is markedly class-based, and can be linked to Riding's movement out of the Jewish, working-class world of her garment-industry parents into the mostly upper-class, non-Jewish world of Anglo-American modernist poetry, where the celebration of the individual author was central. The jewel/needle comparison also reflects Riding's conflict as a woman writer: should she choose the role of the "jeweled" muse, where her idealized body is placed on a pedestal by the male poet, or that of the woman writer, who is perceived as an unfeminine, "needling" witch? In Riding's work, jewels certainly appear more often than needles. And while her self-positioning as a muse might initially suggest that she has chosen a passive role, her consistent preoccupation with examining the power relations between muse and artist through the material object complicates the idea that she has only two options, positing the possibility of a utopian space where, for Riding and the woman artist, "divergence" is "corrected."

NOTES

1. Among those whose art situates them as both appropriators and appropriated: H.D.'s attention to Greek and Roman classicism, biographical accounts of her Greco-Roman dress, and poems such as "Eurydice," in which she retells the Orpheus–Eurydice story from the muse's perspective; Frida Kahlo's use of Mexican dress in her life and in her paintings; Mabel Dodge Luhan's devotion to Native American culture in New Mexico; Gertrude Stein's dedication to Pablo Picasso's cubist ("primitive"-inspired) art.

2. It is important to note that I am selecting writings from across a range of time periods—a primary characteristic of Riding's work is its changing, sometimes contradictory quality. In this way, I trace a concern that emerges at various times throughout her career.

3. Ernst Gombrich's comment "I am what Hitler called a Jew, that's what I am" shows how identity is not necessarily formed from the individual outward. From Marjorie Perloff, *The Vienna Paradox* (New York: New Directions, 2003), 78. In addition to gender, Riding's Jewish background is a significant aspect of her interest in impersonality.

4. Elizabeth Friedmann, *A Mannered Grace: The Life of Laura (Riding) Jackson* (New York: Persea Books, 2005), 12 and 22.

5. Jeanne Heuving, "Laura (Riding) Jackson's 'Really New' Poem," in *Gendered Modernisms: American Women Poets and Their Readers,* ed. Margaret Dickie and Thomas Travisano (Philadelphia: University of Pennsylvania Press, 1996), 211 n. 14.

6. Friedmann, *A Mannered Grace,* xviii.

7. In the past, many critics have perpetuated Riding's reputation as a "witch," drama queen, and mere sidekick to Robert Graves. More recently, this tradition of villianizing Riding has compelled

some critics to avoid incorporating biographical contexts or making cultural/historical critiques of her writing.

8. Deborah Baker, *In Extremis: The Life of Laura Riding* (New York: Grove, 1993), 180.

9. Friedmann, *A Mannered Grace*, 165.

10. Joyce Piell Wexler, *The Enemy Self: Poetry and Criticism of Laura Riding* (Ann Arbor: UMI Research Press, 1990), 90. In her essay "Not Elizabeth to His Raleigh: Laura Riding, Robert Graves, and Origins of the White Goddess," in *Literary Couplings: Writing Couples, Collaborators, and the Construction of Authorship,* ed. Marjorie Stone and Judith Thompson (Madison: University of Wisconsin Press, 2006), a primarily biographical look at Riding, Amber Vogel describes the strained relationship between T. S. Matthews and the poet.

11. All references to Petrarch's *Rime Sparse* are from *Petrarch's Lyric Poems,* trans. Robert Durling (Cambridge, Mass.: Harvard University Press, 1976).

12. Friedmann, *A Mannered Grace,* 93 and 166.

13. For more on Riding's views on poetic tradition, see Lisa Samuels's introduction to *Anarchism Is Not Enough* (Berkeley: University of California Press, 2001).

14. See Susan M. Schultz, "Laura Riding's Essentialism and the Absent Muse," *Arizona Quarterly* 48, no. 1 (1992): 1–24, and "Of Time and Charles Bernstein's Lines: A Poetics of Fashion Statements," *Jacket* 14 (2001), ed. John Kinsella, http://jacketmagazine.com/14/schultz-bernstein.html.

15. Schultz, "Laura Riding's Essentialism," 9.

16. Jo-Ann Wallace, "Laura Riding and the Politics of Decanonization," *American Literature* 64, no. 1 (1992): 120, states that "it is just this refusal to cede interpretive authority or to relinquish intentionality and referentiality which makes Riding's work and project so useful to feminists today, if only because it foregrounds the degree to which a struggle for cultural authority underlies all canon formation."

17. Durling, *Petrarch's Lyric Poems,* viii. I am concerned with the general concept of the muse, but I will specifically address the male poet–female muse relationship. Within this structure the female poet–male muse, as well as female poet–female muse and male poet–male muse relationships, may parallel or differ from the characteristics of male poet–female muse Petrarchanism. For more on modernist women writers and muse making, see Rachel Blau DuPlessis's excellent "Pater-Daughter: Male Modernists and Female Readers," in *The Pink Guitar: Writing as Feminist Practice* (New York: Routledge, 1990).

18. I have decided to use "Riding" for ease of reading. There is no consensus among contempo-

rary critics about which is the "correct" name to use—a situation that in itself reinforces the uncertainty and fluid quality the poet's name possessed during her lifetime.

19. Like Ezra Pound and her other contemporaries, Riding does not, for the most part, employ end-rhymes in her poetry; by "Petrarchanism," I am referring particularly to the poet-muse structure and its relation to literary history and the process and formation of writing, not necessarily to the Petrarchan sonnet form.

20. Laura Riding, *The Close Chaplet* (London: Hogarth Press, 1926). A "chaplet" is a head ornament like laurels or a tiara.

21. Robert Graves, *The White Goddess: A Historical Grammar of Poetic Myth* (Manchester: Carcanet Press, 1997).

22. Laura Riding, "Robert Graves's *The White Goddess,*" in *The Word "Woman" and Other Related Writings*, ed. Elizabeth Friedmann and Alan J. Clark (New York: Persea Books, 1993), 209.

23. Graves, *White Goddess*, 418.

24. Ibid., 503.

25. Ibid., 435.

26. Petrarch, *Rime Sparse*, rime 313.

27. Laura (Riding) Jackson, *The Poems of Laura Riding: A Newly Revised Edition of the 1938/1980 Collection* (New York: Persea Books, 2001), 37. An earlier and slightly longer version of this poem can be found in *The Close Chaplet* as "Virgin of the Hills," 32.

28. Heightening the connections she makes between "word" and "flesh," Riding often expresses a religiously serious devotion to language. See Riding's introduction to *The Poems of Laura Riding* (New York: Persea Books, 2001): "My sincerity as a poet was a sincerity of spiritual literalness of faith in the truth-potentiality of words embodied in the spiritual creed of poetry" (xxxii).

29. Graves, *White Goddess*, 439.

30. Roland Greene, "Petrarchism among the Discourses of Imperialism," in *America in European Consciousness, 1493–1750*, ed. Karen Ordahl Kupperman (Chapel Hill: University of North Carolina Press, 1995), 136.

31. Heather Dubrow, *Echoes of Desire: English Petrarchism and Its Counterdiscourses* (Ithaca, N.Y.: Cornell University Press, 1995), 20.

32. "Pride of Head," in *Poems of Laura Riding*, 10. An earlier version of this poem appears under the title "Head Itself," a subsection of a longer poem, "Body's Head," in *The Close Chaplet*, 22.

33. Roland Greene explores the connection between colonialist discourses and the lyric form in his book *Unrequited Conquests: Love and Empire in the Colonial Americas* (Chicago: University of Chicago Press, 1999).

34. Ella Zohar Ophir, "The Laura Riding Question: Modernism, Poetry, and Truth," *Modern Language Quarterly* 66, no. 1 (March 2005), argues that Riding's autonomy as a poet is political in its resistance to the scientific system: "In [*A Survey of Modernist Poetry* (1927), *Contemporaries and Snobs* (1928), and *Anarchism Is Not Enough* (1928)] Riding comes to identify poetry with individuality, and her defense of poetry becomes an argument for the autonomous authority of the individual mind as against the system-based authority of science. Throughout her work Riding treats science and society as aspects of a single force—as extensions of one another insofar as they are equally inimical to individual thought and expression—and in this way it is not just poetry that comes to be conceived of as radically disjointed from the social and historical world, but the poet as well" (93).

35. Mary B. Moore, *Desiring Voices: Women Sonneteers and Petrarchanism* (Carbondale: Southern Illinois University Press, 2000), 90. It is also worth noting, in connection with Riding, the long-standing stereotype connecting Jews with gold/money. Her use of the gold tiara could indicate an attempt to reclaim this association on her own terms. Riding's story "Socialist Pleasures" deals with her secular Jewish upbringing; the embedded word "Jew" within "jewels"—and Riding's consistent interest in etymology and linguistics—suggests that this aspect of her identity is also present but veiled.

36. "Jewels and After," in *Poems of Laura Riding*, 141; "Auspice of Jewels," in *Poems of Laura Riding*, 277.

37. Ophir, "Laura Riding Question," 109.

38. *Poems of Laura Riding*, 277.

39. Ibid., 141.

40. Joyce Piell Wexler, *Laura Riding's Pursuit of Truth* (Athens: Ohio University Press, 1979), 105–6.

41. Laura Riding, *Progress of Stories* (New York: Persea Books, 1994).

42. "Because of Clothes," in *Poems of Laura Riding*, 321.

8

SPANISH WOMEN'S CLOTHING DURING THE LONG POST-CIVIL WAR PERIOD

Giuliana Di Febo

THE "CHRISTIAN WAY OF DRESSING"

Women's clothes played an important role in Spain during the Civil War (1936–39), which was so dominated by irreducible political, cultural, and symbolic polarizations that dress too became a sign of dichotomy, a way to show which side you were on. For the Francoists, the "vestir cristiano" (the Christian way of dressing) became an important stimulus to recover the traditional feminine role from Republican emancipation. Ultimately, it acquired attributes of a patriotic principle: "You'll build our homeland if you make healthy habits with your Christian way of dressing. Decide, woman."[1]

Vestir cristiano linked patriotic reconstruction to the society's "re-Christianization" in Francoist propaganda. In this light we should read the strongly negative caption to a photograph of a female soldier in blue overalls carrying a rifle: "She dressed as a man and behaved as the worst savage of the wild hordes."[2] Fighting on the Republican side, female soldiers adopted masculine clothes, the mythic "blue overalls." In fact, female participation in armed battle was brief and limited, but it gave rise to a significant amount of iconographic production.[3] If the Republicans presented the image of a fighting woman as one of the principal symbols of female emancipation, for the *nacionales,* instead, the woman "dressed up" as a man represented the most profane expression of the reversal of traditional roles. After the war ended, references to the female soldier as a contaminating figure of the "feminine" continued. This *miliciana* became the final point in a chain of transgressions caused by the policy of female emancipation enacted by the Second Republic. Its demonization also entailed the condemnation of behaviors that questioned Spanish *esencia,* including one of its pillars, the traditional female.

Decrying the negative repercussions to Spain of practices considered to be transgressions (smoking, playing sports, sunbathing, dancing) became a cliché. The harmful effects of Spanish women's bolder acts would often be recirculated in numerous publications produced by religious, political, and creative writers. These writings were characterized by a rhetoric of condemnation and a redundancy of examples that remained substantially the same until the 1960s. It is not surprising, therefore, that, in the 1960s, a description of female soldiers as dissolute reappeared in a speech of the Feminine Section of the Falange: "Women wore soldier uniforms, got drunk in cellars, raised machine guns, and converted themselves into the sad figure of the female militia, which was both bestial and lamentable."[4]

During the entire so-called *postguerra* period, which in reality lasted until the 1950s because of the continuation of extreme backwardness and of the opposition between the victors and the defeated perpetuated by the regime, dress played the role of a symbolic indicator of a feminine model of maternal sacrifice and confinement to the private sphere. Gender difference, emphasized even in Franco's speeches, was codified through legislation that removed women from work and the public sphere and canceled modern and secular Republican laws such as divorce and coeducation.[5] If, at the end of the war, the *Caudillo* desired a renewal that meant "men with more courage and women with less lipstick," the church also promoted an intense campaign for the recovery of feminine "modesty" and "decorum."

The *vestir cristiano* was made explicit through postings on Spanish churches of the

Normas concretas de modestia femenina (Concrete rules of feminine modesty), following the instructions of Archbishop Pla y Deniel:

1. Clothes should not be so tight as to mark provocatively the forms of the body.
2. Clothes should not be so short as not to cover most of the legs; they cannot reach just the knees.
3. Low necklines go against modesty; some are so audacious that they are sinful because of the dishonest intentions they reveal and the scandal they produce.
4. Short sleeves go against modesty if they do not cover the arm at least to the elbow. . . .
5. Not wearing stockings goes against modesty.
6. Wearing clothes that are transparent or punctured goes against modesty if they do not cover the parts of the body that should be concealed.[6]

Rigidly normative, these rules recalled the exhortation formulated by the *Sacra Congregatio Concilii* (Sacred Congregation) of 1930 that had been inspired by the first letter of the apostle Paul to Timothy (1 Tim. 2:9–10): "mulieres in habitu ornato cum verecundia et sobrietate ornantes se."[7] Dress based on modesty and chastity guaranteed a correspondence between inside and outside. As the "mirror of the soul," it was a referential code rendering visible compliance to mass conformity. The prohibitions and the centimeter count were designed to avoid the eternal threat of the feminine body as a source of seduction and sin and therefore of moral disorder. The feminine body was supposed to be, yes, pretty and, of course, well-groomed; but, at the same time, it had to be encapsulated in a carefully controlled decorum. Home economics textbooks and women's magazines propounded the rhetoric of the *hogar* (the home) and were full of advice on how to take care of the skin, hands, and hair. The readaptation of the sixteenth-century model of the "perfect wife" to contemporary needs required all these components. The ancient treatise by Fray Luis de León, *La perfecta casada* (The perfect wife) published in 1583, was resurrected for young women of the marrying age as a compendium of moral virtues that stressed being reserved and resisting frivolous behavior.[8]

"Como es la esposa perfecta," an article published in 1943 in *Y... Revista para la mu-jer* (Y ... A magazine for women) of the Falangist Feminine Section, was emblematic of this tendency. The stereotype of the ideal wife was based on aesthetic attributes—one meter, sixty-five centimeters tall, blonde hair, manicured hands, slender body—and of a behavior marked by the austere tones of the convent: "The perfect wife speaks little and always in a very low voice; she walks slowly and with decorum; she keeps her distance and it is not easy to interact with her except formally. She is reserved and dignified but this does not stop her from being cheerful and brilliant. The perfect wife always wears unobtrusive colors and at night always dresses in black."[9]

The campaign to preserve feminine decorum and modesty also involved those public places where morality was thought to be most at risk. The beach was the object of many denunciations. The priest Enciso Viana claimed it was a place that allowed nudity and therefore the loss of shame: "On the sand toasted by the sun and dampened by the water, the soul denudes itself of its shame as the body removes its clothes."[10] The church's preoccupation with the exposed female body pushed the state to intervene also. In 1941, the Dirección General de Seguridad published a note—which would be repeated for many years at the beginning of each summer—stating that in addition to the rules about the measurements of the bathing suit (a little skirt and covered shoulders were mandatory), sunbathing had to be done in a beach robe.[11]

Dance halls were also heavily criticized because they encouraged the "fervent promiscuity" that was a fruit of modern times. In post–World War II Europe, modern dances became the symbol of a refound liberating freedom; however, in Spain, dance became the object of a crusade conducted from pulpits, through pastoral letters, magazines, and pamphlets often enriched with demonizing images—drawings in which one of the two dancers was a horrific devil. For instance, in a 1946 pastoral letter, *Sobre los bailes, la moral católica y la ascética cristiana* (On dances, Catholic morality, and Christian asceticism), Cardinal Segura intervened in apocalyptic terms against dancing.[12]

The magazine *Ecclesia*, the official organ of Acción Católica (Catholic Action), had previously published an editorial in support of censorship—exalted as a "magnificent work of purging"—in which the list of the enemies of the nation was extended to the modern and the exotic, which meant whatever was strange and transgressive: "[The homeland] is also betrayed by the noisy explosions of black music, exotic dances, extravagant hats, and 'interesting' books."[13] Indeed, the *extranjerizante* fad was condemned as the main cause for the increase in beachgoing and dancing because it incorporated customs and ideas from other countries, thus polluting Spanish national ones, including a push toward greater freedom in relationships and dress. Fashion and clothing bore a great deal of the responsibility for this disarray, becoming the target in the crusade for "public decency."

INDECENT AND EXTRANJERIZANTE FASHION

Fashion, understood as "the empire of the ephemeral" that catches up with the present, inevitably seemed to contrast with the tendency toward immobility and the recovery of tradition permeating Spanish society. Autarchic policies went beyond the economic dimension, invading the field of values and behavior in order to become a barrier against foreign intrusion. The Spanish woman became the object of a campaign directed at defending her from those modernizing and foreign impulses coming from nearby France or, through the movie screens, from faraway Hollywood. The church saw in American cinema one of the causes of "demoralization" and the consequent loss for women of their most important feminine connotations—the sense of domesticity: "stop the growing loss of morals in women (caused largely by American customs introduced through movies) that push young women to be independent thereby disintegrating the family and making young women unfit or less fit for their future role of wife and mother because of exotic practices that defeminize them and distance them from the home."[14]

The propaganda for "national reconstruction" that characterized the postwar period included, therefore, the denunciation of the temptation of modernity represented by fashion that was considered the source not only of waste but also of moral degeneration. These were the years of the exhausting rationing lines (which lasted until 1952), as thrift—*el ahorro*—became for Spaniards a way of life, almost a moral category transferred to the existential field. Women's magazines and home economics textbooks urged women to be scrupulously economical with their clothes: they were taught how to turn coats inside out, how to sew a dress with an Alfa sewing machine, and how to choose material that was stain resistant and inexpensive. As writer Carmen Martín Gaite wrote in her novel *El cuarto de atrás,* it was a period when "not being able to recognize fabric by its name was as scandalous as mistaking your neighbors' last names."[15]

Within the strategy to relaunch national resources, the Feminine Section appealed to female farm workers encouraging them to produce silkworms so that "the decorations of cult, the flag and banners, and the clothes of Spanish women can be made of pure and holy Spanish silk."[16] In the backward Spain of the long postwar period, the problem of clothes was second only to that of food. More than ever, in the 1940s and 1950s, dress played the role of being a marker not only of age and sex, but above all of social division. The priest Salicrú Puigvert, author of many textbooks on female education, was well aware of the multiple meanings dress could assume. To counter the exaggerations of fashion, he recommended an aesthetics of sobriety and utility that clearly defined both sexual roles and social status. This was "honest" fashion as opposed to an indecent one: "For fashion to be honest, hygienic and to conform to an aesthetic sentiment it must have three objectives: serve the human body by protecting it from the rigors of bad weather; be a barrier against concupiscence; establish the relationship between appearance and reality as far as the sex, age, and condition of each person is concerned."[17]

Echoing the tone and the approach of the ancient sumptuary laws,[18] Delgado Capeans also perceived in the nexus fashion/luxury one of the sources of change on different fronts. In the first place, the race toward elegance pushed women out of the private sphere toward greater sociability. Furthermore, the spirit of imitation, which fashion created, resulted in an external homogenization, a "unification of the language of appearance,"[19] that might facilitate social destabilization, "Because ladies, those who occupy the lowest places in the social ladder tend, . . . by a natural law, to imitate those who occupy higher places."[20]

In reality, the denunciation of fashion as a tyranny and as an "idol," along with the attempt to steer dress in an "honest" direction, was a reproposal of an ancient tradition of condemnation present, more or less markedly, in proclamations by church fathers, in the appeals of Girolamo Savonarola to "burn vanity," and in various popes' writings, for example, Leon XIII (cited by Capeans) and Benedict XV's criticisms of "disgraceful" fashion.[21] In Spanish textbooks, this tradition was constantly revivified, often through the filter of the book *Las modas y el lujo* (Fashion and luxury) written by the theologian Isidro Gomá.[22] Published in 1913, this work was cited by many contemporary manuals. Gomá's text, which opened with a citation from *La perfecta casada* by Fray Luis de León about the frivolity and fickleness of women's dress in his time, intended—as the author explicitly declares—to support the *cruzada de la modestia cristiana* (crusade for Christian modesty) begun that same year (1913) by the congregation of the Daughters of Mary of Orihuela.[23] The exhortative tone echoing many eminent writers such as Voltaire, Jacques-Bénigne Bossuet, François Fénelon, church fathers, and Epicurus was clear in the appeals made to women to conduct fashion's imperatives within proper limits because fashion could be extremely harmful. The "abuses" and the harmful effects of fashion and luxury were underlined in contrast to the values that circulated around the definition of womanhood. Decorum and modesty in dress were considered feminine dimensions that expressed spiritual virtues and guaranteed social stability. But these feminine dimensions were continually undermined by the "tyranny of the fashion-plate" that pushed women to be independent and to unlearn their duty—that is, *hacer casa*, literally to make house.

Fashion, in general, was associated with the classic attributes connected to ideas of excess and volubility: extravagant, indecent, exaggerated, indecorous, frivolous. In addition to pushing traditional regional clothes into the background, fashion and luxury were accused of introducing French words and other exotic terms into the language. When luxury became excessive, moreover, it could create social disorder both for the wealthy classes—in that it broke the equilibrium between wealth and the superfluous to the detriment of charity—and for the poor because it made resignation to their lot more difficult. Gomá had understood the power of the worship of the "fashion goddess" as linked to the progress of industrialization and saw in it a mode of sacredness that would clash with ecclesiastic principles concerning the control of feminine seductiveness.[24] Significant traces of his book still remained in some textbooks of the 1950s.[25]

Fashion was the object of many disquisitions noting gender dichotomy not only by religious writers but also by politicians and intellectuals. José María Pemán (who at the time was the director of the Real Academia de la Lengua), inspired by Fray Luis de León, Balthasar Gracián, Friedrich Nietzsche, Georg Simmel, and many other thinkers and writers, advanced sophisticated hypotheses about clothing. For example, he considered fashion as an expression of female fickleness and also of the need to compensate them for their adherence to gender norms, foremost conjugal fidelity. The "danger," therefore, was not in the impulse toward change that fashion produced but in the push it created toward a harmful aggregation that rendered each individual irresponsible: "The danger represented by fashion is the same as the one represented by revolts and mass collective crimes: the elimination of responsibility."[26]

THE MASCULINIZATION OF APPEARANCE

Smoking

The emancipatory push coming from North America, which at the end of the Second World War invaded Europe, influencing lifestyles and promoting among the female masses the adoption of "uninhibited" clothes, was contrasted in Spain by the negation of any form of modernity and "freedom of appearance."[27] Traces of vaguely anticonformist attitudes and dress could be found only in magazines for a small circle of women of the well-off classes. The dominant conformism carefully contained any opening toward external influence. The campaign for modesty and decorum was accompanied by a no less powerful propaganda against the adoption of clothes (pants, pajamas, boots, and sweaters) and attitudes (short hair, sports, smoking) with masculine connotations, which were a means to mime social practices exclusive to the male world. Being attracted to this nonconformist fashion was seen as a negation of dignity and of woman's essence with repercussions for the body. In those years, the attribute *marimacho* negatively implicated women who adopted masculine attitudes. The dictionary of the Real Academia Española defines the term: "a woman who in her corpulence or actions resembles a man."

Pants

In the postwar period, except in cities like Barcelona and Santander that were more exposed to French influence, it was very rare to see a woman wearing pants on the streets of Spain. Pants on a woman recalled the transgressive image of the female soldiers of the still recent past. But more important, they were the most visible and concrete sign of that "masculinization" of appearances so criticized because it was the most evident denial of the dominant representation of women. The prohibition against pants necessarily meant the abolition or strict limitation of all those activities that required wearing them. For example, in her memoirs, Pilar Primo de Rivera, president for life of the Feminine Section of the Falange, mentions the restrictions in certain provinces on women riding bicycles.[28] Sports and gymnastics, which were largely managed by the Feminine Section, were another source of distress. Pius XII's negative judgment about sports, as an occasion for indecent clothes, "exhibition," and "camaraderie," weighed heavily on women's sports activity.[29] The Falangists resolved the problem of female athletes with the antiaesthetic and uncomfortable *pololos*. These pants, which were almost as wide as a skirt and were closed under the knee by an elastic, resembled the *jupe-culotte* of the previous century. Lola Gavarrón ironically described them in this way: "The hated 'pololos' of the school girls and dancers had tight elastics that in cases of precocious obesity could even block blood circulation. But these hygienic considerations didn't worry at all the sargentonas of the Feminine Section."[30]

Fashion in the 1940s

Still, in the domain of clothing, the prohibitions, the crusades, and the appeals for public morality did not impede the publicity and spread of fashion. Many women's magazines, such as *Chicas, Hola, Ellas, Revista para la mujer, Siluetas,* and *Lecturas,* dedicated
a section to fashion. Other more specialized magazines were the mouthpiece for high
fashion. In the early 1940s, the passage from haute couture to fashion on an industrial
scale occurred with difficulty. Boutiques specializing in prêt-à-porter appeared very
slowly.[31]

Balenciaga, who went to live in Paris during the Civil War, premiered his first important *défilé* in 1937 in France, becoming one of the most important fashion designers. Two
years later, in the center of Madrid, he opened the firm EISA, which for years represented
the symbol of elegance, linking together "the refinement of France and the vigor of
Spain."[32] In 1940, five of the most famous Spanish tailors—Pedro Rodríguez, Santa Eu-
lalia, Asunción Bastida, Manuel Pertegaz, and El Dique Flotante—founded the Cooper-
ativa de la Alta Costura in Barcelona that periodically organized *défilés* for a select clien-
tele and other tailors.[33] Their work appeared in the magazines *Alta costura, La Moda en
España, El hogar y la moda,* and *Arte y hogar.* These magazines were obviously for the mid-
dling to upper social groups: they were luxurious and the designs they presented—extremely elegant and refined—were for a select public. But as we are reminded by Carmen
Martín Gaite, *figurines* (fashion plates), familiar both to women who made their clothes
at home and to women who had their clothes made by stylists, were the *trait d'union* between haute couture and its imitation by those less well-off.[34]

Buen Vestir *and Austerity*

La Moda en España, during this period one of the most popular fashion magazines,
through its editorials, captions, and articles offers an interesting view both on the ten-

dencies of high fashion and on the mentality that surrounded it. *La Moda en España's* prestige was assured by its head editor, Carlos Sáenz de Tejada, who was the official painter for the regime. In one of his first editorials (February 1941), signed with the exotic pseudonym Friné, elegance was seen as a sign of moral renewal in addition to signaling a return to normality. *Buen vestir* was presented as an innovative language in contrast to Republican "vulgarity" and "dirtiness," as a recovery of freedom in that "being dressed with bon ton had been an additional motive for being persecuted by the reds," and, finally, as true patriotic commitment: "*Moda en España* by giving advice, publishing tendencies, and offering on its pages, from a strictly national vantage point, the rules of dressing well is performing a mission that can be defined without exaggeration as patriotic. One can cooperate in the work of reconstruction that has been taking place since the Crusade from many different angles."[35] Evidently this patriotic justification was supposed to neutralize the church's criticisms of luxury and waste in postwar Spain.

In reality, through the glossy pages of the magazine, dress revealed its "display value" in that it represented wealth, elegance, and bon ton. The magazine presented a careful liturgy of dress, marking the hours of the day in the manner of a complex ritual. Changing clothes acquired the significance of an unavoidable social code, because "every social moment has its needs."[36] Supplementing the classic distinctions—day dress for shopping, afternoon dress for walking, evening dress for society life—there were other distinctions depending on activities and seasons: clothes for holidays, sports, marriage ceremonies, eighteen-year-old birthdays, gala evenings, and so on. The dominant fashion was a very refined one in which the quality of the materials, often leading to an inevitable introduction of French words *(velours, piqué, crêpe georgette, foulard)*, was linked to an attention to details: the style was classic but skillfully enhanced by drapes, frills, and curls. For many years, the forms of the body were emphasized in all kinds of clothes, from severe *tailleurs* to multicolored summer dresses, by "wasp waists," the strong delineation of the shoulders, and the shortening of skirts (but not of evening gowns) to just below the knees. Slight décolletages in day dresses began appearing around 1942. As for furs, alongside the domestic sheepskin relaunched by economic autarchy, one could see more and more often muffs, collars, beaver coats, *ocelot, renard-argenté*, and *astrakan*.[37]

FIGURE 8.1 Francisco Franco (and wife), *Life Magazine,* November 10, 1938. Time Life Pictures/ Time and Life Pictures/Getty Images.

Much magazine space was dedicated to underwear. Underskirts with very slender shoulder straps were advertised alongside long and luxurious silk, satin, or crepe nightgowns with elaborate bodices. As the comment beside an advertisement illustration reads, "the clothes one cannot see" are the reflection of external dress, and "Beautiful and well-cared-for underwear is a sign of sincere sensibility because it would be a horrible sin of disrespect to place among rags the envelope of the soul."[38] But *buen vestir* also concerned housewives so that they could do housework and still maintain "a delicate coquetry."[39] Graceful aprons, shoes with very high heels, and hair carefully gathered projected the image of a "housewife" who used utensils and pots as if they were porcelain vases, was dressed perfectly to receive guests when she knitted or embroidered, and was ready to wear her precious housecoat as soon as she got out of bed. She was a housewife who always had the objective of maintaining her husband's interest in deference to the famous Spanish proverb "The well-behaved wife keeps the husband from going to another door," which was often repeated in manuals written for women.[40]

The scansion of the day and of the seasons through clothes was often accompanied by the illustration of complex strategies of seduction and rejuvenation. In addition to the usual dieting recipes, there was an abundance of advice to young women on how to increase beauty through the use of Spanish creams—*venus, mirugia, cafarena, numantina*—and through practices to postpone the time when men's admiration waned. Forty-five was the transition point to the fateful age. The magazine recommended, together with "suave attitudes," the use of clothes that were extremely sober in their form and colors.[41] A woman over forty always had to be very careful of the danger of appearing ridiculous.

Fashion, therefore, was characterized by good taste at every age and at every moment of the day. White during the day and black in the evening was, for years, a sign of distinction. Immediately after the Civil War, dresses for evening social occasions were dominated by a blaze of tulles, organza, silk, taffeta, and high-quality material cut into princely gowns. These dresses were inspired by the collections of Pedro Rodríguez, Cristobal Balenciaga, Raphael, and in particular of those of the French designers Lucien Lelong, Jeanne-Marie Lanvin, Pierre Balmain, and Jacques Fath.

When German occupation ended, France again became the center of fashion. From Paris came the surprisingly low-cut dresses that, often appearing in magazines, became a sign of social self-celebration destined for a small circle who appear free from moralistic preoccupations. The "night dresses," decorated with bodices of paillettes, with silk belts, and with skirts with "big flounces" or hints of a train, evoked fairy-tale atmospheres. "Going out at night" became, for the elegant woman of postwar Spain, a pretext to evade and exorcise the austerity proclaimed in other European countries: "To satisfy this desire tailors offered the most beautiful materials; materials that were also highly decorated evoking the thousand and one nights of the fabulous times of prosperity."[42] References to postwar European austerity came from a correspondent in England who informed readers in March 1945 of the limitations England was experiencing in the clothing industry due to rationing of textiles and a shortage of factory workers.[43] But in the Spain of the *ahorro*, one could read that an evening dress needed fourteen meters of taffeta to be made.[44]

Modernity

The magical word "modernity," frequently cited in Friné's articles, came to mean an acceptance of the latest style in textile, form, gradation of color, and the adoption of uninhibited and anticonformist attitudes. Up to 1944–45, movies—the ones that got through the rigid net of censorship—were an important showcase for fashion, not only in the field of clothes. Hollywood stars became models to imitate. They represented a fundamental reference point that united traditional femininity (with all its potential seductive powers to capture men) with emancipatory attitudes. *La Moda en España* was an important vehicle for this novelty. In 1942, for example, Brenda Marshall, who appeared in the film *La guardia de noche (Footsteps in the Dark)*, was photographed with a long white crepe dress with a very low neckline, while Judy Garland was captured in her daily life as a housewife wearing a simple checkered housecoat.[45] In the article "What a Woman Has to Do to Get Married," actress Patricia Dane provided ten rules on how to catch a husband. The rules amounted to a complex game of techniques and strategies to attain the longed-for marriage.[46]

Film stars strengthened the timid tendency toward sports and gymnastics. In the article "The Stars Practice Sports," actresses gave their advice: Norma Shearer recommended swimming, Joan Crawford suggested tennis to make muscles more flexible, while Jeanette MacDonald declared that she strengthened her lungs through horseback riding and Myrna Loy mentioned tennis, bicycling, and skiing. Greta Garbo's mythic walks with her pants of "masculine cut" were also noted.[47] Physical exercise and sports found space in the magazine because they satisfied aesthetic and health needs and the desire to play. Swimming, tennis, horseback riding, and bicycling became part of vacation diversions and pastimes, or a means to stay slim especially during the summer months when the female body on beaches was exposed to the judgmental look of men.[48] Once again obeying fashion introduced innovation: the one-piece bathing suit, which had already been inaugurated on French beaches, appeared in 1946 along with the sundress. And it was pants, even if used sparingly, that marked the timid openings to modernity.

As early as 1941, in an editorial, Friné recommended the use of long pants but with many restrictions.[49] So as not to be masculine and not to take anything away from the fascination of the female silhouette, the pants had to be long, wide, perfectly cut, and worn with wide Canadian or Saharan jackets, or be a culotte model. In the captions there were often instructions on how to make the dress article more feminine: "Very wide pants so that people can't tell they're not skirts when you are walking in them."[50] In 1947, Paris was still looked at as a reference point for the daily use of pants: "In Paris and in some other important French cities that follow the fast rhythm of the city on the Seine, many women wear pants on the streets. And these pants, so masculine, do not provoke any scandal or chaos."[51]

Praise of the Hat and the Sinsombrerismo of Spanish Women

Despite these nods to contemporary fashion, the hat remained the most reassuring proof of attachment to tradition and social belonging; wearing hats even became the symbol of deference to the regime's aesthetic. The hat, a fundamental piece in the "hierarchy of appearance" and a completion of female dressing based on *buen tono,* was the object of many articles in the magazine. It appeared in many different forms depending on the fashion, the season, and the moment of the day. In the immediate postwar years, the exotic turban continued to be seen along with a multiplicity of forms: coquettish Italian straw hats or *canotiers* decorated with flowers and ribbons, sumptuous piqué or felt hats enriched with veils or wide brims, and the *cucurucho* that covered the ears in the Catherine de Medici style. These were elegant and elaborate but were not worn for protective or for practical reasons. Instead, they often disappeared behind a downpour of veils, half-veils, flowers, and feathers. They were recommended to connote the "distinguished lady" and were to be worn at every public social occasion.

Once again, Hollywood promoted this accessory: Rosalind Russell, "the most elegant woman of America," was shown during the ritual of her personal milliner placing an

PLATE 1 Plate from portfolio. From *Sonia Delaunay:
Ses peintures, ses objets, ses tissues simultanés, ses modes*
(Paris: Librairie des Arts Décoratifs Publications, 1925).

PLATE 2 [FACING] Giacomo Balla, "Futurist Embroidered Waistcost,"
1924–25. Courtesy Biagiotti Cigna Foundation.

PLATE 3 [ABOVE] Giacomo Balla, "Sketch for a Fan," 1918.
Courtesy Biagiotti Cigna Foundation.

PLATES 4, 5, 6, 7 Jewish Stars embroidered
by Hungarian tailors. Author's collection.

PLATE 8 [ABOVE] Maria Damon, *Terra Divisa/ Terra Divina: (T/E/A/R)*, 2009.

PLATE 9 [FACING] Cover of *Report for a Corpse* by Henry Kane (New York: Dell Publishing Company, Inc., 1949). Cover by Gerald Gregg.

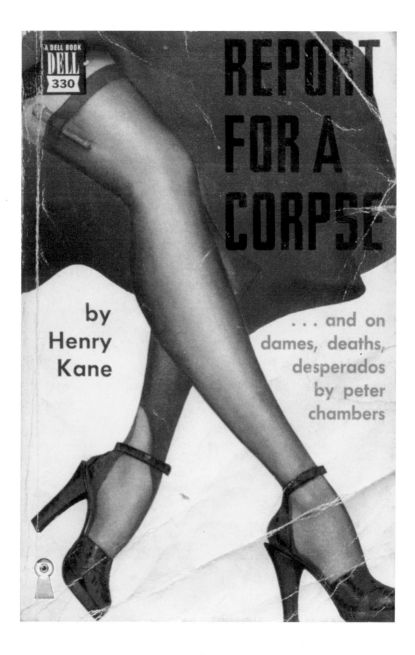

REPORT FOR A CORPSE

by
Henry
Kane

... and on
dames, deaths,
desperados
by peter
chambers

Arab-inspired turban on her head.[52] But, starting in 1943, the numerous criticisms of what was termed *sinsombrerismo femenino* (women's hatlessness) indicated a fear of decline in hat wearing by Spanish women: a dangerous influence of French women who regularly went out bareheaded. In *Moda, sinsombrerismo* could signal concessions to the bad taste of the enemies of the regime: "In addition, I agree completely with those people, who have dealt with this topic, who claim that a woman who goes out with an uncovered head only produces the feeling, even if this isn't in the least her intention, that she is making concessions to the bad taste of the enemies of our regime."[53]

In 1946, from London and New York, came the fashion for smaller and more practical hats. It was the moment of the *boinas*—Rembrandt style, with shorter half-veils and small brims that underlined graceful and thoughtful faces. The forms changed, but the preoccupation that hats were falling into disuse remained. In June 1947, Eva Perón's visit to Madrid elicited demonstrations of gratitude for the wheat sent by Argentina to Spain. It was an opportunity for *La Moda en España* to interview the countess de Foxa, a Spanish lady returning from Argentina in the plane with Eva Perón. The interviewer reported: "We have ascertained that a hat is unavoidable for the Argentinean woman no matter what her social condition is and no matter what time of day or occasion it is. Cooks go out to shop for food wearing hats, and ladies of high standing who go out to eat at a friend's house, I mean for dinner, also wear hats."[54]

However, the mantilla also held a privileged position in the fashion of the 1940s. Being a prestigious symbol of Spanish tradition, it was a mandatory article of clothing at weddings of the upper classes; but it was also an essential part of ancient Andalusian female seductiveness that later spread to all of Spain. The following celebratory stanzas are dedicated to the "playful, moving, / sinful, and penitent" mantilla, with its multiple connotations and in its popular dimension: "In your feminine and seductive simplicity, / you continue to be / such a lady / and so part of the people."[55]

Nineteen forty-seven was a significant year for *La Moda en España*. In the editorial for the March issue dedicated to its female readers, new sections on fashion were announced.[56] Furthermore, these new sections would feature prestigious writers and cor-

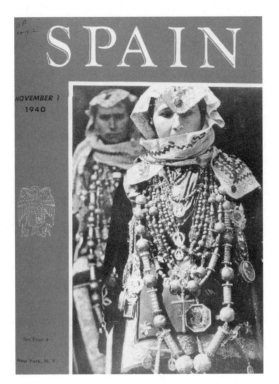

respondents in the capitals of Europe and the United States. There was news of Christian Dior's New Look, and in the July issue very chaste shorts worn on beaches suddenly appeared.[57] It was, therefore, an emblematic year where both recovery of tradition and modernizing openings coexisted and marked the slow evolution in fashion—at least as it was written—for "the elegant Spaniard of the middle class." More than ever, the pages of the magazine reflected an unreal female image that tried to reconcile pomp with moralism, domesticity with worldliness, and tradition with modernity in Franco's Spain. This image is well represented by the bodiless silhouettes of Carlos Sáenz de Tejada, whose dreamy looks are lost in emptiness.

1. Rafael Abella, *La vida cotidiana durante la Guerra Civil*, vol. 1, *La España nacional* (Madrid: Planeta, 1974), 117: "Harás patria si haces costumbres sanas con tu vestir cristiano. Decídete mujer."

2. Raquel García González, "El taller del soldado en Valladolid," in *Las Mujeres y la guerra civil española* (Madrid: Ministerio de Cultura, 1991), 183: "Se vistió de hombre y actuó como el más salvaje de las hordas desencadenadas."

3. Mary Nash, "La miliciana: otra opción de combatividad," in *Mujeres y la guerra civil española*, 97–108.

4. *La mujer en la nueva sociedad* (Madrid: Editorial del Movimiento, 1963), 38: "Las mujeres se vistieron con monos de soldado, se emborracharon en las cantinas, enarbolaron las metralletas y se convirtieron en esa triste estampa, al mismo tiempo bestial y lamentable de la 'miliciana.'" On the Feminine Section of the Falange, see María Teresa Gallego Méndez, *Mujer, Falange y Franquismo* (Madrid: Taurus, 1983); Rosario Sánchez López, *Mujer española, una sombra de destino en lo universal: Trayectoria histórica de la Sección Femenina de Falange (1934–1977)* (Murcia: Universidad de Murcia, 1990).

5. On the condition of women during Franco's regime, see Geraldine Scanlon, *La polémica feminista en la España contemporánea (1868–1974)* (Madrid: Siglo XXI, 1976); Aurora G. Morcillo, *True Catholic Womanhood: Gender Ideology in Franco's Spain* (Dekalb: Northern Illinois University Press, 2000); Giuliana Di Febo, "'Nuevo Estado,' nacionalcatolicismo y género," in *Mujeres y hombres en la España franquista*, ed. Gloria Nielfa Cristóbal (Madrid: Universidad Complutense de Madrid, 2003), 19–44.

6. The "Concrete rules of feminine modesty" were in reality ten. In Carlos Salicrú Puigvert, *Cuestiones candentes acerca de la moralidad pública* (Barcelona: La Hormiga de Oro, 1944), 285.

7. Sacra Congregatio Concilii, "Instructio," in *Acta Apostolicae Sedis: Commentarium officiale* (Rome: Typis Polyglottis Vaticanis, 1930), 22:26.

8. The text had already been republished in an economical edition during the Civil War as Fray Luis de León, *La perfecta casada* (Madrid: Austral, 1938) followed by many other editions. On this work, see the stimulating essay by María Angeles Durán, *La jornada interminable* (Barcelona: Icaria, 1986).

9. "Como es la esposa perfecta," *Y . . . revista para la mujer* 61 (February 1943), 43, 54–55: "La es-

posa perfecta habla poco y siempre en voz muy baja, anda despacio y con decoro y no es ni dada a familiaridades ni fácil de llegar a su intimidad. Es reservada, tiene dignidad, lo que no evita que sea alegre y brillante. La esposa perfecta viste siempre de colores discretos y por la noche siempre va de negro."

10. Emilio Enciso Viana, *Muchacha* (Madrid: Studium, 1959), 135: "En la arena tostada por el sol y humedecida por el agua, el alma se desnuda de la vergüenza, a la vez que el cuerpo se desnuda del vestido."

11. Rafael Abella, *La vida cotidiana en España durante el régimen de Franco* (Barcelona: Argos Vergara, 1985), 78.

12. Ibid., 77.

13. "Más precisiones," *Ecclesia* 12 (1942), 3: "[A la patria] se la traiciona también con los explosivos de gran retardo de la música negra, del baile exótico, del sombrero estrafalario, y del libro 'interesante.'"

14. *Ecclesia* 235 (1946), 595. Cited in E. Nicolás Marín and B. López García, "La situación de la mujer a través de los movimientos del apostolado seglar," in *Mujer y sociedad en España (1700–1975)*, ed. Rosa M. Capel Martínez (Madrid: Ministerio de Cultura, 1982), 375: "atajar la creciente desmoralización de la mujer (proveniente en gran parte de las costumbres americanas introducidas por el cinematógrafo), independizando a la joven, desintegrando a la familia, inhabilitando o menoscabando la futura consorte y madre con prácticas exóticas que la *desfeminizan* y tornan descentrada del hogar."

15. Carmen Martín Gaite, *El cuarto de atrás* (Madrid: Destino, 1981), 12: "no reconocer las telas por sus nombres era tan escandaloso como equivocar el apellido de los vecinos."

16. *La mujer en el campo*, pamphlet edited by the Feminine Section of the Falange (Murcia, 1941), 5.

17. Carlos Salicrú Puigvert, *La educación: estudio normativo acerca de las obligaciones que impone la vida social* (Barcelona: La Hormiga de Oro, 1951), 276: "La moda para ser honesta, higiénica y responder a un sentido estético ha de orientarse hacia tres finalidades del vestir: servir al cuerpo humano preservándolo de los rigores de la intemperie, poner un dique a la concupiscencia, establecer la relación entre la apariencia y la realidad por lo que se refiere al sexo, edad y condición de cada uno."

18. On this point, see Rosita Levi Pisetzky, "Le leggi suntuarie," in *Il costume e la moda nella società italiana* (Turin: Einaudi, 1989), 30–36.

19. This expression is in Daniel Roche, *Il linguaggio della moda* (Torino: Einaudi, 1991), 51.

20. Ricardo Delgado Capeans, *La mujer en la vida moderna* (Madrid: Bruno del Amo, 1941), 154: "Porque, señoras, los que se hallan en los últimos puestos de la escala social . . . tienden por ley natural, a imitar a los que ocupan puestos superiores."

21. "La moda delle nostre figlie davanti l'immagine del Cristo morente," *Azione Muliebre*, 24, nos. 8/9 (August–September 1924), 454–55, in Michela de Giorgio, *Le italiane dall'Unità a oggi: Modelli culturali e comportamenti sociali* (Bari: Laterza, 1992), 226.

22. Isidro Gomá y Tomás, *La modas y el lujo ante la ley cristiana, la sociedad y el arte* (Barcelona: Tipografía Católica, 1926). Gomá y Tomás was consecrated archbishop of Toledo in 1933 and two years later primate cardinal. An eminent theologian, he had a fundamental role during the Civil War. In July 1937, he promoted the *Carta colectiva del episcopado español* (Collective charter of Spanish bishops) (which had many repercussions on Catholicism worldwide) in which the reasons for the church's support of the military insurrection were given and in which religious persecution was denounced.

23. Ibid., 7.

24. Ibid., 125–30.

25. One example is the book written for the young women of Acción Católica by Matilde Zamanillo, *En la mies del señor. Diversas tareas femeninas* (Santander: Bedia, 1958).

26. José María Pemán, *De doce cualidades de la mujer.* In *Obras completas* (Madrid: Escelicer, 1947), 3:837: "El peligro de la moda es el mismo que el de los motines y los crímenes colectivos de masas: la disolución de la responsabilidad."

27. De Giorgio, *Le italiane dall'Unità a oggi*, 209.

28. Pilar Primo de Rivera, *Recuerdos de una vida* (Madrid: Ediciones Dyrsa, 1983), 279.

29. Pius XII, "A una folta delegazione della Gioventù Femminile di Azione Cattolica," in *Discorsi e radiomessaggi di Sua Santità Pio XII* (Vatican City: Tipografia Poliglotta Vaticana, 1955), 3:89.

30. Lola Gavarrón, *Piel de ángel: Historias de la ropa interior femenina,* with a prologue by Luis Berlanga (Madrid: Tusquets, 1988), 272: "Los aborrecidos 'pololos' de colegialas y bailarinas, con ceñidas gomas que, en casos de obesidad precoz, hasta cortan la circulación sanguínea sin que

estas consideraciones higiénicas inquieten lo más mínimo a las sargentonas de la Sección Femenina."

31. An exception was represented by the Caruncho family, which in 1939 opened a boutique in Madrid and inaugurated homemade prêt-à-porter; see Lola Gavarrón, *Mil caras tiene la moda* (Madrid: Penthalon, 1982), 104–12.

32. Cecil Beaton, "La mode des années Balenciaga," in *Hommage à Balenciaga* (Paris: Herscher, 1985), 36: "les raffinements de la France et la viguer de l'Espagne."

33. *Espanya: 50 anyos de Moda* (Barcelona: Ajuntament de Barcelona, 1987); there are references to fashion also in María Luz Morales, *La moda: El traje y las costumbres en la primera mitad del siglo XX, 1935–1947,* vol. 11 (Barcelona: Salvat Editores, 1956).

34. Carmen Martín Gaite, *Usos amorosos de la postguerra española* (Barcelona: Anagrama, 1987), 122.

35. Friné, "Perfiles de la moda," *La Moda en España. Revista de figurines mensual,* February 1941, 3: "*La Moda en España,* dando consejos, publicando orientaciones y trayendo, con un carácter estrictamente nacional, a sus páginas las directrices del buen vestir, cumple una misión que no es exagerado titular de patriótica. Desde todos los ángulos se puede cooperar a la obra de reconstrucción en que estamos empeñados después de la Cruzada."

36. *La Moda en España,* July 1943, 8.

37. Gavarrón, *Mil caras tiene la moda,* 147.

38. *La Moda en España,* January 1943, 20: "La ropa interior bella y bien cuidada es un indicio de sincera sensibilidad, porque sería horrendo pecado de menosprecio albergar entre harapos la envoltura del alma."

39. Ibid., March 1942, 20.

40. Ibid., February 1944, 7.

41. Ibid., April 1943, 47.

42. Ibid., November 1946, 18: "Para halagar este deseo brindan los modistas los tejidos más hermosos; los más adornados también, evocadores de 'Las mil y una noches' de los del tiempo fabuloso de la prosperidad."

43. Rosario, "Crónica de Londres," *La Moda en España,* March 1945, 10.

44. *La Moda en España,* August 1947, 2.

45. Ibid., January 1942, 11.

46. "Lo que debe hacerse para logar casarse," *La Moda en España,* January 1943, 6.

47. "Las 'estrellas' practican los deportes," *La Moda en España,* February 1943, 11.

48. *La Moda en España,* July 1946, 14.

49. Friné, "Perfiles de la moda," *La Moda en España,* July 1941, 4.

50. *La Moda en España,* July 1943, 14: "El pantalón, con mucho vuelo, para que al andar no se aperciba que no es falda."

51. Friné, "Tendencias y perfiles," *La Moda en España,* January 1947, 5: "En París y en algunas capitales francesas que marchan al ritmo acelerado de la ciudad del Sena, muchas mujeres usan pantalones para la calle, sin que este atuendo—tan masculino, promueva el menor alboroto."

52. *La Moda en España,* September 1942, 24.

53. Friné, "Perfiles de la moda," *La Moda en España,* February 1945, 7: "Y es más, coincido totalmente con algunas personas que se han ocupado del asunto, al afirmar que la mujer, con ir destocada, sólo consigue causar la sensación, aunque este no sea su propósito, ni mucho menos, de hacer concesiones de mal gusto a los enemigos de nuestro régimen."

54. Marichu de la Mora, "Reflexiones sobre la moda en Argentina con motivo de un viaje," *La Moda en España,* July 1947, 18: "Y averiguamos que el sombrero es una prenda imprescindibile para una argentina, sea cual sea su condición social y sea cual sea la ocasión y la hora del día. Las cocineras salen a la compra con sombrero y las señoras de la sociedad, si van a comer a casa de unos amigos, me refiero a comer por la noche, van también de sombrero."

55. Luis Fernández Ardavin, "La mantilla," *La Moda en España,* April 1945, 14: "Juguetona, tornadiza, / pecadora y penitente, / . . . / Prenda que, en tu sencillez / femenina y seductora, / sigues siendo tan señora / y tan del pueblo a la vez."

56. *La Moda en España,* March 1947, 1.

57. Ibid., July 1947, 1.

9

THE YELLOW STAR ACCESSORIZED
IRONIC DISCOURSE IN FATELESSNESS
BY IMRE KERTÉSZ

Zsófia Bán

The application of visible stigmas (or, more mildly, distinctive signs) is a time-honored practice in all kinds of societies for a large variety of often despicable reasons and still lingers on as one of the favorite pastimes of what is known as human civilization. The designs and the aims may vary, but the impulse has lost none of its old momentum.[1]

> On the breast of her gown, in fine red cloth, surrounded with an elaborate embroidery and fantastic flourishes of gold-thread, appeared the letter A. It was so artistically done, and with so much fertility and gorgeous luxuriance of fancy, that it had all the effect of a last and fitting decoration to the apparel which she wore; and which was of a splendor in accordance with the taste of the age, but greatly beyond what was allowed by the sumptuary regulations of the colony. . . . Her attire, which, indeed, she had wrought for the occasion, in prison, and had modeled much after her own fancy, seemed to express the attitude of her spirit, the desperate recklessness of her mood, by its wild and picturesque peculiarity. But the point which drew all eyes, and, as it were, transfigured the wearer,—so that both men and women who had been familiarly acquainted with Hes-

ter Prynne, were now impressed as if they beheld her for the first time,—was that SCAR-
LET LETTER, so fantastically embroidered and illuminated upon her bosom. It had the
effect of a spell, taking her out of the ordinary relations with humanity, and enclosing
her in a sphere by herself.[2]

One may wonder, of course, why someone like Hester Prynne, thus punished, humiliated, and ostracized by her community, would make such an effort to transform the token of her "sin" into such a flamboyant affair. Would it be to have the "effect of a spell,"
as Nathaniel Hawthorne wrote, in order to take her "out of the ordinary relations with
humanity," and to enclose her "in a sphere by herself"? The development of the plot
seems to contradict this as, instead of being enclosed, Hester becomes reintegrated into
the community on a different, higher level, and people gradually start to regard her
stigma "as the token, not of that one sin, . . . but of her many good deeds since."[3] Or
would it, rather, be a sign of rebellion, a sign of nonacceptance of her punishment, and
thus the values of her community? Hawthorne's description of Hester's stance contradicts this too; Hester does acknowledge her deed as an act of transgression, albeit not as
one that is necessarily sinful. ("What we did had a consecration of its own.")[4] It seems
then that the luxurious embroidering of the sign functions as a subtle method with
which she defuses the visual mine it is originally meant to be. By proudly enhancing the
visual aspect of the stigma, she transforms it into something that succeeds in making a
substantial statement about herself, that is, into something that becomes a visual com-
plement—an accessory—to her very essence. The embroidered scarlet letter, just like
any well-chosen accessory, is able to make relevant statements concerning its wearer's
view of herself and the world around her. Hester's accessory, however, is one of a kind,
as it is transformed into an irremovable, unchangeable sign, a sort of "hyperaccessory."[5]
It becomes, as it were, a part of her; it becomes second nature. Instead of the secondary
status normal accessories tend to have, it acquires a primary, elevated, moreover unique,
exclusive role, like the pope's miter, for instance, or a queen's crown and scepter. In other
words, it acquires the status of regalia, the symbols and emblems of rank and power.

In what follows I wish to examine the stigma/accessory relation as it appears in the Nobel laureate Hungarian author Imre Kertész's chef d'oeuvre, the novel titled *Fatelessness*.[6] This will also allow me to look at how the author revives the topos of stigmatization and more specifically that of *visual* stigmatization to represent individual freedom versus coercion. Kertész's book is one of the most outstanding and unique examples of Holocaust literature, a testimony written by an author who, as a fourteen-year-old boy, experienced and miraculously survived the ordeal of the concentration camps. If his survival was miraculous in Buchenwald, his continuing *second* survival after the war (in the light of the countless suicides committed as an aftermath to that experience) is explained by Kertész with the revelatory logic of his specific geopolitical situation:

> What saved me from suicide (from the example of Borowski, Celan, Améry, Primo Levi, and others) was that society, following the experience of the KZ proved, in the form of so-called Stalinism, there could be no grounds whatsoever for freedom, liberation, great catharsis, etc., for all those things about which intellectuals, thinkers, and philosophers in more felicitous parts of the world were preaching, and in which they no doubt believed; which for me guaranteed the continuation of imprisonment, and thus excluded even the possibility of any delusion.[7]

The historical experience of repetition, of the segue from one total dictatorship to the next, is what gave Kertész and all those who lived in Eastern Europe the knowledge that totalitarianism was not an extrahistorical accident but something inevitable. This is the kind of knowledge, the kind of experience that irrevocably informs culture, that, moreover, itself functions as a culture, as Kertész professes in his seminal essay, "The Holocaust as Culture."[8]

Fatelessness has often been regarded as a novel of development in which a child, a teenager, undergoes the process of socialization in a concentration camp. His situation leads him to see the world of the camps as one governed by some kind of logic, which he continuously and dutifully tries to legitimize as his only way of endowing it with any kind of meaning. It is also his only way of adjusting to it, and thus of survival, for if he is able to maintain an illusion of normalcy, then there are only "given situations" that have to be solved, one at a time. The imposition of some kind of logical necessity onto the events happening to him is his only hermeneutical tool with which to perform an escape from the *horror vacui*, the total meaninglessness of his experience. There is a significant scene in the beginning of the novel in which the protagonist (Köves) has a conversation with a girl living in the same house who belongs to his circle of friends. She shares with them a problem that has been nagging her, connected to the obligation of wearing the yellow Star of David.[9] When she elaborates the idea that the difference between Jews and non-Jews must be an inherent one ("It was her view, in fact, that 'we Jews are different from other people,' and that difference was the crux of it, that's why people hate Jews"), Köves tries to convince her of the opposite, that it is a difference imposed on them externally.[10] Eventually, the girl seems to accept his argument (based on the tale of the prince and the pauper), whereupon she breaks down and starts crying. "But she exclaimed bitterly, in a voice that choked as it went on, something along the lines that if our own qualities had nothing to do with it, then it was all pure chance, and if she could be someone else than the person she was forced to be, then 'the whole thing has no sense,' and that notion, in her opinion, 'is unbearable'" (37). After Köves returns from the camp he retrospectively rehabilitates the girl's stance (or at least claims to understand it better) and retroactively imposes a similar logic on his experience in order to escape the "unbearable" to which the girl had referred. In other words, he eventually chooses to claim his experience as his own, acknowledging that even if he was not in control of the events, his actions were his own and constituted his life.

Until the concluding pages of the book, all of this, however, is presented by Kertész as being carried out by the boy in a strictly undeliberated way, without any teleological content, but simply performed out of pure survival instinct. The author's tour de force resides precisely in the highly disturbing rhetorical representation of "normalcy" throughout the novel, delivered to the reader by way of the protagonist's first-person narration. The narrator's perspective is represented as hauntingly instinctive, unreflective—without, however, being unintelligent. It is the rhetorical representation of a recognized and acknowledged *total* situation, total in the sense that there is no position outside it. The dysfunctional nature of freedom, morality, ethics, and legitimate authority in this world allows only for the participation of what Kertész calls a "functional person"[11] who, instead of constantly viewing and judging his condition from the perspective of metaphysical horror, simply "takes the next step" that is to be taken in the given situation. This behavior, which during the boy's days at the concentration camp was unreflective, instinctual, becomes at the end of the novel the cornerstone of his philosophy allowing him to endow his fate with meaning and to go on living. Once he decides to claim his experience as his own after his return home, his dead father's old friends cannot persuade him to "forget the terrors" so that he may live freely, so that he may start a new life. This assumption perplexes the boy, as he sees no chance for that.

> I would only be able to start a new life, I ventured, if I were to be reborn, or if some affliction, disease, or something of the sort were to affect my mind, which they surely didn't wish on me, I hoped. "In any case," I added, "I didn't notice any atrocities," at which, I could see, they were greatly astounded. What were they supposed to understand by that, they wished to know, by "I didn't notice"? To that, however, I asked them in turn what they had done during those "hard times." "Errm, . . . we lived," one of them deliberated. "We tried to survive," the other added. Precisely! They too had taken one step at a time, I noted. (256–57)

The old men do not seem to grasp his meaning, especially when the boy gives them the example of people having taken steps forward in the queue at the camps, while waiting for the doctor to decide whether they should be immediately gassed or "given a momentary reprieve." "'Where does all this fit in?' they asked, 'and what do you mean to say by it?'" This is the boy's reply:

> Nothing in particular, I replied, but it was not quite true that the thing "came about"; we had gone along with it too. Only now, and thus after the event, looking back, in hindsight, does the way it all "came about" seem over, finished, unalterable, finite, so tremendously fast, and so terribly opaque. And if, in addition, one knows one's fate in advance, of course. Then indeed one can only register the passing of time. A senseless

kiss, for example, is just as much a necessity as an idle day at the customs post, let's say, or the gas chambers. Except that whether one looks back or ahead, both are flawed perspectives, I suggested. . . . "It's about the steps." Everyone took steps as long as he was able to take a step; I too took my own steps, and not just in the queue at Birkenau, but even before that, here, at home. I took steps with my father, and I took steps with my mother, I took steps with Annamarie, and I took steps—perhaps the most difficult ones of all—with the older sister. I would now be able to tell her what it means to be "Jewish": nothing, nothing to me at least, at the beginning, until those steps start to be taken. None of it is true, there is no different blood, nothing else, only . . . given situations and the new givens inherent in them. I too had lived through a given fate. It had not been my own fate, but I had lived through it.[12]

It is in the course of this conversation that the boy (by now long initiated into adulthood) comes to the revelation that if there is fate, then there is no freedom, but if there is freedom, then "we ourselves are fate." He tries, at all costs, to defend this revelation, it being his only chance to give some meaning to what has happened to him thus far:

It was impossible, they must try and understand, impossible to take everything away from me, impossible for me to be neither winner nor loser, for me not to be right and for me not to be mistaken that I was neither the cause nor the effect of anything; they should try to see, I almost pleaded, that I could not swallow that idiotic bitterness, that I should merely be innocent. (260–61)

Clearly, it is not innocence that is at stake here. In Zeitz, in the concentration camp where the protagonist spends the most time, one of the inmates, another Hungarian, approaches him with the following:

"Do you know what this here," pointing to his chest, "this letter 'U,' signifies?" Sure I did, I told him: "*Ungar*, Hungarian." "No," he answered, "*Unschuldig*," meaning "innocent," then gave a snort of laughter followed by prolonged nodding of the head with a brooding expression, as if the notion were somehow highly gratifying, though I have no idea why. Subsequently, and quite often in the beginning, I saw the same on others in the camp from whom I also heard that wisecrack, as if they derived some warming, fortifying emotion from it.[13]

Strength, for the boy, does not, cannot surge from the knowledge of being innocent. Quite the contrary, were he to acknowledge the validity of such a term under the circumstances, it would only serve to weaken his morale and to prevent him from "taking the next step." Pure innocence would mean stasis and ultimately death; instead, his goal is to become "a model prisoner." As the quotation above also shows, at the time of the events this idea is something purely instinctual, or more precisely, *functional*. "I might have tried to break up time in my novel, and narrate only the most powerful scenes. But the hero of my novel does not live his own time in the concentration camps, for *neither his time nor his language, not even his own person, is really his*. He doesn't remember; he exists," explains Kertész in his Stockholm lecture.[14] Not until the very end of the narrative does the boy consciously identify with his earlier, unreflective actions, and then holds on to them, literally, for dear life.

In her essay on "The Holocaust and the Generations," philosopher Ágnes Heller emphasizes this same unreflectiveness:

> During the Holocaust the victims, essentially, were not thinking either. If I recall that year when my family and I were living in the extreme situation of the Holocaust, I cannot remember any kind of reflection. Things simply happened to us. We expressed this with the following words: the yellow star came, the confinement in the ghetto came, the entrainment came . . . they came . . . like something fateful, which we had expected to come. Even those who managed to escape acted only on instinct.[15]

In *Fatelessness*, this behavior and attitude of temporal, linguistic, and psychological disengagment is expressed on various rhetorical levels. Probably the most striking device in the novel used for this purpose is the haunting, at times definitely annoying, or even enraging, repetitive use of the word *naturally*. Practically everything the boy relates is complemented by words such as *naturally* or *understandably*, words lexically aiding the hermeneutic feat he accomplishes. This feat is to interpret the given situation as a limiting frame that closes off the rest of the world and that, consequently, functions quite literally as a frame of mind. No less important, this device also facilitates the rhetorical feat the *author* accomplishes, which is to heighten the effect of horror by detachment. The boy's description of their journey to Buchenwald in the boxcar is a good example of both:

> For those who complained about the lack of space there were plenty who reminded them, quite rightly, to remember that the next time there would be eighty of them. And basically, if I thought about it, when all was said and done, there had been times when I was more tightly packed: in the gendarmerie stable, for instance, where the only way we had been able to resolve the problem of fitting ourselves in was by agreeing that we should all squat crosslegged on the ground. My seat on the train was more comfortable than that. If I wanted, I could even stand up, indeed take a step or two—over toward the slop bucket, for example, since that was situated in the rear right-hand corner of the wagon. What we initially decided about that was to use it as far as possible only for purposes of taking a leak; but as time passed, entirely predictably of course, it was forcibly brought home to many of us that the demands of nature were more powerful than any vow, and we boys acted accordingly, just like the men, to say nothing of the women. (72–73)

At the end of the book, this framing, which previously had been represented on a purely rhetorical level, is foregrounded as a matter of discussion. When the boy finally returns to Budapest, from where he was deported, he meets a journalist on a streetcar who comes to his aid when he is unable to purchase a ticket. The journalist starts to interrogate him, wanting to know what it was like in the camps:

> "Did you have to endure many horrors?" to which I replied that it all depended what he considered to be a horror. No doubt, he declared, his expression now somewhat uneasy, I had undergone a lot of deprivation, hunger, and more likely they had beaten me, to which I said: naturally. "Why, my dear boy," he exclaimed, though now, so it seemed to me, on the verge of losing his patience, "do you keep on saying 'naturally,' and always

about things that are not at all natural?" I told him that in a concentration camp they *were* natural. "Yes, of course, of course," he says, "they were *there*, but . . . ," and he broke off, hesitating slightly, "but . . . I mean, a concentration camp in itself is *unnatural*," finally hitting on the right word as it were. I didn't even bother saying anything to this, as I was beginning slowly to realize that it seems there are some things you just can't argue about with strangers, the ignorant, with those who, in a certain sense, are mere children so to say. . . . "Would you care to give an account of your experiences, young fellow?" . . . "But what about?" "The hell of the camps," he replied, to which I remarked that I had nothing at all to say about that as I was not acquainted with hell and couldn't even imagine what that was like. He assured me, however, that it was just a manner of speaking: "Can we imagine a concentration camp as anything but a hell?" he asked, and I replied, as I scratched a few circles with my heel in the dust under my feet, that everyone could think what they liked about it, but as far as I was concerned I could only imagine a concentration camp, since I was somewhat acquainted with what that was, but not hell. (247–49)

This passage summarizes some of the focal ideas of the book. One is the questioning of the *concept of the natural,* suggesting that it is a cultural construction, as is madness, for instance, as discussed by Michel Foucault in *Madness and Civilization.*[16] Being placed in the concentration camps as a fourteen-year-old, without any substantial previous socialization, Köves undergoes this process of constructedness in the only world he knows. He has no means of comparison, which leads us to the other central issue of the novel, namely the *use of language.* The novel not only suggests that the natural is a cultural construction, but also conveys the idea that it is a logical construction, in the sense that what is natural may also be logical *within the given system.*

Some of the statements in Ludwig Wittgenstein's *Tractatus Logico-Philosophicus* (1921) seem to have striking relevance to ideas in the above passage. For the boy, the given situation is regarded as a system within which the individual elements logically correspond to each other, and for him there isn't—there cannot be—anything outside that system. "5.555 Where, however, we can build symbols according to a system, there this system is the logically important thing and not the single symbols; 5.5557 The application of logic decides what elementary propositions there are; 5.5571 If I cannot give elementary propositions a priori then it must lead to obvious nonsense to try to give them."[17] The situation of the Holocaust is evidently one in which it is impossible to "give elementary propositions a priori," because its "logic" contradicts all previous a priori elementary propositions. Nevertheless, the journalist makes attempts at doing so, and this is (logically) received by the boy as childish nonsense. The journalist obviously believes in the universality of a system and thus of elementary propositions, whereas the boy's experience contradicts this. Furthermore, when the journalist makes a reference to hell as a metaphor ("manner of speaking") for the camps, without having knowledge of the camps (nor of hell, for that matter), then the metaphorical use of language becomes purely hypothetical, as there is no knowledge to sustain comparison. When many expressed the idea that there can be no art—neither literature nor any other form of art—about the Holocaust, it was, among other things, the metaphorization of the elementary and concrete that was refuted as superficial and facetious. To return to the earlier question of "innocence," in these terms the boy's knowledge (of the camp) limits his language (he can neither speak of nor imagine hell), and the limits of his language delineate the limits of his world. "5.6 The limits of my language mean the limits of my world." In this sense, innocence is no more part of his language than hell. The journalist—a user of language by profession—entertains the illusion that there is freedom in the use of language, while the boy's experience tells him that there is none. Consequently, the boy throws away the piece of paper on which the journalist put down his name and address. There can be no collaboration between them, they cannot write an article together, as the journalist suggested, since they lack a common language. This lack of a common language applies to the reader as well and manifests itself, for instance, in the scandalous use of certain words, like happiness, in such a context:

> There is nothing impossible that we do not live through naturally, and keeping a watch on me on my journey, like some inescapable trap, I already know there will be happiness. For even there, next to the chimneys, in the intervals between the torments, there

was something that resembled happiness. Everyone asks only about the hardships and the "atrocities," whereas for me perhaps it is that experience which will remain the most memorable. Yes, the next time I am asked, I ought to speak about that, the happiness of the concentration camps. If indeed I am asked. And provided I myself don't forget. (262)

These are the last lines of the book, and by writing it, the author fulfills the boy's resolution.

Such is the theoretical context in which I wish to discuss what I mean by the accessorization of the yellow star. While examining how this process takes place, I will show its relevance for the issues of assimilation, familiarization, and determination. In the beginning of *Fatelessness,* the narrative makes clear that the compulsory wearing of the yellow Star of David causes some psychological discomfort for Köves, the protagonist: "It was a slightly uncomfortable feeling going around with them [the boy and his parents] like that, as a trio, yellow stars on all three of us. The matter is more a source of amusement to me when I am on my own, but together with them it was close to embarrassing. I couldn't explain why that was, but later on I no longer took any notice of it" (9–10). Here, I refer the reader to the text of the Hungarian ministerial decree quoted earlier, according to which the star should not simply be yellow but a highly specific *canary yellow.* While obviously enforcing the wearing of a striking, eye-catching hue, the wording also tellingly reveals the psychology of the subtext, namely that the authorities wish to regulate the lives of these people in every possible way, down to the minutest detail.[18]

Besides causing psychological discomfort, it also makes the wearer conscious of certain otherwise natural acts: "It was a clear, balmy morning, considering it was still just early spring. I was about to unbutton myself but then had second thoughts: it was possible that, light as the head breeze was, my coat lapel might flap back and cover up my yellow star, which would not have been in conformity with the regulations. There were by now a few things I had to be more on my guard against," says the boy in the beginning of the novel (5). The wearing of such a visual stigma thus affects not just the mind, but also the body, triggering self-surveillance and self-censorship, except instead of the natural reflex, which is to hide a stigma, the boy's actions here are coordinated in order to keep it visible at all times. The boy, when resolving to be more circumspect, falls into the trap of wanting to be a good citizen, albeit in a society that enforces immoral, unethical laws.[19] Likewise, he later on wants to be a model prisoner at the camp. The changing of the laws, the changing of the system, is not his competence. What *is* his competence is how well he can obey the law, how well he can assimilate to society and be a good citizen. In Hungary, Jews have traditionally been very highly assimilated, most of them placing their national identity much before their Jewish identity. The boy's behavior can thus be read not just as part of Kertész's authorial strategy, but also as a reference to this historical tradition. Hence, as the boy himself remarks in the passage quoted above, he later stops paying attention to the issue of the star on their clothing not just because he becomes used to it but, more important, because it becomes accepted by him as part of the system; in other words *it becomes natural*. The defamiliarization of the Star of David, achieved by transforming it into a visual stigma, becomes refamiliarized by the boy's assimilationist tendencies. And this is also how the yellow star becomes, as it were, accessorized. The boy and his parents go to a shop seeking items the father would need at the labor camp. This is how the boy describes the shop:

> As it happens, I know the shop, because it is situated close to where we live, but I had never been inside before. It is actually a sort of sports goods shop, though they sell other merchandise as well. Of late it has even been possible to get their own make of yellow stars there, given that now there was a big shortage of yellow fabric, of course. (As for our own needs, my stepmother had taken care of that in good time.) As best I could make out, it was their innovative twist to have the material stretched over some cardboard base, so that way, of course, it looked more attractive, plus the arms of the stars weren't cut in such a ludicrously clumsy fashion as some of the homemade ones that were to be seen. I noticed that they themselves had their own wares adorning their chests, but in such a way as to seem that they were only wearing them in order to make them appeal to customers. (10)

The ambition—described here from the boy's point of view!—to make the star *more attractive* cannot, I assume, be read as anything but an effort to transform the star into an accessory, into something that will look good and will thus enhance the appearance of its wearer, like any high-quality pair of shoes or gloves. The dangers implied in this process obviously concern not just the Jewish population, but anyone who comes to share this feeling of "naturalization."[20] This is one of the most insistent *subtextual* communications conveyed by Kertész's indirect rhetoric in the book. In the passage above, the accessorized star is made to carry the tension created by the difference between the narrator's and the author's points of view—a tension sustained throughout the book by the author's relentless use of the rhetoric of indirectness or irony.

A similar rhetoric is used by Ernö Szép, one of the outstanding Hungarian writers of the interwar period, in his unique, diary-like chronicle of his ordeals at a labor camp in 1944, at the age of sixty. He writes the following on how the dwellers of his building in the Budapest ghetto related to the star:

> All summer long I had watched how those yellow stars were cared for; washed and ironed, cleaned with spot remover if stained, then reversed and sewn back on. And some ladies and gentlemen used lemon yellow, some yellow ochre, depending on what went well with the coat. And certain finicky dames and dandies wore yellow silk, much more elegant than the linen or cotton ones.[21]

Not coincidentally, the tone is strikingly reminiscent of Kertész's in his own book. While the horrors in Szép's account are softened by the sustained ironical and puzzled tone, the magnitude of the horrors related is not diminished. Quite the contrary, the tone rather emphasizes the absurdity, immorality, and intolerability of the situation. This kind of indirect or inverted, ironic discourse is highly characteristic of East-Central European thought in which black humor, understatements, and the downplaying of ill fate serves to outline the "intended" inverse meaning. As I see it, in *Fatelessness*, Kertész turns directly to this tradition and reappropriates it for his own purposes. The passage quoted above from *The Smell of Humans*, in which the yellow star is transformed into an acces-

FIGURES 9.1, 9.2, 9.3, 9.4, 9.5

Jewish Stars in various shades of
yellow embroidered by Hungarian
tailors. Author's collection.

sory, is complemented by a later passage in which Szép, to while away the time while marching to the labor camp, surveys real accessories, the hats and caps worn by those trudging in front of him:

> I kept myself amused by surveying the various headpieces worn in front of me. Gray hats and beige hats; beige was the most numerous, this colour having been the fashion for the past few years. One or two elderly gentlemen wore hats with those very narrow brims, such as worn by young punks. But there were a few black hats visible—strange, in warm October weather. You could see plenty of caps as well: golfers' caps, touring caps for the sportier types. Oh, those fine wool travel caps, once in my foolish youth I bought one of those for a trip abroad. But I saw ahead of me many other types of caps, cheaper kinds worn by so-called "little men"—retailers, artisans, workers, street vendors and poor peasants. Herr Director T. (who wore a cap whenever he went out on rubble clean-up details) kept me entertained once by giving an account of the cap industry: how small manufacturers bought up the remnants of inexpensive fabrics and linings, what a lively and competitive industry this was, and what a huge part of society Europe-wide and worldwide wore caps instead of hats. And that was not even counting all those students, scouts, soldiers, railroad employees, sailors, pilots, doormen and others who did not wear hats as a rule. If you were to hold a headcount you would find that more people on earth wore caps than hats.[22]

These musings have a double-edged effect: while they serve to anchor the narrator in the real, normal world, offering him the illusion that this world still exists, they also highlight—for him, as well as for the reader—the inconsistency, irrationality, and hopelessness of such an assumption. The accessories reeled off here are portentous, metonymical markers of a suddenly sunken world. In the context of the events related, these hats and caps were manufactured in Atlantis. They are also harbingers of those other accessories captured on film and photographs: the shoes standing in heaps in Auschwitz.

Besides this rhetoric of irony, the accessorized yellow star also appears in the context of a discourse less popular and less rooted in East-Central European discourse, that of decadence. The decadent trend, launched in European literature (and life) primarily by

Joris-Karl Huysman's hugely popular novel À rebours (1884), was never as obsessive in Hungary as it was in France or England, for example, where it bloomed into a veritable lifestyle, exemplified by the life and works of Huysman's best pupil, Oscar Wilde. Since Huysman's book was only translated into Hungarian in 1921 (by one of the best Hungarian poets and writers, Dezsö Kosztolányi), the reception of this trend was rather belated in Hungary. "Vivre? les serviteurs feront cela pour nous" is the typical bon mot from a contemporary dramatic poem that became one of the slogans of the decadent movement.[23] While this philosophy had reached the height of its popularity at the fin de siècle, by the interwar period it lost much of its original luster. In an era laden with somber issues and problems, such a frivolous worldview, regarding life, morals, and everyday problems as petty, seemed at best irresponsible, not to say immoral. Hence, by the period of World War II, the cultivation of decadence, illness, and languor went irrevocably out of fashion.

Dezsö Szomory, one of the most popular playwrights and writers of the interwar period in Hungary, spent seventeen years in Paris in his youth, at the time when the decadence mania had reached its apogee. He fled to France in 1889 as a deserter of the Austro-Hungarian army, and thus lived there in exile. Szomory became strongly influenced by the decadent spirit and aesthetics, and upon his eventual return to Hungary when he was granted a pardon, he became one of its few authentic representatives and practitioners, a role he retained until his death. It became a mask for him that, like Dorian Gray's, was impossible to remove after a time. There is a famous anecdote about Szomory who, as a Jew, was obliged to wear the yellow star during the war. Andor Kellér, writer and publicist, his faithful helper and admirer, relates it in his book on Szomory as follows:

"Hello," he said. "I've run out of cigarettes. The maid has left; I can't send her to the tobacco shop. Be so good as to bring me cigarettes. A pack of Vitéz."

"Of course. But you come along, too, Dezsike. Let's walk a little. It's another half-hour till curfew."

He looked at me indignantly, and then pointed to his star. "With this on my chest? A yellow star on a gray jacket? The disharmony of colors is the death of elegance. I am ready to die, but I will never show poor taste."[24]

The aesthetics of decadence allowed Szomory to pronounce such sentences without the slightest whiff of irony. He completely identified with his role, even at the price of ridicule and derision that was often his lot, for decadence and aestheticism in those days could, at best, come off as camp. The insistence on an attitude fundamentally alien to the given place and time may function as an unconscious mode of psychological resistance, which shields its practitioner from the contemplation of his situation. But it can also be seen as a highly conscious mode of resistance in the sense that it does not accept the logic of the imposed system, that is, the normalization of its absurd requirements, and insists on adhering to one that is totally and radically alien to it. Fascism, as Walter Benjamin pointed out, is "the aestheticization of politics," and here Szomory resists this with an extreme aestheticization of life.[25] And even though such a stance has an undeniably tragicomical effect, it does make a relevant statement concerning the total "loss of taste" that Fascism meant.

Szomory's example is thus one of determined adherence to a lifestyle and way of thinking that sets him apart from the crowd, whereas in Kertész's *Fatelessness* we get the *inverse* of this strategy: the boy's intense wish to conform to the situation and accept what it has to offer. Instead of the rhetoric of decadence or the rhetoric of tragedy, we are offered the rhetoric of irony—that of the *author,* not the narrator. As discussed above, Kertész rhetorically naturalizes and familiarizes the boy's plight in order to heighten the alienating effect. The yellow star, as I have argued, is often a device or, shall we say, an accessory to this rhetoric of naturalization. In fact, at certain crucial, though barely noticeable moments, Kertész goes even beyond that and invests it with desire. In the beginning of the narrative there is a highly subtle example where the boy is describing Annamarie, the girl he falls in love with: "She too is fourteen years old, or thereabouts. She has a long neck and is already starting to round out under her yellow star" (13). Not only do these simple words naturalize the situation in general, not only do they familiarize the yellow star transforming it into an accessory, but they also, perplexingly, sexualize it, in spite of everything. And when I write "in spite," I mean it quite literally, for here love and sexual desire is *in spite* of everything around them; of everything that, in turn, has spite for things like love. The star becomes a part of the girl's body, integrated by the boy's desire;

it becomes, as it were, an object of desire. This seems to affirm the dictum that "clothes do not make the man," for in this instance it is the (wo)man that "makes" the clothes; and the boy's gaze acknowledges this difference.[26]

At a later stage in the book, this early experience gives way to revision of this dictum. Before reaching Zeitz, their final destination, the boys are first transported to Auschwitz where, luckily, they spend only a few days. In this scene, they are already shaved, and they have received their prisoner's clothes; in other words they have all been robbed of their civilian identity and distinctive features:

> The boys and I for a long time at first just examined and stared in wonderment at one another, turning each other around. But I also noticed a young-looking man nearby who at length and with absorbed attention, yet somehow hesitantly, was inspecting and patting his clothes from top to toe, as though he wished merely to convince himself about the quality of the material, its genuineness, so to say. After that, he glanced up, like someone who suddenly has a remark to make, but then, seeing all at once only clothes of the same kind around him, finally says nothing after all. (100)

Not long after this, the news starts spreading in the camp that they are soon to receive hot soup. Besides commenting in a puzzled tone on the childlike joy with which the other inmates receive this simple news, the narrator adds the following:

> I also considered it very likely that the information might well have derived from that prisoner who had immediately appeared to become our guide, not to say host, at this place. He too, just like the prisoner at the bath-house, had a snugly fitting outfit, a head of hair, which to me in itself already seemed truly unusual, and on his head a soft cap of dark blue felt, what one would call a beret, on his feet elegant tan shoes, and on his arm a red band to give his authority immediately visible expression, and I began to realize that it seemed I ought to revise a notion I had been taught back home to the effect that "clothes do not make the man." He likewise had a red triangle on his chest, and that too showed everyone straightaway that he was not here on account of his bloodline but merely for his way of thinking, as I was able to learn not much later. (103)

Terrible as it is, in this context even hair is transformed into an accessory, just like the dark blue cap and the beige shoes that enhance the general good looks of this man. In a situation where they are stripped, literally, of their original identity and condemned to uniformity, the thought that clothes *do* make the man does not seem to be unfounded. This realization on the boy's part still seems to support his conviction elaborated earlier in the debate with the girl at home, according to which difference is imposed externally, whereas the girl thought it must be something inherent, something we carry in ourselves. According to the boy's argument supported by the story of the prince and the pauper who exchange their fate with each other out of pure curiosity, even fate itself can be worn as a kind of accessory that will put us in one group as opposed to another. This is what happens with the more privileged prisoners in the concentration camp. "Philosophy" is here deemed a lesser sin than "blood," but in another situation it could very well be the other way around. This is precisely what the girl, at the time of their debate, finds "totally unbearable." But as the boy eventually realizes at the end of the book, the steps we take in a given situation are ours, these are what constitute "fate," these are what constitute our lives. It is not a question of the possibility or impossibility of going against the laws that others impose on our lives in certain dark moments of history. It is about realizing and accepting that incredibly difficult and burdensome thought: that whatever happens *is* our life. That there is, actually, no such thing as "fatelessness."

NOTES

1. See, for instance, a fairly recent example, when in May 2001, Hindus in Taliban-ruled Afghanistan were ordered to wear a distinctive sign on their shirt pockets, distinguishing them as non-Muslims. The Ministry for the Promotion of Virtue and Prevention of Vice, which runs the religious police, specified that the label should be a yellow cloth. The decision, obviously reminiscent of Nazi policy during World War II, triggered international protests.

2. Nathaniel Hawthorne, *The Scarlet Letter* (New York: Bantam, 1981), 149.

3. Ibid., 149. See also how the letter A acquires different interpretations in the course of the story,

like Able, Angel, etc., all bearing positive connotations, as opposed to the negative, condemnatory content of the original.

4. Ibid., 179.

5. Concerning its irremovability, see the scene in which Pearl throws a fit ("The Child at the Brook-Side") and does not want to acknowledge Hester as her mother until Hester is willing to fasten the discarded letter back onto her dress: "Now thou art my mother indeed! And I am thy little Pearl!" (ibid., 193).

6. Originally published in Hungarian as *Sorstalanság* (Budapest: Szépirodalmi Könyvkiadó, 1975).

7. From Kertész's essay titled "Haza, otthon, ország" [Nation, home, country], in *A gondolatnyi csend, amíg a kivégzőosztag újratölt: Monológok és dialógok* [Moments of silence while the execution squad reloads: Monologues and dialogues] (Budapest: Magvető, 1998), 9, my translation. In his Nobel Prize lecture (Stockholm, 2002), he complements this thought by stating, "If I look back now and size up honestly the situation I was in at the time, I have to conclude that in the West, in a free society, I probably would not have been able to write the novel known by readers today as *Fatelessness*" (translated by Ivan Sanders).

8. Kertész, "A holocaust mint kultúra," [The holocaust as culture], in *A gondolatnyi csend*.

9. In Hungary, the ministerial decree ordering the compulsory wearing of the yellow Star of David dates from March 31, 1944. The first paragraph of the decree states: "(1) As this decree comes into force, every Jewish person who has completed his sixth year—without regard to sex—is obliged, when going out, to visibly wear on the left upper part of his clothing a six-pointed, canary yellow–colored star having a diameter of 10 × 10 centimeters, made of cloth, silk, or velvet. (2) The distinctive sign described above must be fastened—by sewing—onto the clothing in a way as to prevent its easy removal."

10. Imre Kertész, *Fatelessness*, trans. Tim Wilkinson (New York: Vintage, 2004), 35. Further references appear in the text.

11. A term used in Kertész's initial notes in *Gályanapló* [Galley boat-log 1961–1991] (Budapest: Holnap, 1992).

12. Kertész, *Fatelessness*, 258–59. The older sister here is the girl who in the beginning of the book discusses with him her dilemma concerning the difference between Jews and non-Jews, referred to earlier in this essay.

13. Ibid., 142–43. In *The Scarlet Letter*, the letter A (standing for Adultery), originally meant to

signal Hester's guilt, is gradually transformed into an indictment of the world around her without, however, making her innocent. Being innocent is beside the point if the prevailing laws are flawed. "In an immoral world to be moral is immoral as well," writes Kertész in his piece titled *Jegyzőkönyv* [Record of evidence] (Budapest: Magvető-Századvég, 1993), 16.

14. Translated by Ivan Sanders. Emphasis added.

15. Ágnes Heller, *Auschwitz és gulag* [Auschwitz and gulag] (Budapest: Múlt és Jövő Kiadó, 2002), 82–83, my translation.

16. Michel Foucault, *Madness and Civilization: A History of Insanity in the Age of Reason* (Milton Park: Routledge, 2006).

17. Ludwig Wittgenstein, *Tractatus Logico-Philosophicus,* with an introduction by Bertrand Russell (London: Routledge, 1990). Translated from the German by C. K. Ogden in 1922.

18. The star was not necessarily yellow in all countries; for instance in Poland it was blue (and it was not sewn on but worn on a white armband).

19. In this respect, Kertész's bildungsroman clearly does not follow the typical trajectory of the genre, where the protagonist moves from conformity to autonomy through rebellion.

20. The difference, however, is not to be ignored: in the case of Jews this danger was lethal, while with others, "merely" moral.

21. Ernö Szép, *The Smell of Humans,* trans. John Batki (Budapest: CEU Press–Corvina, 1994), 50. Apparently not everyone cultivated the canary yellow of the decree.

22. Ibid., 64–65.

23. Count Philippe-Auguste Villiers de l'Isle-Adam, *Axël* (1885–86), trans. H. P. R. Finberg (London: Jarrolds, 1925).

24. In Andor Kellér, *Író a toronyban* [Writer in the tower] (Budapest: Szépirodalmi Könyvkiadó, 1958), 126, my translation.

25. Walter Benjamin, "The Work of Art in the Age of Reproducibility," ed. Howard Eiland and Michael W. Jennings, trans. Edmund Jephcott and Harry Zohn, in *Selected Writings,* 3: *1935–1938* (Cambridge, Mass.: Harvard University Press, 2002), 122.

26. Again, I have to refer here to the similar process that takes place in *The Scarlet Letter.*

TERRA DIVISA/TERRA DIVINA: (T/E/A/R)

Maria Damon

Terra Divisa/Terra Divina: (T/E/A/R), referring to the Scottish/English "Debatable Lands," is bisected by conflict on the diagonal: brown and green for the earth and its cycles of rest and renewal or, more violently, death and rebirth. I used lettering from Scots and English children's samplers. That these are made by children and now collected by adults adds to the conflictual status of "outsider" or "naïve" art.

The large, ornate T and A are from a Scottish sampler from the 1750s, described in my pattern booklet as "a step toward the majestic illuminations to follow."[1] The A takes pride of place and space: it's the largest letter, spilling over its borders. It resonates with the American literary classic, Nathaniel Hawthorne's *The Scarlet Letter*, about a woman who dares to live outside society's rules by having a child by a man who was not her husband. As penance she is forced to embroider an A (for Adultery) on her clothing. As an assertion of her artistry and humanity, she makes the A as ornate and elaborate and gorgeous—a "majestic illumination" for sure—as she can. But to take it one step further: the story of Scottish bard Màiri nighean Alisdair Ruaidh (ca. 1615–1706) reminds me that A is, of course, also the Artist, so Nathaniel Hawthorne, descendant of the Judge John Hathorne who condemned the Salem witches, carries a closet identification with his heroine Hester (and her real-life foremothers) despite his complaints to his publisher

FIGURE 10.1 Maria Damon, *Terra Divisa/Terra Divina: (T/E/A/R)*, 2009.

in 1855 about the "damned mob of scribbling women" whose popular fiction compromised his craft. Màiri's stated desire to be buried face down so that her expressive arts would be forever and redundantly condemned to silence (death is not enough; the punishment, as Michel Foucault and Hawthorne remind us, must be spectacular, even if, as in this case, no one can actually see it, as it is underground) prompted me to turn the A upside down.

The smaller E and R are from an English sampler made in an orphanage in the 1840s. I thought I should include an English "font" as representative of the other side of the border dispute. My pattern booklet includes English samplers from 1590, but they were a bit too stark and small scale for my needs; moreover, the pathos of English orphans being taught to do this dying art (by 1840 the advent of industrial textile manufacture, even industrially produced embellishment, meant that this form of production could only be a disciplinary measure rather than a useful pedagogical transmission of practical skills) indicated this as the right choice. Children who have been torn from their families and/ or their social place to be institutionalized suffer a diasporic border war of their own, internal as it may be. The original sampler lettering did not include the outlining of the letters; I added that to make the scale more appropriate for the balance of the piece.

I noticed near the end of the project that the pattern booklet I used—Van Valin's *Alphabets from Early Samplers*—is published by the Scarlet Letter.

NOTE

1. Marsha Van Valin, *Alphabets from Early Samplers: Sixty-Four Examples from Samplers Dating from circa 1590 to 1868, with Charts and Authentic Color Schemes* (Sullivan, Wis.: Scarlet Letter, 1994), 13.

11

BLACK HATTITUDE

Jeffrey C. Stewart

A hat heightens the body, but it also elevates the soul. Especially elevating is a cocked hat on a man or woman with attitude. You have seen them: Black men with a swagger in their step, a hat broke at an outrageous angle, tilted like a landscape of a world about to fall off its axis, ambling down the street like they own it, even if they haven't a quarter in their pockets. Yes, it is a performance, but it is also a tightrope act, balancing deficits and demerits of the economies of past slavery against the hypocritical world that replaced it. A man's hat cocked to the side makes him more than he is—a knight in helmeted armor, ax on his head, cutting through an unforgiving world that has already dismissed him. Already discarded her. I say "her" because it was Zora Neale Hurston who first articulated the politics of hatdom as a methodology of emancipation from the discourses of oppression that Alain Locke tried but failed to exorcize from African-American studies with *The New Negro: An Interpretation* (1925).[1] During the 1930s and 1940s, Hurston penned a series of novels and memoirs in which she offered some ways to pry the Negro's response away from the typical reflex of victimhood. When facing down racial ignorance, Hurston sought to elude the racial reactivity that almost always ensnarled the unsuspecting Black humanist. In contrast to verbal retaliation, she developed a technology of dress that allowed a subtler, more nimble reflexivity whereby the Negro subject answered the blow to her ego by dismissing the adversary wordlessly. Or, to put it in a Hurston-like epigram, when the grip of race is tight, make sure your hat is right.

Zora Hurston discussed the temptation to get caught in race failure when she recalled a painful encounter at a doctor's office in "My Most Humiliating Jim Crow Experience."[2] Ironically, but tellingly, her "most humiliating Jim Crow experience came in New York instead of the South as one would have expected." Hurston had been sent by her patron, Mrs. Charlotte Mason, to "a certain White specialist at her expense." Here is where the well-meaning White ally can cause the Negro friend the most trouble. The ally sees racism as epiphenomenal, a quirk, or an anachronism afflicting those ignorant people "over there," not the social formation of identities "right here." As Hurston quickly discovered, the New York doctor was not happy to find a brown Zora sitting in the reception room of his very white office. "He did not approach me at all, but told one of his nurses to take me into a private examination room. The room was private all right, but I would not rate it highly as an examination room. Under any other circumstances, I would have sworn it was a closet where the soiled towels and uniforms were tossed." When the doctor entered, he asked a couple of questions "desultorily" about what ailed Hurston and then wrote a prescription to get her out of his office pronto. For most human beings such an experience wounds, and it wounded Hurston. But she would not give him, his nurse, or herself the satisfaction of being publicly hurt—or angry. "I did not get up and sweep out angrily as I was first disposed to do." Once the doctor finished going through the motions of an examination, "I got up, set my hat at a reckless angle and walked out, telling him that I would send him a check, which I never did. I went away feeling the pathos of the Anglo-Saxon civilization . . . for I know that anything with such a false foundation cannot last."[3]

Here is the key insight about the hat set at a "reckless angle" on a Black head—it signifies Hurston's impunity, functioning as a shield against the brainwashing that attempts to inculcate in its would-be victims the idea of their inferiority, that somehow they deserve the rude treatment segregationists dish out to them. Just when the emotion connected to such abuse began its assault on her psyche, she reached for her hat, cocked it at an angle that says "kiss this," and sauntered out of the vortex. That hat cut through the space of race and freed Zora from the emotion with which her Hippocratic oath–violating segregationist wished to trap her. By not retaliating verbally, Hurston refused to confirm that the doctor had "got to her"; instead, her gesture turned the tables and cut through the stink of wet linen and funky attitude that sequestered her in a laundry room. Detaching from her emotions allowed Hurston to observe his performance "as an objective person" and retain a sense of agency, really a sense of choice, to do as she wished and not be dictated to by her adversary. And her hat concretized her attitude into an unforgettable slicing through the room as she left, no doubt stunning the doctor and his nurse.

"Who does she think she is?" probably escaped from one of their mouths. In their reaction would be her microvictory. In the clutches of a scenario designed to turn her into an object of White male power, Hurston's cocked hat represented him as the inferior because he had violated the professional, no, human, norm of how you treat another person. In short, she had outed him. And while he tried to sort out his response, she fled the scene of his crime. Of course, it was still Hurston's "most humiliating Jim Crow experience," but it was only the "most" humiliating of a string of incidents that had given her the moral discipline to deal with this one. She had learned that it was not what you said, but what you did, and so she chose a gesture—the cocked hat—that sent an unmistakable message, "I am still here, Black and proud," as her body and its cutting edge, her hat, swept out of the room. Responding to racism with a "reckless angle" had allowed her to "change the joke and slip the yoke"—as Ralph Ellison put it in his memorable line—and escape a racial encounter with her self-worth intact.[4]

Hurston's musings epitomize Chela Sandoval's theoretical exploration of the way the oppressed in America have developed a methodology of survival and assertive subjectivity in societies devoted to objectifying, especially, the colored masses.[5] Yet the challenge for our phenomenology of hats is not only to track its operation under oppression, but also to think about hat wearing beyond simply the racial-oppression response paradigm. Zora Neale Hurston is interesting in this regard as a kind of Janus-faced intellectual, someone who documents the Black subject pushing back against racism but refuses to reduce Black culture to simply shoring up the soul against Whitey. Regardless of whether she is facing the gaze of a doctor or a publicity shot, she seems to have a particular talent for wearing hats at just the right angle, actually the most extreme angle she can wear them on her head, as if how they are "broke" to the side tells us how much attitude she is carrying *every* day. And that attitude is what keeps her going in a world that doesn't give a damn whether she or anyone else lives or dies.

We must be careful here. The zeal with which we expose the racial technology of a gesture in a racially charged situation needs to be tempered with an awareness that any gesture can have multiple intentions and, perhaps most important, be infused with various meanings by an observer. A case in point is Hurston's angling her hat to create a desired effect. What is that effect, really? Let's consider it from a different perspective. In the fashion history book *Coups de têtes extravagants,* a record of accessories, especially hats and gloves, designed for women by haute couture designers, the authors include a history of hats from ancient to modern. Under one of the photographs in the book of a woman wearing a hat broke to the side, the book's caption reads: "Portrait d'une tres

FIGURE 11.1 Carl Van Vechten, *Zora Neale Hurston,* 1935. Printed by permission of Van Vechten Trust.

grande dame au chapeau."[6] The grande-dame pose suggests that gender and class are both weapons and obstacles to Hurston's assertion of her identity and figure prominently in her choice of the hat as her weapon of self-deliverance. As a woman wearing a woman's hat, Zora Neale Hurston could appropriate a grande-dame aesthetics for her defense. Even the extreme angle of the hat fits within this stereotype, since the extremely sophisticated woman of the world has the right to break the superficial rules of "correct dress" upheld by the petite bourgeoisie, partly because she operates according to worldly rules of dress and etiquette unknown to the provincial philistines around her. The grande dame's chapeau set at a "reckless angle" allows Hurston to announce that she is not only a lady, but a great lady, whose superiority to her audience should be understood. "And I am your superior," her hat announces to her doctor, "because I have behaved like a lady (not getting loud and angry, like some common person would) while you have not acted like a gentleman." Hurston has used the rhetoric of gendered class gesture to shift the focus from biology to one of behavior, because by those standards, he *is* the inferior.

To be fair, class and gender consciousness may have figured in the doctor's Jim Crow reaction. After all, Zora Hurston was sent into the situation by a real grande dame, Mrs. Mason, with whom the doctor may have forged a relationship based on her extreme wealth and social position. Having inherited millions from her deceased surgeon husband, Mrs. Mason lived in the grand style, her Park Avenue apartment spanning the entire floor of the building. Her wealth insulated her so well from the economic effects of the Great Depression that she was able to spend thousands of dollars on her pet Harlem Renaissance projects, including paying Hurston two hundred dollars a month to conduct folklore research in the rural South. Indeed, the doctor may have constructed his practice around the idea that he would treat only the wealthy and the socially prominent and may have believed that Mrs. Mason had recommended to him someone from her class and social position. Then, in walks Zora—not even, in his thinking, a middle-class person, but a n_____. Finally, after crafting a ritual he thought would put her permanently in her place, he was stunned by her departure. His reaction was probably not only racial, but also gendered and class based, that is, "who does this lower-class woman think she is?"

Indeed, we know from Hurston's letters, biographies, and novels that her life was lived as much in conflict with men, and their attempts to contain her behavior, as with Whites. Her string of White female patrons suggests that she experienced much less conflict with women, even the rich, White women who were often her greatest supporters. And such women had modeled for her the kind of grande-dame strategy she adopted in defense of her ego in the doctor's office. Of course, we know that such judgments are racialized, since withholding lady *status* from Black women is based on race. But gender configures how race is lived in America, and Black women like Hurston have mastered a mimicry—to borrow Homi Bhabha's term—a repetition with a difference of how rich White women extricate themselves through class-specific behavior from gender segregation in America.[7]

We see a bit of Hurston's gendered "attitude" in the photograph where she poses in front of a window celebrating the Federal Writers Project shortly after the 1937 publication of her most feminist book, *Their Eyes Were Watching God*.[8] Here, her hat is not sitting at a "reckless angle," but it is angled ever so slightly to confer on her otherwise proper, almost Sunday, dress the hint of the bohemian that lurks below her constructed self-image as a middle-class Black woman. Indeed, her clothing and the book she is holding seem to be in conversation with one another, which becomes more provocative when we realize that the book she is holding is an anthology, *American Stuff*, that published writing by two of her most outspoken critics, Richard Wright and Sterling Brown. Her hat, her veil, but mostly her hat's angled posture mirror the skeptical attitude on her face as she looks inside a book that advertised the work of Black male writers and not her own. When we recall that part of these authors' negative attitude toward her work derived from their distaste for her overtly feminist narrative in *Their Eyes Were Watching God*, we can feel the need for that angled hat—another shield from the opinion registered by the book that she is holding that her "stuff," the writing of a Black woman who celebrated independent Black women in her novel, was not worthy of inclusion as *American Stuff*.

Indeed, Hurston's tensions with other authors were not reserved for males: Hurston felt herself marginalized in the African-American literary canon because she was not solidly middle class in education and breeding like Jessie Fauset and Nella Larsen, not

light-skinned like they were, and not disposed to writing about middle-class Black female angst, as they were.[9] As the only Black woman novelist of her generation to walk the streets of the ghetto and the dusty roads of the rural South in search of material, and to write in a dialect of the Black lower class in America, she found that her excavations were deemed difficult to consume by the generation of Black intellectuals, male or female, who set critical opinion and taste. Interestingly, unlike such other Black women writers as Fauset, Larsen, Gwendolyn Bennett, and Georgia Douglas Johnson, among others, Hurston did not stop writing or publishing, even though she could not draw on the kind of psychic social support that they enjoyed from the educated Black bourgeoisie. Hurston kept working and publishing into the late 1940s, and something of that determination to self-expression comes through in this photograph and the expressiveness of her hat— not so much a crown, as one would wear to church, but a helmet. Indeed, her whole outfit has a shimmering quality to it—perhaps it is a silk dress or suit—that suggests a dress of arms the battle-tested Zora dons before posing as the grande-dame Black woman of literary talent who willed herself out of the Black working class into the elite of successful authors in twentieth-century America. Here we can add one more element to the racial, gender, class nexus we have found in the tilted hat—her triumphant individual will, first expressed by Zora as a little girl, who, her father complained, always wanted to wear "de big hat," to act just like White folks, to be "ambitious" and become the speaking subject transcendent from the mass.[10] The tilted hat signifies the coming into voice of Hurston, but also the voicing of the subaltern, the silenced in American culture generally, whose technology of speaking through the semiotics of sartorial splendor she appropriates as her own. Even when she became a writer, Hurston realized that she still needed a methodology of speaking without words, that is, the unexpected expressiveness of a cocked hat. What Zora Neale Hurston had done was distill all of the class, gender, and Black attitude she had observed in a life of race, class, and gender transitions into a Black-hatted posture whose angle and intensity combined yet transcended them all. For in the end, her Black hattitude was enlisted to do one thing really well: privilege Zora-ness through her hats.

Something about the rake of a cap or hat communicates a devil-may-care attitude, or worse, a subversive rebelliousness against public civility. In the late 1980s, I remember a White male colleague of mine recalling an incident on the streets of Georgetown, the chic-clothing and nightly entertainment enclave of Washington, D.C. "These guys were walking down the sidewalk—you know the kind: with their caps turned to the side—and blocked my side of the sidewalk as I tried to pass. I had to wait for them to go by before I could pass. Really!" At the time, it was clear to me that he meant Black youths, as they were the only ones indulging that turn of the hat. But by the early 1990s, White youths, especially young men, often in white jeeps listening to rap music, had adopted the style of turned-around caps to exhibit their own rebellious attitude toward middle-class civility. In short, while African-American culture, a culture developed out of adversarial encounters with White America, had employed the cocked hat to cut through the bullshit of American racism and assert superiority on an urban street, rebellious White youths observed, read, and assimilated such technologies of the oppressed to signify their own alterity. Even more often, such youths donned the mask of alterity for a while, then they "grew up," entered corporate America, and discarded the evidence of their former subversion. Indeed, they did not need to discard it, because once generally adopted by the White mainstream—even middle-class White girls now wear their caps with brims at the back—the signified is emptied of its adversarial meaning and becomes a sign of its opposite, of in-group status, a suburban style, and then, of course, finally a cliché.

Where did the turned-cap gesture originate? That is more difficult to determine. Some say it emerged in America with the sport of baseball, specifically by catchers, who turned the cap around so they could wear the catcher's mask that clipped over the forehead. Here, the early African-American participation in the Negro leagues may have migrated the gesture out of the ballpark, especially when Josh Gibson became, perhaps, the greatest African-American hitter and a catcher.

But some discrimination within the range of turned-cap wearing may be helpful here. In contrast to simply the hat with the bill turned to the back, perhaps more prevalent in the visual culture of Black America is the cap-wearing style my colleague noticed on the streets of Georgetown in the 1980s—the cap turned to the side. And more, perhaps, it is important to link that gesture with an attitude, expressed on the face of the wearer, that sediments the meaning of the hat as worn. One can find that culture in the 1920s. Perhaps its most enduring representation occurs in Augusta Savage's best sculpture, *Gamin*, a sculpture of a young African-American male, in which the hat is turned to the side just enough to resonate with the attitude of skeptical questioning etched on the young man's face. Here, Savage has captured a personality that during the nineteenth century, and particularly with White urban youth, would be described as a street urchin. Yet the attitude revealed on the face, I would argue, captioned by the hat, speaks to the particularity of Black urban youth in the 1920s. Rather than bright and cheery, as some romanticized versions of the White urchin from that period are, or surly, angry, and depressed as contemporary images of Black American youths often are, this portrait suggests a skeptical rather than cynical attitude toward his future, which, seemingly, he eyes

FIGURE 11.3 Augusta Savage (American, 1892–1962), *Gamin*, ca. 1929–30. Hand-painted plaster, 44.5 × 24.2 × 20.4 cm. The Cleveland Museum of Art. Purchase from the J. H. Wade Fund 2003.40.

in the distance. Certainly, this young man is unconvinced that America will treat him with justice; but, at the same time, there is a hint of invulnerability, perhaps best expressed in the slightly off-kilter hat position, that says, "Yeah. I transcend oppression, I refuse to even notice it!" This hat announces the Negro as an active, thinking personality, because it concretizes an attitude of continued self-assertion in spite of efforts to turn him into an object of another person's racism, sexism, or paternalism. That hat is a tool of survival for the self, and with this young man of the 1920s, it also captures a gleam of hope, a willingness to challenge society to make a place for him, even if his self-protection system tells him it probably is not forthcoming, at least in his lifetime. What endears, in a sense, in these early to mid-twentieth-century representations of Black hattedness is a still-retained flexibility in the face of struggle, a flexibility that in contemporary African-American working-class youth culture is more fleeting.

I want to conclude with a discussion of a photograph that first prompted me to think about the compressed energy in how a hat is worn by Black people in America. Taken by

Wayne F. Miller in Chicago in 1947, *Lunch Break* was part of a series of photographs that Miller, on a Guggenheim grant, took to document "The Way of Life of the Northern Negro" between 1946 and 1948. Its image is of a man sitting on the street with his buddies with his hat turned three-quarters of the way around to the back. That image takes us out of looking at hat styles as a response to racism and brings us into the intimacy of community formed in working-class America. Of course, this is a segregated job site in Chicago, one of the most segregated cities in post–World War II America. But this photograph lets us into a gendered world, that of working-class Black men on the job, that perhaps is emblematic of the subaltern in America, who are a majority, not a minority, but whose presence or voice is seldom seen and heard in the grand narrative of America. The photograph conveys the energy of the men's fraternity and encourages us to imagine what has just occurred that has led to such animation among these men. The man to the left suggests one possible narrative, since he is poised to leap into what appears to be an ongoing, humorous conversation, perhaps one in which these workers have combined both a critique of the status quo in some sense—the bosses, the job they are working on, the arrogance of their foreman, the stupidity of how the job is being run,

FIGURE 11.4 Wayne Miller, *Lunch Break,* 1947. Printed by permission of Magnum Photos.

the utter incompetence of their superiors—with some humorous remark or "signifying" on that commentary that has both raised a serious point and also skewered the most likely authority figure with some deflating, hilarious language that is now lost to us.

We can imagine this because the man on the left, out of the action, is trying to get into the exchange to make his contribution to it, perhaps a more serious contribution than that just offered by the man who centers the composition, whose smirking, playful grin, sparkling eyes, and "recklessly angled" brim suggest that *he* has just delivered the critique as joke that has made the others laugh and that he is still enjoying. In this scene, therefore, the man with the side-turned hat is subversive of authority, but also mirthmaking, a man who has retained from his adolescence, perhaps, a devil-may-care detachment from colluding adulthood even as he has matured into an evidently hardworking man. He has become a worker but has not left behind the rebellious mind of his teenage years, even as he has submitted his body to the discipline of industrial labor as a millworker or street construction worker. He is a man who has also, significantly, submitted himself to the demands of fitting into and working with a group or gang of men. He has become a buddy, but also a spokesperson whose off-kilter personality is concretized in his radical-angled cap. He has adjusted to what it means to be a productive Black man in a world quickly moving toward that postindustrial erasure of the kind of labor he and his buddies do, and his comment may have embodied their collective anger at their collective predicament. Most important, his turned-to-the-side hat anchors his uniqueness and individuality even as he immerses himself in the joy of fraternizing with the fellows.

This, in fact, is the work the Black stylized hat does in American public culture, whether it is used as defensive armor or provocative affirmation. It allows a Black man or woman to assert him or herself as an individual despite the pressures to be reduced to a race, class, or gendered collectivity, and to resist the tendency of everyone in America to be turned into a commodity. Despite the protections of group identity, the rakish hat worn on a Black head suggests the ability, the freedom, and the confidence to dispense with all that for a second and impose her or his will on the world as a subject without peer.

We see such confidence in Zora Neale Hurston, and we see it in this unidentified Black worker on his lunch break. Turning toward the camera, he is aware that a White photographer has intruded into their midst, yet he seems not to care. He is a subject in this world who demands the camera make him the subject of this photograph even if his face may never be the face of what is usually called America.

NOTES

1. Alain Locke, "The New Negro," in *The New Negro: An Interpretation* (New York: Albert and Charles Boni, 1925), 3–8.

2. Zora Neale Hurston, "My Most Humiliating Jim Crow Experience," in *Folklore, Memoirs, & Other Writings* (New York: Library of America, 1995), 935–36.

3. Ibid., 936.

4. Ralph Ellison, *Shadow and Act* (New York: Vintage, 1995), 45–59.

5. Chela Sandoval, *The Methodology of the Oppressed* (Minneapolis: University of Minnesota Press, 2000).

6. Monique Herzog and Cathy Strub, eds., *Coups de têtes extravagants* (Strasbourg: Opéra du Rhi, 1997), 58.

7. Homi K. Bhabha, "Of Mimicry and Man: The Ambivalence of Colonial Discourse," *October* 28 (1984): 125–33.

8. Zora Neale Hurston, *Their Eyes Were Watching God* (New York: Harper Collins, 1990).

9. Compare *Their Eyes Were Watching God* with Jessie Fauset's *There Is Confusion* (Boston: Northeastern University Press, 1989) or Nella Larsen's *Quicksand* (New Brunswick: Rutgers University Press, 1986).

10. Zora Neale Hurston, *Dust Tracks on the Road* (New York: Harper Collins, 1996), 29.

12

BARBARA STANWYCK'S ANKLET
THE OTHER SHOE

Paula Rabinowitz

> *The shoes are always open to the unconscious of the other.*
> JACQUES DERRIDA, *The Truth in Painting*

FETISH, ICON, SYMBOL?

Why, from Karl Marx and Vincent Van Gogh in the nineteenth century through Martin Heidegger, Charlie Chaplin, and Walker Evans in the twentieth, have men tracked aesthetic value, social standing, and the meaning of labor through the boots of workers, while women, following Sigmund Freud's consideration of the shoe as fetish object, have understood shoes to signal freedom and constraint—at once powerful symbols of mobility and icons of and for desire? I speak of two modes of desire: for the commodity itself, objects of use—products, equipment, as Heidegger called them—no matter how apparently excessive; and within its representation in paintings, photographs, films, novels, advertisements. These, as Jacques Derrida goes to great lengths to point out, are not the same thing; yet because of the oddity of this particular object, an object in need of another for it to be put to proper use, desire doubles back on itself collapsing differences between materiality and representation.

Shoes as emblems of death and icons of sex collide within the tawdry mise-en-scène of film noir. When femme fatale Phyllis Dietrichson (Barbara Stanwyck) descends the stairway to meet insurance salesman Walter Neff (Fred McMurray) in Billy Wilder's 1944 film *Double Indemnity*, the camera lovingly focuses on her gleaming white legs, feet sheathed in a puffy high-heeled mule above one of which drapes a gold anklet. Moments later, seated cross-legged before Neff, Phyllis waves her foot ostentatiously in his face, distracting him enough that he mentions: "That's a honey of an anklet you've got there." She removes her foot and straightens up primly, but the scene evokes the power of the woman's foot to control a man. The anklet, no matter how thin its gold chain appears, is always one-half of the shackles that snare him. Cinderella got her prince because only she among all his subjects could fit into the tiny glass slipper styled for her by her fairy godmother. The anklet, that piece of jewelry adorning one leg, at the bottom of the body rather than the top, calling the eyes to travel down the length of the body and fix on one foot, foregrounds the fetishistic quality of women's footwear, especially, as in the case of Cinderella as well, the isolated, single bare foot and its adornment. Derrida points out the important differences between a pair of shoes and a single one: the pair, useful, regular, and normal, a heterosexual couple; the lone shoe, perverse, bisexual, destabilizing.[1] Of course, an anklet is not a shoe; it's the shoe's other, suspended above the foot, without any purpose besides being pure honey, an ornament and accessory—a sweet reminder of what lies above, below, and within it. This one filigreed with the name Phyllis, from the Greek for leafy green bough.

The iconic pan from the floor up to the star's face tells us everything we need to know of her character.[2] For instance, when the camera, with Cornel Wilde, first gazes at Ida Lupino draping one shoeless bare leg over the boss's desk before traveling up to a close-up of her face in the 1948 film noir *Road House*, we know that despite whatever nasty banter ensues they will eventually become lovers. Wilde moves across the room toward the desk dividing them, watching Lupino smoke and play solitaire, and picks up her shoe—a platform sandal, designed to replicate Stanwyck's anklet and open-toed mule, displaying "toe cleavage" and a bound ankle.[3] She snatches it from him and hides it be-

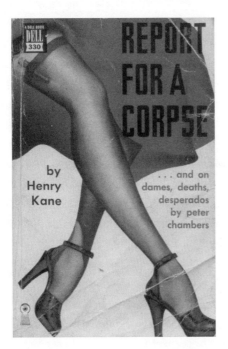

FIGURE 12.1 Cover of *Report for a Corpse* by Henry Kane (New York: Dell Publishing Company, Inc., 1949). Cover by Gerald Gregg. This is one example of the spread of the ankle-bound platform shoe throughout 1940s American popular culture.

hind her back as one would any intimate article found lying about in plain sight. Ida Lupino's shoe is out there in a public display so raw she might as well have been naked before his and our eyes. Worse, her naked display is not only of her sex, but of his as well. The single shoe "combines in a system the two types of object defined by Freud: elongated, solid or firm on one surface, hollow or concave on the other."[4] Shoes, for Freud, like "a whole number of dream-symbols are bisexual and can relate to the male or female genitals, according to the context."[5] Hollywood's Hays Code forbade overt nudity and other representations of sex, sending directors and cinematographers to search out legible symbols. Like Walter Neff, they knew where to look.

For women in the movies, especially postwar B movies, shoes, usually high-heeled pumps, click along the hard concrete sidewalks. They sing a chorus combining vulnerability—we know she cannot run too fast in them—and menace: her relentless approach or retreat alerting us to her ever-presence. They tap the cobblestones like armor. In Jacques Tourneur's 1942 *Cat People,* Serbian designer Irene (Simone Simon) pursues her American rival, the wholesome "new kind of other woman" Alice (Jane Randolph), through a Central Park tunnel at night. The camera pans from one set of black pumps to another. As the clicking magnifies and echoes within the space and the sounds merge, Alice is overtaken with a terror that lifts only when she is startled by an oncoming bus that she boards even though it takes her back the wrong way. In the 1944 film, *Phantom Lady*'s Kansas (Ella Raines) threatens a bartender (Andrew Tombes Jr.) by following him after sitting immobile night after night in his bar. Her slender trench-coated figure waits for him under the streetlight, and again we see only her black pumps swiftly pursuing him through the night, their rhythm matching the man step for step. By all logic, high-heeled women should not constitute a threat, but they do. The opening shot of the British noir film *Yield to the Night* (1956) follows Mary (Diana Dors) as she paces across a square, nabs a cab, and descends into an alleyway; her clicking heels foreshadow the gun shots she will unload into her lover's girlfriend (who has removed one high heel to shift gears) that land her in prison. The opening sequence of *Caged* (1950) shows Marie (Eleanor Parker) seated in the paddy wagon among an assortment of jaded prostitutes, her demure and plain flats setting her apart from them; however, by the time she is re-leased on parole she has been transformed. She signals her "new" life outside, on the streets, by entering a car full of men and crossing her legs so that her high heels are vis-ible and her knee available for fondling. The black-heeled pump was an essential element of postwar working women's attire. These aggressive shoes clattering across the city pavement—dealing death and desire in their wake—banished forever the iconic last scene in Josef von Sternberg's 1930 *Morocco* of Marlene Dietrich shedding her high-heeled pumps in the Sahara sands, the camera lingering over them disappearing in the dust as, barefoot, she joins the camp followers marching into the desert behind her lover, Legioner Tom Brown (Gary Cooper), to an erratic drumbeat across Africa. The cross-dressing Marlene, who in top hat and tails blatantly kisses a woman on the lips triggering Cooper's fascination, is annihilated, undone, and now among the "crazy" women who live and die for love.

These examples from midcentury films noirs, in contrast to Vincent Van Gogh's invocation of work boots as a sign of poverty, speak to women's aggressive mobility in wartime and postwar urban spaces. The physical movement and sexual predation available to women emerge visually from their shapely legs and aurally from the sound of their heels beating the pavement. They walk the streets, streetwalkers, turning public spaces relentlessly into scenes of crime and themselves into objects of desire. As streetwalkers, their shoes are also of use: they work/walk the pavement nightly; however, the icon of the high-heeled pump rarely registers as working apparel. It is a marker of sexual violation, not labor. Yet an economy of desire is always first an economy, a point exaggerated to absurdity in Samuel Fuller's 1964 noir spoof, *The Naked Kiss,* in which prostitute Kelly (Constance Tower) beats her pimp by pummeling him with her black patent leather purse while standing over him in her matching stilettos before retrieving the money he owes her. She disappears into small-town America to enter her new life as a nurse for disabled children, only to discover that she cannot escape corruption: in Grantville, cops pimp for the brothel across the river, and the leading citizen and philanthropist is a pedophile. To protect the young women and girls of Grantville, Kelly again uses her black leather purse as a weapon, murders the town's madam, and then kills the pervert with his black Bakelite telephone receiver (both repeating her shoes, one in its material, the other in its form), only to end up in jail when her pimp presses charges for assault—the shoe was prologue.

In his discussion of "Fetishism" Freud puts it quite simply: "I announce that the fetish is a substitute for the penis. . . . To put it more plainly: the fetish is a substitute for the woman's (the mother's) penis that the little boy once believed in and—for reasons familiar to us—does not want to give up."[6] The fetish is the simultaneous sign of disavowal (of woman's castration) and attachment (to the fantasy of the female phallus) and is often connected to this contradiction by its partial nature; thus the foot or the shoe—seen first from below as the child looks up to find the absent phallus—suits at once "both the disavowal and the affirmation of the castration."[7] "The fetish, like a 'screen memory,' represents this phase [a submerged and forgotten phase of sexual development] and is thus a remnant and precipitate of it."[8] "What is substituted for the sexual object," says Freud in "Three Essays on Sexuality," "is some part of the body (such as the foot or hair) which is in general very inappropriate for sexual purposes, or some inanimate object which bears an assignable relation to the person whom it replaces and preferably to that person's sexuality (e.g. a piece of clothing or underlinen). Such substitutes are with some justice likened to the fetishes in which savages believe that their gods are embodied."[9] Thus the shoe, which like the foot holds power "as an age-old sexual symbol which occurs even in mythology," is a "corresponding symbol of the *female* genitals."[10] Age-old and savage, the fetish is antimodern.

Possession and disavowal overvalue the fetish as relics of an image of plenty destroyed, never quite admitted, and so reinvested with godlike power. Freud's description of the fetish locates the trauma of castration within the "little boy" and presents the fetish object as *his* substitute. Can women fetishize the shoe? Or is it instead shoes that stir desire? As phallic mother substitute, they, like the phallic mother, present an ambivalent homosexual identification with the female phallus as female genitalia. The shoe, as Freud admits in "On Dreams," especially the high heel, is both phallus and its lack. As such it fulfills Victor Turner's definition of ritual symbols. These incorporate contradictory social practices: "symbols are social facts, 'collective representations,' " he says in *The Forest of Symbols,* that are "multireferential," at once "sensory" and "ideological," whose "empirical properties" include "(1) condensation; (2) unification of disparate meanings in a single symbolic form; (3) polarization of meaning."[11] The shoe and the pair of shoes have almost nothing in common, no matter how redundant the two are (but of course not, they're as different as right and left). Hence freedom and death, sex and labor, accessory and necessity, object and symbol: magic, a mysterious thing. "Yes yes, we're magicians," assures Vladimir as he and Estragon struggle to get Estragon's boots on in *Waiting for Godot.*[12]

As lowly objects, abject objects, shoes remain as reminders, remainders of death. The lone shoe lying in the middle of a street following the shooting of Red Army Faction leader Rudi Dutschke is a melancholy memento, its photograph part of the collective archive of 1968.[13] The piles of shoes lining the railroad tracks of Auschwitz that appear in Alain Resnais's *Night and Fog*, like the catalogue of photographs of articles of clothing, mostly shoes—remains of the slaughtered men of Srebenica—are monuments of horror, reminders of the destruction of twentieth-century genocides. Articles meant to take the wear and tear of daily use, shoes remain intact after other personal effects, and with them, their owners, have disintegrated, disappeared. "The Still Life as a Personal Object," from which Meyer Schapiro argues with Martin Heidegger over a pair of shoes, are the very shoes, as Derrida notes, left behind in the flight from the soil still clinging to one's work boots for an urban exile. *Nature Morte,* indeed, death follows their footsteps.[14] Shoes, as symbolic objects themselves, travel across three fundamental planes of human experience: work, sex, death.

"A MAGICAL OBJECT"

"The fetishism of commodities has its origin . . . in the peculiar social character of the labour that produces them." Marx continues, "It is value, rather, that converts every product into a social hieroglyphic."[15] His example of this oxymoronic process of collective indecipherability goes as follows: "When I state that coats or *boots* stand in a relation to linen, because it is the universal incarnation of abstract human labour, the absurdity of the statement is self-evident. Nevertheless, when producers of coats and *boots* compare those articles with linen, or, what is the same thing, with gold or silver, as the universal equivalent, they express the relation between their own private labour and the collective labour of society in the same form." It is this "fantastic form," this "mist-enveloped region," this "mysterious thing" that fetishizes the commodity, separating it from its use-value as a product of human labor into an abstract value of exchange equivalent to all others and masking the "social character of the labour that produces them."[16] Walter

Benjamin notes that Karl Korsch pushed Marx's insight into the fetishism of commodities to account generally for "human self-alienation ... by revealing *all* economic categories to be mere fragments of one great fetish."[17] As a religious practice, "fetishism seem[s] to appear only among peoples who have already attained to a certain degree of civilization."[18] In those "mist enveloped regions of the religious world" where "the productions of the human brain appear as independent beings endowed with life, and entering into relation with one another and the human race," fetishism, notes Marx, emerges as a transition after totemism.[19] Relying on the same primitivist ideas animating Freud's work on the fetish, Marx also views its power as suspiciously ancient.[20] It depends, according to Marx's reading of Robinson Crusoe's story, on circulation, that is, on alienation and the division of labor, and on consumption, the appropriation and incorporation of objects as values. In a characteristic gesture, Benjamin, quoting Theodor Adorno as Wiesengrund, describes the fetishized commodity as a "phantasmagoria ... a consumer item in which there is no longer anything that is supposed to remind us how it came into being. It becomes a magical object, insofar as the labor stored up in it comes to seem supernatural and sacred at the very moment when it can no longer be recognized as labor."[21] Again, anxiety about the non-Western, primitive, irrational basis of fetishism—"we're magicians"—the commodity and its consumer, like the fetish and its worshipper, are suspiciously feminized, or at least emasculated as Samuel Beckett's Gogo and Didi.

Unpacking his library, Benjamin notes the peculiar fascination with ownership that certain items produce for consumers within bourgeois culture. These items, like books or shoes, are those that can form a "collection"; collections produce "collectors" for whom "ownership is the most intimate relationship that one can have to objects."[22] Collections, like genres, operate on the principle of repetition with a difference, as every item resembles its other, yet must be distinct at the same time. Susan Stewart calls this "the total aestheticization of use value."[23] For Stewart, this aspect of collecting acts to annihilate history; however, a shoe collection must always retain its historicity—that is the trap of fashion, it's of a moment, au courant. The collector acts like a criminal in his/her relentless pursuit of the missing items, rare editions, and so forth. "Every passion borders on the chaotic, but the collector's passion borders on the chaos of memories" such that "the life of the collector [is] a dialectical tension between the poles of disorder and order."[24] Within a commodity fetishistic culture, then, ownership becomes both a sickness and its cure. Furthermore, collectors oscillate between stasis—one needs someplace to put the objects collected—and movement. Travel is essential to collecting: Benjamin remarks that he made his "most memorable purchases on trips, as a transient. Property and possession belong to the tactical sphere. Collectors are people with a tactical instinct; their experience teaches them that when they capture a strange city, the smallest antique shop can be a fortress, the most remote stationery store a key position."[25] In short, the collector is always one who walks; she needs a good pair of shoes.

Calling Benjamin our greatest theorist of the object, critic Douglas Mao argues that the "feeling of regard for the physical object as object—as not-self, as not-subject, as most helpless and will-less of entities, but also as fragment of Being, as solidity, as otherness in its most resilient opacity—seems a peculiarly twentieth-century malady or revelation . . . one of the minor trademarks" of modernism.[26] For Mao, the object, and desire for it, cannot resemble the fetish and fetishism as charted by either Marx or Freud, despite Benjamin's obvious reliance on their sources. Suggesting that "solid objects" were under siege as the concrete and particular gave way to the vast abstract systemizing of science, Mao sees a melancholy rescue of the object in the Anglo-American high modernist writers, such as Virginia Woolf. *Orlando*'s feat of Restoration consumption in redecorating the ancestral home is matched when, as a modernist poet, she drives to the department store in pursuit of various household necessities, including "boy's boots, bath salts, sardines" only to be foiled by the plethora of stuff spilling across the aisles she glances as the elevator lifts her to the loaded counters. Orlando, however, seems to confirm Marx, even in her choice of words: "In the eighteenth century, we knew how everything was done; but here I rise through the air; I listen to voices in America; I see men flying—but how it's done, I can't even begin to wonder. So my belief in magic returns."[27] Yet she fails to return with any of her shopping list items—so many products, incommensurate

FIGURE 12.2

The Gold Rush (Charles Chaplin, 1925).

things, the solid melts into air. Woolf implies that for the modern woman, by definition a shopper, commodities are interchangeable and inconsequential; however, Woolf's modern woman is educated, a woman of privilege, even if her mansion has become a museum.

OTHER SMALL OBJECTS

Charlie Chaplin's Tramp cooks and serves his boiled boot to fend off starvation on the Klondike in *The Gold Rush* (1925). His careful dissection of the boot, picking each hobnail out as a finely trained waiter might debone a trout, and precise twirling of the laces into a mound of spaghetti call forth the animal quality of shoes—made of leather, absorbing the odors of the feet (one aspect that makes them so likely to become a fetish according to Freud)—and thus close to edible; yet their proximity to the filthy ground and their sweaty smells make them abjectly inedible. Chaplin had his boots constructed from licorice—sometimes called shoe-leather—and thus ate them with relish. In the section of *The Arcades Project* on the Saint-Simonians, Walter Benjamin quotes from a "revealing" Leon Halevy poem, "La Chaussure":

This people, whose head and hand you fear,

Must march, must march—no halting!

It's when you stop their steps

They notice the holes in their shoes.[28]

"They notice the holes in their shoes" only when they have time to contemplate their poverty, that is, when they no longer even have work and become excess. This impoverished proletariat, presocialist and anarchic, like the Tramp, as Roland Barthes finds him, is "still hungry . . . expressing the humiliated condition of the worker."[29] Work boots full of holes have no use. They no longer can be considered "equipment," in Heidegger's sense, and like their unemployed wearers signify a miserable excess in their lack. Those gone to extremes—forced to eat their own shoes, self-devouring, and empty—are useless as either producers or consumers within capitalism.

> Of shoes: ordinary workshoes may be called "typical": only if you remember that old sunday shoes, tennis sneakers, high tennis shoes, sandals, moccasins, bare feet, and even boots, are not at all rarely used: it should be known, too, that there are many kinds of further, personal treatment of shoes. Mainly, this: Many men, by no means all, like to cut holes through the uppers for foot-spread and for ventilation: and in this they differ a good deal between utility and art. You seldom see purely utilitarian slashes: even the bluntest of these are liable to be patterned a little more than mere use requires: on the other hand, some shoes have been worked on with a wonderful amount of patience and studiousness toward a kind of beauty, taking the memory of an ordinary sandal for a model, and greatly elaborating and improving it. I have seen shoes so beautifully worked in this way that their durability was greatly reduced.[30]

James Agee's treatise on the clothing of the tenant farmers of Hale County, Alabama, like his fellow "spy" Walker Evans's photographs of George Gudger's Sunday shoes drying before the "altar" of the decorated fireplace or his work boots airing in the sun, refutes Agee's call to avoid considering their work as "Art," as he compares the blues of the farmer's overalls and work shirts to "the blues of Cezanne"[31] and Evans quotes Van Gogh's peasant boots. Each emphasizes the beauty of these objects so thoroughly tied to use-value, yet conveying the most private longings for aesthetics:

> There is great pleasure in a sockless and sweated foot in the fitted leathers of a shoe made of most simple roundnesses and squarings and flats, of dark brown raw thick leathers nailed, and sewn coarsely to one another in courses and patterns of doubled and tripled seams, and such throughout that like many other small objects they have great massiveness and repose and are, as the houses and overalls are, and the feet and legs of the women, who go barefooted so much, fine pieces of architecture. . . .They are worn out like animals to a certain ancient stage and chance of money at which a man buys a new pair; then, just as old sunday shoes do, they become the inheritance of a wife.[32]

These clay-encrusted objects placed symmetrically before the fireplace are emblems of labor, of poverty, and they are symbols of the essential uniqueness and dignity the reporters find in the lives of America's forgotten. "Clay is worked into the substance of the uppers and a loose dust of clay lies over them. . . . The shoes are worn for work."[33]

According to Emanuel Swedenborg, shoes signify "all the things which would be natural and corporeal uncleanness."[34] Men's shoes, claims Gertrude Jobes, served as "ancient means of binding a contract," because the removal of the shoe meant "loss of legal rights," which corresponds to religious interdictions against wearing shoes in sacred places because they possess "contagion from the secular."[35] Yet Jean Servier "observes that 'to walk shod is to take possession of the ground.'"[36] These images of land and its ownership entrust the shoe with powers at once menial and imperial. The workingman's shoe carries the earth in its ancient creases and thus remembers that labor is its equipment. In their iconic usage, the work shoe becomes attached to lowly peasant labor in the fields; whether Martin Heidegger registers Van Gogh's boots as belonging to the farmer's wife or Meyer Schapiro insists that they are "clearly" the painters' own, we know they must be read as figuring some form of abject masculinity. As Agee points out,

women's work shoes began as men's, only becoming their wives' (or daughters' or mothers-in-law's) possessions after they near disintegration. This becomes clear in the two Evans's photographs where women are shown wearing shoes—the family portrait of the Woodses in which Miss Molly wears a battered pair of boots, and the picture of Margaret Ricketts washing dishes in an old pair of men's shoes. The destination of worn boots means that they are not firmly latched to masculinity—or that the masculinity to which they are attached is hardly secure; it is the province of "humble" men tied to the earth; their movement is toward dissolution—the eventual wearing away of the leather soles, but not before they have been transferred onto women's feet. Heidegger relied on Van Gogh's paintings of peasant shoes as a secondary way to consider the movement from equipment (as a pure useful thing) to its apprehension in the truth of an artwork. Tellingly, Heidegger reads Van Gogh's shoes as belonging to the farmer's wife—hand-me-downs, already used, secondhand equipment, leftovers.

According to Joseph Kockelman's rendering, those shoes evoke for Heidegger a loneliness and rugged tenacity of earth and the "wordless joy of having once more withstood want" through the endless repetition of wearying fieldwork.[37] This "heavy pathos of the primordial and earthy" denied what for art historian Meyer Schapiro was the central point of Van Gogh's paintings—that the still life objects were the *artist's* personal belongings, his self-representation.[38] Heidegger frequently referred to shoes and shoemakers as exemplary of a being-in-a-world in which materials and labor create meaning.[39] In short, workingmen's boots, as useful products, and shoemakers—producers of use-values par excellence—aestheticize, even romanticize, human drudgery as survival. In one of the remarkable moments in Art Spiegelman's *Maus,* Vladek describes how he survived liquidation by claiming to know how to repair boots, thus securing himself a source of income by fixing a guard's broken sole. Without any skills, except hustling and a good memory, Vladek lands a position in the shoe shop and earns enough to bribe various capos into transferring his wife Anja into a barracks near him in Birkenau. Ever practical, not only does he describe the story to Artie, he draws a picture for his son, showing how to repair a boot.[40]

What all this thingness of equipment and beauty of utility and earthy broken shoes and so forth have in common is a remarkably consistent image of the peasants' shoes and the toiling shoemaker as central icons of survival, of noble yet lowly subsistence, of a beauty and truth to be found in the very scraped bottoms of the filthy boots that trudge the heavy furrows to bring forth the meager means of human subsistence, to establish the ground for mid-twentieth-century philosophical musings on death, art, time, work, and being. Shoes connect the laborer to the earth, and to toil and deprivation. Like evocations of the land and rural life, as antidotes to industrialism (or even as evocations of productive work in general), these images of solidity, earthiness, and use are sentimental; both left-wing iconography of labor or Fascist icons of soil would redeem a bereft manhood. Men's work boots reek of hard labor; and while Agee and Evans revered this, Preston Sturges was mocking it in his 1941 satire of proletarian social realism *Sullivan's Travels.*

But enough with the heavy trod of hobnails and creaky mud-encrusted leather! Yes, men's boots and shoes evidence the nobility of soil and the grind of stoop labor. Shoes, even men's work shoes, have other uses, signal other kinds of work, too. In the 1950s, Nikita Khrushchev banged on the United Nations table with his hefty black oxford declaiming, "We will bury you!" His denunciation of American capitalism—made in New York City, capitol of capital, was a reminder of his peasant origins; yet the shoes were resolutely corporate in their anonymity. Van Gogh and Agee and Evans evoked the individuality of the work shoe, molded by years of wear to the foot; but the black leather oxford was meant, like the organization man who wore it, to fit in and disappear. The opening shot of Alfred Hitchcock's *Strangers on a Train* (1951) tracks the rushing commuters' shoes crisscrossing up and down the aisle until they come to rest when Bruno (Robert Walker) and Guy (Farley Granger) bump into each other, two men outside the heterosexual corporate economy (as wealthy gay man and professional tennis player, respectively) who wear more distinctive footwear. In Robert Aldrich's *Kiss Me Deadly*, another 1950s thriller that explicitly refers to the Soviet nuclear threat, Mike Hammer (Ralph Meeker) is able to discern the killers who have gotten hold of the "great whatsit" by recognizing their distinctive wing tips, a sign of precarious masculinity.[41]

SIX-INCH HEEL WITH ANKLE STRAP

Women's shoes, especially those meant for dress-up, are so much more useful; even Mrs. Gudger put on "black lowheeled slippers with strapped insteps and single buttons" on Saturday, market day at Cookstown.[42] The work they do is invisible as work; yet they too point to sites of labor. For Agee, shoes are wombs—the worn leather molded to the sweated bare foot—and none more surely convey terror and desire than the spiked high heel, vagina dentata. Mrs. Gudger's demure flats hint, with their straps and buttons, at the sexual intimacy connected to the removal of shoes. A March 2000 *New York Times* article pictured a Tristan Webber sandal, with four-inch tapered heel featuring spikes protruding from the instep and straps and the heel, over the caption "Shoe or weapon?"[43] Pierre Silber's advertisement for a "$35 six-inch spike available in sizes 6–14" offers a woman's shoe destined for a transgendered foot walking across skin, not pavement.[44] The woman's shoe as weapon begins Fuller's campy film noir *The Naked*

Kiss, but it is also a pivotal scene in Herbert Biberman's 1954 left-wing labor film *Salt of the Earth.* In this saga about a New Mexico miners' strike and the increasing activism of the miners' wives, Esperanza (Rosaura Revueltas), wife of macho strike leader Ramon (Juan Chacón), breaks free from her husband and children to join the women who have taken over the picket line after a court injunction prohibits the men from marching. Handing her newborn infant to a stunned Ramon when the sheriff's deputies draw their guns at the women, Esperanza "stops for a second, slips off her right shoe as [deputy] Vance [(E. A. Rockwell)] knocks the other woman down, pulls his revolver from his holster. Esperanza whacks him over the wrist with her shoe, knocking the weapon out of his hand."[45] Esperanza joins the women's group and forcefully helps lead the strike, leaving Ramon to take over the domestic chores. This labor melodrama, made during the height of McCarthyism by blacklisted actors, screenwriters, and directors, condenses many left-wing feminist and labor ideals in this one scene, tapping into latent fears of female autonomy and the vagina dentata. After this episode, Esperanza is rarely home as housewife; she carts her kids to the picket line or else leaves them with Ramon to feed.

Shoes facilitate women's social mobility. In *Salt of the Earth,* a simple flat bests a gun, averting violence; but a hooker's spiked heel can almost kill a man as Constance Towers demonstrates. So we arrive at the third "meaning" of the shoe—as symbols of travel, especially the journey to freedom and/or death.[46] Twice in Sandra Cisneros's prose poem *The House on Mango Street* (1983), the narrator, another Esperanza, astutely notes her sexual vulnerability as a girl on the verge of adolescence, hopeful child of Mexican immigrants living on the edges of urban poverty. Both of these moments occur through her recognition of her unsettled footing within her world. This footing, literalized in the form of shoes, oscillates between a clunky 1950s girlhood, epitomized by bulbous saddle shoes, those sturdy markers of practicality bought by Depression-era mothers to last a whole school year, and her blossoming sexuality. Forced to wear these school shoes to the fancy party for which Esperanza is dressed in a new frock, her ceremonial coming out—a dance with her uncle—is thus forever marred by the twin signs of poverty and gawkinesss. No party shoes accessorize this dress. Yet Esperanza has glimpsed the power of impractical shoes when she and her friends try on a few discarded pairs of dyed high heels and wobble around the block eliciting catcalls from the men and boys hanging on the street corners. Thrilled and terrified by their newly acquired swaying hips, the girls toss the heels as soon as they discover that men now see them as sexually desirable. With these two scenes, two crucial aspects of footwear in modern times are represented: that class position is instantly recognizable by looking at the soles of all folk, and that women's desires are tied to their (in)ability to move within them. Ultimately Esperanza dreams of leaving the confines of Mango Street, changing her name to Ze Ze the X, and possessing a house of her own emptied of all furnishings save blank paper and a pair of shoes neatly stored by her bedside.[47]

Women's decorative shoes, especially high heels, like Cinderella's glass slippers and Esperanza's yellow heels, reveal female sexuality. They become weapons and as such also convey those attracted/attached to them toward danger, even death. The Little Mermaid suffers on legs sharp as knives as she searches the land for her prince, suffering in silence. Women appear vulnerable in these wobbly unstable objects, but they elevate themselves to greater height, commandeering space through the constant clattering of their heels on the hard surfaces of the city streets and work places (whether office buildings or bedrooms). As objects of desire for both men (who, unlike the aristocracy until the eighteenth century, now only watch them) and women (who can both watch and wear them), these icons also slide across genders, leading inevitably to death. Not the inexorable, slow death of decay, but rather a sudden, violent death.[48] "These boots are made for walking," sang Nancy Sinatra in her thigh-high white boots, "and one of these days they're gonna walk all over you." Through work or sex, shoes journey to death; but the path they take, at least partially, runs through freedom. Pursuit is dangerous; but it's better than bondage. The broken feet of aristocratic Chinese women curtailed their movement, forcing them to take small mincing and painful steps unless carried. Shoes move us across space; desire for mobility leads us to death.

In the Hans Christian Andersen fairy tale, the Little Mermaid, pursuing her desire for her beloved prince, succumbs to a witch's brew that allows her to silently walk on legs that felt like knives piercing her body, only to be left mute and alone. In "The Red Shoes," a young girl's desire for shiny red shoes, inappropriately worn to church and funerals, leads to her being controlled by her independent red shoes. Try as she might to take off the perpetually moving shoes, they remain fast on her feet, dancing her frenetically past the coffin of the old woman who had cared for her. Only when an executioner chops off her feet, leaving her crippled, can she stop dancing and repent her vanity. Broken in spirit, like the little mermaid, she dies blessed. These terrifying stories of female lust link female desire to mobility.

Carolyn Steedman recalls a recurring dream she had as a child of a woman in a New Look coat entering a doorway, her severe black pumps clicking along the sidewalk just out of young Carolyn's reach. Steedman's meditation on "the politics of envy" dictating the terms of her mother's brutal life's landscape depended on a thorough understanding of the connection between female mobility and clothing. Buy a good pair of pumps, a New Look coat, and a smart suit, and a working-class woman, skillfully shedding her accent, could transform her destiny.[49] Leaving her ratty Lancashire mill town for the precarious possibilities open in London during the Depression, Steedman's mother used her sexuality to secure another future for herself and her two daughters. Fundamental to her mobility—geographic and class—was her ability to wear the proper articles of clothing fitting her desires. The trajectory from Lancashire to London depended on learning how to move in the smart pumps of postwar women's autonomy. Like the many femme fatales in film noir who traverse the dark city streets of San Francisco, New York, and Los Angeles in search of power, pleasure, and money, Steedman's postwar London mother knew how to dress for success.[50]

Success for the young middle-class girl growing up in this postwar world was mapped out, as Charlotte Nekola remarks in her memoir, *Dream House,* by "the progression from childhood to full womanhood . . . Mary Janes to flats to pumps with a small tasteful heel, and finally to the realm of pure sex and authority, 'spike' heels." Remembering an incident when she moved her "convertible" strap on her Sunday dress-up Mary Janes so that her girlish shoe would magically appear as a mature flat, Nekola describes how this gesture "instantly transformed [her], now a sinful Cinderella with some new shoes of big-girl life."[51] However, when she showed her mother her magnificent maturity, she was chastised with disapproval. Like the old woman who tries to steer Karen from the red shoes, Nekola's mother insists Charlotte keep the strap tightly fixed around her instep, maintaining the freedom of her "native girlhood" as long as possible.[52] Cisneros's Esperanza and her girlfriends beat a quick retreat from "Cinderella" to their native girlhood after their triumphant "tee-tottering" in the "lemon shoes and the red shoes and the shoes that used to be white but are now pale blue" castoffs of "the family of little feet" because the threat of their sexual allure—men were suddenly whistling and offering each a dollar for a kiss—would inevitably lead to dangers: sex, pregnancy, marriage.[53] Or worse: Barbara Stanwyck's anklet and heels, her cigarette and whiskey, her cat glasses and gun, would indeed turn you into a femme fatale—murderous, deadly, and doomed to die in a hail of bullets.

Growing up in the 1950s, many young girls studied these films, found on late-night television, as documentaries of lives our parents might have lived if not for the fortunes of free education from City College and the G.I. Bill enabling the institution of the white nuclear family in the suburb. Office of War Information photographer Esther Bubley had recorded these actual noir women who rode midnight buses and trains across the country in search of war work, residing in rooming houses. Her bus trip throughout the Midwest and the South undertaken in 1943 took her to such unlikely locales as an Ohio coffee shop shaped like a giant coffeepot now housing a large family, but primarily it took her to bus stations where she photographed single women sleeping on benches waiting for the 5 a.m. to Memphis, their black pumps dangling from their swollen feet. These intimate images of migrant women, solitary and vulnerable, are matched by those of single women seated alone at a bar waiting for a pickup. Bubley's single working women in transit during World War II presaged the "evil women [who] were women of psychological difficulties . . . who lived entirely in scenes of blood, murder, suicide, and physical and psychiatric violence of all kinds. Barbara Stanwyck's career . . . [was] built on the portrayal of this type of gangster woman." These women's crime films were so popular, noted one of C. L. R. James's female informants, "a sensitive and well-read observer," because "they are the only performances that seem to be *real*."[54]

Quoting documentary photography and dramatizing the pleasures, powers, and terrors of women's aggressive mobility, made visually and aurally explicit in the erotic high-heeled slippers and anklet of Phyllis Dietrichson in *Double Indemnity*, the relentless clatter of Kansas's black pumps in *Phantom Lady*, and Kelly's vicious spiked heels in *The Naked Kiss*, film noir turns women into magicians. If commodities could speak the secrets therein, they might tell us just what a woman does want—shoes! Wedgies, platforms, sandals, thongs, mules, flats, pumps, loafers, heels, slingbacks, sneakers, not to mention boots.

1. "A pair of shoes is more easily treated as a *utility* than a single shoe or two shoes which aren't a pair. The pair inhibits at least, if it does not prevent, the 'fetishizing' movement; it rivets things to use, to 'normal' use; it shoes better and makes things walk according to the law." He goes on to question what either Martin Heidegger or Meyer Schapiro would have "done with" a painting with only one shoe, especially a single high heel as in René Magritte's *La Lune* or Richard Lindner's *The Shoe*. "Would they have been able to produce . . . ?" Jacques Derrida, *The Truth in Painting*, trans. Geoff Bennington and Ian McLeod (Chicago: University of Chicago Press, 1987), 332–33.

2. "Shoes. Dream shoes. Shoes to power the imagination. We sat spellbound before *Mildred Pierce*. Our eyes followed her feet . . . her shoes. . . . Inevitably black, they featured three-inch talons, a slightly raised platform, and a delicate strap encircling the ankle. Her shoes were a sign—but of what?" ask Shari Benstock and Suzanne Ferriss in the introduction to their collection *On Fashion* (New Brunswick, N.J.: Rutgers University Press, 1994), 1. "Shoes," they declare, "are hot." They went on to explore the vital question: "What is it in our culture that has led to this fascination with shoes?" in their subsequent comprehensive collection *Footnotes: On Shoes* (New Brunswick, N.J.: Rutgers University Press, 2001), 1, 3.

3. Thanks to Cora Leland for bringing the term "toe cleavage" to my attention, which comes from the interdiction against sandals outlined in the dress code governing employees at Arthur Ander-

son and other accounting firms in the United States. See Colin McDowell, *Manolo Blahnik* (New York: HarperCollins, 2000), which quotes Blahnik as confirming that "the first two cracks" of toe cleavage is a "very important part of the sexuality of the shoe." Quoted in Penelope Green, "Fall Reading, From Head to Toe," *New York Times,* September 4, 2000, B10. Not only films, but their print double, pulp paperbacks, displayed this motif as is clear from the cover to Henry Kane's *Report for a Corpse* from 1949.

4. Derrida, *The Truth in Painting,* 269.

5. Sigmund Freud, "On Dreams," in *Standard Edition of the Complete Psychological Works of Sigmund Freud,* ed. and trans. James Strachey (London: Hogarth, 1959), 5:633–86, 684. Hereafter noted as *Standard Edition.*

6. Sigmund Freud, "Fetishism," in *Standard Edition,* 21:152–53.

7. Ibid., 156.

8. Sigmund Freud, "Three Essays on Sexuality," in *Standard Edition,* 7:154, n. 2 (added 1920).

9. Ibid., 153.

10. Ibid., 155 (emphasis in original).

11. Victor Turner, *The Forest of Symbols: Aspects of Ndembu Ritual* (Ithaca, N.Y.: Cornell University Press, 1967), 28, 29, 30.

12. Samuel Beckett, *Waiting for Godot* (New York: Grove Press, 1954), 44.

13. The picture appears in Astrid Proll, ed., *Baader-Meinhof: Pictures on the Run, 67–77* (Zurich: Scalo, 1998), 35. Thanks to Christina White for bringing it to my attention. Its caption reads in English: "Rudi Dutschke's shoe in Kurfurstendam shortly after shots had been fired by a right-wing assailant, 11th April 1968."

14. On the "ideological" and historical differences between these two men, see Derrida, *The Truth in Painting,* 281. Martin Heidegger, "The Origin of the Work of Art," in *Poetry, Language, Thought,* trans. Albert Hofstadter (New York: Harper and Row, 1971), 15–87. Meyer Schapiro, "The Still Life as a Personal Object—A Note on Heidegger and Van Gogh," in *The Reach of Mind: Essays in Memory of Kurt Goldstein,* ed. Marianne L. Simmel (New York: Springer, 1968), 203–9. Derrida's long essay on this "debate" appears in the "Restitutions" section of *The Truth in Painting.* It became the jumping off point for Fredric Jameson's *Postmodernism; or, The Cultural Logic of Late Capitalism* (Durham, N.C.: Duke University Press, 1991); see pp. 6–11 as well as other less widely read texts, some of which are noted below.

15. Karl Marx, *Capital*, trans. Samuel Moore and Edward Aveling (New York: International Publishers, 1967), 1:72, 74.

16. Ibid., 76 (emphasis added), 72.

17. Walter Benjamin, *The Arcades Project*, trans. Howard Eiland and Kevin McLauglin (Cambridge, Mass.: Belknap Press, Harvard University Press, 1999), 662.

18. Emile Durkheim, *The Elementary Forms of the Religious Life*, trans. Joseph Ward Swain (New York: Free Press, 1969), 203.

19. Marx, *Capital*, 72.

20. For critiques of these sentiments, see a cryptic set of questions by Derrida in *The Truth in Painting:* "What if Heidegger were already questioning beyond this already coded thematics? What if he were also wary of the concept of fetishism according to Marx or according to Freud? And what if he wanted to take the whole of this problem up again, and the whole question of the thing in truth which exercises the notion of fetishism?" (334). See also the analysis of "the rhetoric of iconoclasm" in W. J. T. Mitchell, *Iconology: Image, Text, Ideology* (Chicago: University of Chicago Press, 1986), 151–208.

21. Benjamin, *Arcades*, 669.

22. Walter Benjamin, "Unpacking My Library," in *Illuminations*, ed. Hannah Arendt, trans. Harry Zohn (New York: Schocken, 1968), 67.

23. Susan Stewart, *On Longing: Narratives of the Miniature, the Gigantic, the Souvenir, the Collection* (Durham, N.C.: Duke University Press, 1993), 151.

24. Benjamin, "Unpacking My Library," 60.

25. Ibid., 63.

26. Douglas Mao, *Solid Objects: Modernism and the Test of Production* (Princeton, N.J.: Princeton University Press, 1998), 4.

27. Virginia Woolf, *Orlando: A Biography* (Harmondsworth, England: Penguin, 1942), 212.

28. Benjamin, *Arcades*, 594.

29. Roland Barthes, *Mythologies*, trans. Annette Lavers (New York: Hill and Wang, 1972), 39.

30. James Agee and Walker Evans, *Let Us Now Praise Famous Men* (Boston: Houghton Mifflin, 1941), 262–63.

31. Ibid., 267.

32. Ibid., 270.

33. Ibid.

34. Emanual Swedenborg, *The Heavenly Arcana disclosed, which are in the Sacred Scripture, or Word of the Lord: here, first, those which are in Genesis; together with wonderful things seen in the world of spirits and in the heaven of angels,* Rotch edition (New York: New Church Board of Publication, 1893), 3:223.

35. Gertrude Jobes, *Dictionary of Mythology, Folklore, and Symbols* (Latham, Md.: Scarecrow Press, 1962), 2:1440.

36. Quoted in Jean Chevalier and Alain Gheerbrant, *A Dictionary of Symbols,* trans. John Bruckman-Brown (Oxford: Blackwell, 1994), 876.

37. Joseph J. Kockelman, *Heidegger on Art and Art Works* (Dordrecht, Netherlands: Martinus Nijhoff, 1985), 127.

38. Schapiro, "Still Life as a Personal Object," 206.

39. See Otto Poggeler, "Heidegger on Art," in *Martin Heidegger: Politics, Art, and Technology,* ed. Karsten Harries and Christoph Jamme (New York: Holmes and Meier, 1994), 114.

40. Art Spiegelman, *Maus II: A Survivor's Tale: And Here My Troubles Began* (New York: Pantheon, 1991), 60–63.

41. Marjorie Garber, *Vested Interests: Cross-Dressing and Cultural Anxiety* (New York: Harper-Collins, 1993), 44–45 cites *Information for the Female-to-Male Crossdresser and Transsexual,* which relies on John T. Molloy's note that "for the small man . . . the best shoes are traditional wingtip" and on Nancy Friday's mention in *My Secret Garden* of female transvestites' interest in "wingtip shoes" to suggest that wing tips were part of the "imitation man look."

42. Agee and Evans, *Let Us Now Praise Famous Men,* 258.

43. Elin Schoen Brockman, "A Woman's Power Tool: High Heels," *New York Times,* March 5, 2000, sec. 4, p. 2.

44. Advertisement for pierresilber.com in *New York Times.*

45. Michael Wilson, *Salt of the Earth,* screenplay 1953 (Old Westbury, N.Y.: Feminist Press, 1978), 61.

46. In his *Studies in Iconology: Humanistic Themes in the Art of the Renaissance* (New York: Harper and Row, 1962), Erwin Panowsky defines iconography as the study of "the subject matter or meaning of works of art" (3).

47. See "The Family of Little Feet," "Chanclas," and "A House of My Own," in Sandra Cisneros, *The House on Mango Street* (New York: Vintage, 1991), 39–42, 46–48, 108.

48. The discovery of the bloody size-12 Bruno Magli shoeprints left on Nicole Simpson's walk-

way became a spectacular example of this. The search to identify the tread was undertaken by a Japanese firm specializing in shoe-print recognition at crime scenes. The facts that only a few hundred pairs of this size existed worldwide and that O. J. Simpson owned one of them, however, were not sufficient evidence to convict.

49. Leslie Kaufman, "A Walk on the Wild Side Stirs the Shoe Industry," *New York Times,* July 9, 2000, sec. 3, pp. 1, 8, notes that in the United States, women's shoe sales have been remarkably consistent since the end of World War II. During the 1990s despite the consumer boom, women's shoe sales have grown steadily at only 1.8 percent per year, consistent with figures from the 1940s, excluding a spike during the 1980s when athletic footwear became popular. However, during the 2008–9 "Great Recession," "sales of shoes are soaring." Stephanie Rosenbloom, "A Not So Guilty Pleasure," *New York Times,* national ed., November 6, 2009, B1, 6.

50. See Carolyn Steedman, "Landscape for a Good Woman," in *Past Tenses: Essays on Writing, Autobiography and History* (London: Rivers Oram Press, 1992), 21–40. See also her book of the same title.

51. Charlotte Nekola, "Good Mothers, Bad Daughters," in *Dream House* (New York: Norton, 1993), 48.

52. Ibid., 49.

53. Cisneros, *House on Mango Street,* 40.

54. C. L. R. James, *American Civilization,* ed. Anna Grimshaw and Keith Hart (New York: Blackwell, 1993), 131.

13

THE CINEMATIC JEWEL
FETISHIZING THE GOODS

Vito Zagarrio

NECKLACES, EXCHANGES, DOUBLES

Jewels in film are multivalent narrative devices, some of the most intense metaphors of its narrative structure. Think about classic comedies where jewels are the happy source of many plots: for instance *Trouble in Paradise* (1932), one of the sophisticated comedies that better characterize the so-called Lubitsch touch. The story unfolds between Venice and Paris, two of the classic destinations of American tourism: an international gentleman thief (Herbert Marshall) meets a skilled and pretty thief (Miriam Hopkins), and together they decide to defraud a rich Parisian lady (Kay Francis). The unexpected happens, though, and the thief falls for the lady, thus generating a series of mishaps, until the more normal relationship with the other thief prevails, and together they can practice dexterous thieving. Hans Dreier, the set designer, runs wild with an eccentric design often influenced by stereotypes: Venetian gondolas abound and even become diegetic (by looking at a gondola ashtray one of the characters recognizes the thief); the luxurious apartment of the Parisian lady overflows with objects as does the Venetian hotel where the film begins. However, for the most part, jewels are the objects of everyone's desire—protagonists and spectators alike—and the narrative ploy that allows the story to progress: the eyes of our famous thief fall on the necklace of the sophisticated lady during a concert, as the camera zooms in on the woman's neck and on her richly ornate purse (it is actually a dolly shot) coveted by Marshall's binoculars. In two exhilarating sequences, the irresistible thieving couple Marshall and Hopkins engage in a steal and tell competition: in a Venetian hotel and in a Parisian taxi, out of nowhere, come a wallet, a pocket watch, a necklace, and even a garter (the girl, embarrassed, checks under her skirt).

In the Italian counterpart of these comedies, for instance, *Batticuore (Heartbeat)* by Mario Camerini (1939), Assia Noris, in the unprecedented part of a thief with a heart of gold, is involved in a mystery that develops through a double switch: on the one hand, the thief, caught stealing a pin, is forced to impersonate the niece of a foreign diplomat; on the other hand, a series of misunderstandings develops around a pocket watch with a "compromising" photograph inside. It is one of the many Italian examples in which the jewel is the engine of a plot based on switches and doubles.

A small safe emptied of its jewels provides the opening shot of Alfred Hitchcock's *To Catch a Thief* (1955), where Cary Grant interprets the part of a retired international thief hired by the police to catch a new "Cat." Even though it is a typical Hitchcock thriller, there is much Lubitsch-style humor: here too we are in France in a stereotypical French Riviera populated by rich American tourists. On the neck of one of these, the mother of a magnificent Grace Kelly, we find a necklace desired by all. On another neck is another precious ornament on which hinges the much less easy-going classical Hitchcock plot of *Vertigo* (1958). In one climactic moment, the same necklace appears on Kim Novak's neck ("the woman who lived twice," in the Italian translation of the film's title) and on Carlotta Valdez, the mysterious "woman in the painting," ancestor-double, alter ego, or metaphoric projection of the protagonist. The double presence of the jewel is the diegetic element that triggers the game of doubles in the film: "the woman who lived twice," the double suicide, the double death, the double flashback. In the mirror image of the portrait and the jewel (along with the hair style, Kim Novak's blonde chignon), Carlotta Valdez is reincarnated in the present-day Carlotta, ambiguous and disconcerting as the jewel she displays.

Treacherous, too, is Lucia, one of the Valastro sisters in Luchino Visconti's *La terra trema* (*The Earth Trembles*, 1948), on the surface a (neo)realist film that in fact unfolds along the lines of a romantic, impossibly formalist, melodrama. For a jewel, Lucia has sold herself to the slimy Maresciallo who courts her. In the first part of the film, when N'toni's family was poor but happy, Lucia fantasizes about necklaces and earrings, "i pennenti" (i.e., pendants). Now that misfortune has hit the family, when the protagonist is punished by Fate for having tried to become independent from wholesalers, his sisters are also crushed by misfortune: Mara does not fulfill her dreams of love with the little brick mason, and Lucia gives in to the advances of the man in uniform. During a dramatic exchange, Mara reproaches her for the family's dishonor. In one of the most intense scenes in the film, when the grandfather is dying in his bed, a guilt-ridden Lucia creeps along the pink wall, hanging on to it as if to defend herself, holding onto the jewel for which she paid too dearly.

More jewels and more necks: on Madonna's neck, in *Desperately Seeking Susan* (Susan Seidelman, 1985), hangs the cross that will immortalize the ambiguous and desecrating singer of "Like a Virgin," queen of visions between Catholic fetishes and hyperlaic symbols. Instead of jewels, on Charles Bronson's neck in *Once upon a Time in the West* (Sergio Leone, 1968) hangs a small harmonica, which gives him his nickname. An atypical ornament, a weird necklace that contains a fetish as well: the harmonica is what the villain Henry Fonda forced into the mouth of the mestizo "chico" when Fonda used the boy's shoulder as a scaffold to hang his brother, and what the boy, once adult, rips from his neck and forces into the dying "gringo's" mouth. In his earlier classic, *Per qualche dollaro in più* (*For a Few Dollars More*, 1965), the jewel is again a crucial device: a musical timepiece worn as a necklace with a woman's picture inside determines Lee Van Cleef's vengeance against the villain Gian Maria Volonté. More conventionally, the jewel can add to male charm: for instance, Burt Lancaster's smiling face framed with the pirate's earring on one lobe in *The Crimson Pirate* (Richard Siodmak, 1952).

As one can see, the diegetic and symbolic presence of the ornament, the jewel, the necklace, the earring, is constant in many widely different types of film, from Hitchcock to Lubitsch to Visconti, in many genres, from comedy to murder mysteries to action films; in fact, there is a restless search for diamonds or treasures, in pirates' trunks or Pharaohs' tombs, "romancing" a stone or a "jewel of the Nile" (which can even turn out to be human). I would like to draw attention, though, to a specific film that deserves a closer theoretical discourse: what I define as the "fetish" in *Riso amaro*.

THE FAKE NECKLACE

Riso amaro (*Bitter Rice,* 1949) by Giuseppe De Santis immediately calls to mind *La terra trema:* acclaimed "neorealist" film, it forms part of an indivisible trilogy along with *Caccia tragica* (*Tragic Hunt,* 1947) and *Non c'è pace tra gli ulivi* (*Under the Olive Trees,* 1950). (However, a new reading would impose new categories and definitions, and perhaps a redefinition of the idea of neorealism.) Watching it today, its quite ambitious political-cultural aims are apparent.[1]

When De Santis shot *Riso amaro,* only a few years had passed between his first film (*Caccia tragica,* set after the Resistance and World War II) and this new product. Yet the cultural climate had changed completely: there had been national elections on April 18, 1948, when the dream of a Popular Front and the utopia of a revolution born out of the Resistance died. What had not died for the communist sympathizer De Santis, though, is the "Northern wind," that political aspiration that rereads social conflicts in Italy from the standpoint of the working class. Not dead, also because of the time lag, since the film was conceived before the defeat of the Left. Therefore, he set the issue of the laboring subproletariat in *Riso amaro* in the North, in the rice fields around Vercelli in Piedmont.[2]

In fact, hovering in the background is the world of the *mondine* (rice weeders), seasonal women workers hired every year to pick rice. It is not by coincidence that the opening of the film is choral: a radio journalist helps the audience discover a world in ferment, as (female) rice field workers symbolically meet a demonstration by the (male) factory workers of Fiat. The Northern and Southern questions mix, just as social and "genre" films mix from the very beginning, as happens in *Caccia tragica*. Milling amid the crowd are police agents and two "bandits," Walter (Vittorio Gassman) and Francesca (Doris Dowling), back from stealing a very expensive necklace, as can be surmised from the sales cries of newspaper boys. Right away, the subplot of the film is disclosed, in which the necklace becomes both a narrative engine and a clear fetish, as defined by the first volume of Karl Marx's *Capital*.[3]

Jean Renoir's lesson and French political realism come to mind as models for De Santis. In fact, if we examine *La règle du jeu* (*Rules of the Game*, Renoir, 1939) filmed on the eve of the world conflict that would, indeed, change "the rules of the game," upsetting the balances and values of people, we realize the importance of fetishes. In *La règle du jeu*, there are small signs, clues, objects that offer the means for a rereading of the film and of Renoir. They are objects-symbols, objects-fetishes, that also prompt a rereading of Marx's chapter on "commodity fetishism": just as money is a fetish of goods for its exchange value, so too are social roles fetishes, symbolic representations, as men end up wearing "character masks," masks imposed by their social class and their function within it. Marx's theory can be extended to those symbols that can become emblems of the capitalist production system. We do not know whether Renoir had read that specific chapter of *Capital*, but he surely knew Marx, as *La vie est à nous* (*The People of France*, 1936) shows. He fills his *Règle du jeu* with objects-fetishes,[4] small icons of capitalism, refined and subliminal versions of the comic nuts, bolts, and pulleys of Charlie Chaplin's 1936 *Modern Times*.

Something similar happens ten years later in *Riso amaro* where the plot hinges on the stolen necklace mentioned at the beginning of the film. (De Santis has a soft spot for "American" narrative devices.) The necklace is the focal point: the police search for the thieves, and the press amply publicizes the hunt. Both the necklace and Walter are coveted by Silvana (a gorgeous Silvana Mangano), one of the smarter *mondine* who soon becomes their leader, who begins a seduction game with the man and a challenge with the woman thief. Francesca sneaks into the deserted warehouse where the rice weeders sleep and becomes the leader of a group of illegal workers (the *clandestine*), who clash with the regularly hired girls. The scene in which the two groups of women (legal and illegal ones) challenge each other is memorable: staged as a battle, at first through songs directly provoking and answering provocations in rhyme (led by Silvana and Francesca), and then through open physical fighting.

Then Marco appears (Raf Vallone, a constant in De Santis's films), a young draftee who falls for Silvana. Couples switch shortly thereafter. Walter, too, chased by the police, has found shelter in the rice fields and sleeps in the rice warehouses *(magazzini)* where Francesca gives him food. In his hiding place, he thinks up the next robbery: stealing the tons of harvested rice using trucks. To accomplish his plan he uses Silvana, whom he seduces in a dark scene with sadistic and masochistic undertones. Silvana, once she has given in to Walter's advances, becomes his accomplice and is willing to flood the rice fields. The night party celebrating the end of the harvest is the perfect occasion to distract everybody and facilitate Walter's escape. As the fields are flooded, Silvana is elected queen of the party ("Miss *mondina* 1948"). In the general havoc, Silvana watches immobilized, almost in a trance, the final fight between Walter and Marco, who now sides with the newly redeemed Francesca. The showdown takes place in a butcher shop, where the western-style duel is again carried out principally by the two women, assuming masculine roles, as the wounded men watch impotently. In the end, it is Silvana who shoots Walter, once she realizes that the necklace, the engine of the whole action, is fake and Walter has tricked and used her. De Santis shows Walter dying, hanging from a butcher's hook like a piece of dead meat, as in a Grand Guignol show, and Silvana killing herself, as in a melodrama. She throws herself from the high scaffolding built for the party. In the morning, the rice weeders all throw a handful of rice over her body, which soon becomes a funerary "tombstone," a monument to beauty and pain.

Here, too, De Santis subverts genres, mixing popular cinema and sophisticated auteur work, social messages and Hollywood codes: the final western duel, for instance, with the two women taking on manly roles through the phallic gun, precedes the famous ending of Nicholas Ray's *Johnny Guitar* (1954) by a few years; the initial scene of the arrival of the *mondine* train mixes documentary style and detective story; the boogie-woogie scene that reveals Silvana Mangano to the audience is an homage to all Hollywood star-system stereotypes. But there is more: there is the Orientalist reference to rice fields that seem to pop out of an Asian painting and the straw hats unrealistically thrown in the air in the background as festive confetti. There is melodrama (the "high" Visconti kind, and the "low" Raffaello Matarazzo kind), with strongly sexual undertones (such as the scene in which Silvana gives in to Walter, laughing hysterically as he whips her). There is the subtly Marxist symbolism of the necklace or the dummies brought by the soldiers for target practice (like Brechtian *Karactermasquen*) when Raf Vallone appears on the screen. And there are the media—the gramophone, the microphone, the woman's magazine, the radio, American music—all components of a Western mythology that gets mixed up with communist ideology.

In any case, the engine of this postmodern pastiche before its time is the necklace that travels from hand to hand (Walter's to Francesca's to Silvana's), yet never lands on anybody's neck, eventually breaking the necks of two of them, to end up in the gutter. It is, therefore, highly symbolic, a strong narrative vehicle, the mythopoetic engine of melodrama, but also an unsettling analytical tool to dissect consumerist society. As in Renoir's films, the object of reification—in this case the jewel—is the indicator of the larger issue of commodity fetishism as the basis of our society: civil society is as false as the necklace, based on a bluff, on the false convention of the vicious cycle goods-money-goods. Human relationships are false, as are the feelings based on the idea of exchange. Love is false—so are class relationships.

The fake necklace in *Riso amaro* instantiates the American myth that permeates De Santis's work, perhaps unconsciously, even while he disputes it. The director speaks about the "American" elements in *Riso amaro* as possible indictments of a Western way of life:

This is the theme of *Riso amaro*: an indictment of the corruption that, in a seemingly innocent way, a sort of American ideology has brought to Western Europe. Such ideology has managed to spread its poisons even in the healthiest strata of the population,

FIGURES 13.1, 13.2, 13.3

Riso amaro (Giuseppe
De Santis, 1949).

especially among young people who encounter it through the captivating filter of boo-gie-woogie, chewing gum, and easy luxuries. It has been, and it certainly still is, a kind of opium for the least aware young people who, after the moral and material destruc-tion of war, persist on living to the fullest. . . . The rice weeder Silvana is passionately fond of comics, mad for boogie-woogie, avid consumer of chewing gum; she cuts out of glossy magazines pictures of actresses she idolizes. . . . Good fortune and everything else take shape in Walter, typical embodiment of the Americanized European man. It is no accident that Mangano has been called the "Italian Rita Hayworth" by journalists all over the world, and that is exactly the kind of woman I wanted to show.[5]

Actually, the "American ideology" that has formed De Santis's generation seeps into his tastes and imagination: chewing gum and boogie-woogie are not the only clues of this (unconscious?) infatuation with the "air of the West." There is also the whole media sys-tem, composed of radios and loudspeakers, newspapers and typewriters, trains and trucks. And, deep down, that declaration of cinematic affection for Silvana Mangano as an Italian Rita Hayworth cannot help calling to mind the charm that Hollywood cinema, with its star system and erotic components, has always had for this director.

On the one hand, Hollywood codes; on the other hand, civic questions and social drama in the so-called trilogy of the earth tend to short-circuit and create a peculiar sense of conflation. There are the western topoi: the good and the bad with no nuances, such as Michele and Giovanna on one side and Daniela/Lili Marlene on the other in *Caccia tragica,* Marco and Walter in *Riso amaro,* Francesco and Bonfiglio in *Non c'è pace tra gli ulivi;* perverse or sensual women like Daniela or Silvana echo film noir's femme fatales. There is a happy ending (much more obvious in *Caccia tragica* with Alberto's "forgive-ness," and in *Non c'è pace tra gli ulivi* than in *Riso amaro* where the triumph of the good is juxtaposed to Silvana's suicide). But there is also Alessandro Blasetti's realism (see the sequence of *saltarello* in *Non c'è pace tra gli ulivi* that recalls the peasant festival in *Terra madre*) and Alexander Dovzěnko's (the rice fields or the countryside of the Bassa Padana are shot like the pastures of *Zemlja* [*Earth,* 1930]) and Visconti's neorealism (peculiar and atypical as the one in *La terra trema*), and a bit of comedy in the many character actors (such as the dissonant note of Salvatore Capuano in *Non c'è pace tra gli ulivi*) who call to mind their American counterparts.

All the components of De Santis's film grammar are tied to Hollywood as well with a specific purpose in mind, a coherent development from screenplay to editing. The stylistic constants of De Santis's directing are clear: the tracking shot as ideological interpretation of reality that also demonstrates his sheer directorial talent; the panfocus (i.e., the cinematic effect produced mostly through a wide angle) as another essential factor of an all-encompassing and, hopefully, nonmanipulative approach to reality; boom and dolly as musical scansions of the director's score; the fundamentals of an education in images; the formalism of the shot as awareness of the power of cinema, but also the heritage from the maestros (Visconti, Renoir, and John Ford above all); abstract acting, theatricality of narration, and a taste for excess—and on and on.

In *Riso amaro*, actors sometimes move on command, magnificent objects of obsession to the will of a skilled omnipotent puppet master. Take the first shot that reveals Mangano's body: Gassman and Dowling look out of the train where they are hiding, their gazes lost on the horizon, as a few notes of boogie-woogie are heard. On that rhythm, the camera tracks slowly and reveals a series of comic characters inside a sleeping car smugly observing the *mondine*. It is as if De Santis, with a simple camera movement and art direction, said everything about class differences within the capitalist system: on one side the rich bourgeoisie; on the other the proletariat, the rice weeders, inexorably divided. But this message would be boringly didactic if within it there weren't Silvana, at the end of the tracking shot, dancing by the gramophone with a line of extras on the horizon, to give depth to the scene: this is cinema, where fiction and realism mix, where social commentary and Hollywood musical meet.

All this is strung along the fake necklace coveted by two women. Jewels: ambiguity, double-crossing, transitoriness, a pretext to subvert the whole notion of what is real. This is what turns "rice" (in the untranslatable double meaning in Italian of "rice" and "laughter") "bitter."

1. See *Non c'è pace tra gli ulivi: Un neorealismo postmoderno*, ed. Vito Zagarrio (Rome: Edizioni di Bianco & Nero, 2002); *Rosso fuoco: Il cinema di Giuseppe De Santis*, ed. S. Toffetti (Turin: Museo Nazionale del Cinema, 1996); Stefano Masi, *Giuseppe De Santis* (Florence: La Nuova Italia, 1982); A. Martini and M. Melani, "De Santis," in *Il neorealismo cinematografico italiano*, ed. Lino Miccichè (Venice: Marsilio, 1975). About the director, see also the volumes published by the Associazione Giuseppe De Santis, 1: *Giuseppe De Santis, maestro di cinema e di vita* (Fondi, 1999); and 2: *Caccia tragica: Un inizio strepitoso* (Fondi, 2000).

2. See Carlo Lizzani, *Riso amaro* (Rome: Officina edizioni, 1978).

3. See Karl Marx, *Das Kapital: Kritik der Politische Oeconomie*, vol. 1: *Der Produktionprocess des Kapitals* (Hamburg: Otto Meissner Verlag, 1867), Part I: "Commodities and Money," Chapter 1: "Commodities," 3: "The Equivalent Form of Value."

4. See my essays, "La regola del 'gioco,'" in *Film e realtà*, ed. Riccardo Redi (Pesaro: XIV Rassegna Internazionale Retrospettiva, 1995); and "Play—Film—Play: Il Cinema & il gioco," *Igitur* 3 (2002).

5. Giuseppe De Santis, "Confessioni di un regista," *Rivista del Cinema Italiano* 1–2 (January–February, 1953). A lecture given by De Santis at the Gabinetto Viesseux in Florence, in the spring of 1951 (my translation).

14

ENCHANTED SANDALS
ITALIAN SHOES AND THE POST–WORLD WAR II
INTERNATIONAL SCENE

Vittoria C. Caratozzolo

> *To all those who must walk.*
>
> SALVATORE FERRAGAMO, 1957

GRADIVA: SHE WHO WALKS IN BRIGHTNESS

In an essay on women's footwear, Italo Calvino stresses that in order to appreciate the formal quality of a shoe, we must examine it from the ground upward:

> its form (its means and end) is determined by the need to place both heel and toe firmly on the ground and at the same time, lift them up, detaching them from and posing resistance to the dust, dirt, or debris lying beneath. This is why its streamlined shape, shiny surface, and light consistency are not accessory qualities but essential ones.
>
> . . . The seductive power of a woman's shoe is perverse in this respect: it mingles the height of refinement with direct contact with what is degrading, accepted without shame.[1]

This double tension informing the sophisticated technology of shoe manufacture also animated the wounded gaze of those women, real and imagined, who at the end of the Second World War began, with timid yet renewed ardor, to reconsider their physical appearances. In June 1944, the war had not yet ended, but Rome, liberated by the Allied forces, found its streets flooded with gaily dressed young women. Fleeing from the air-raid shelters, they savored the heady foretaste of the peacetime to come celebrated in the colorful print dresses they wore, enhanced by the amber tones of their skin.

This was the scene as viewed through the eyes of Bettina Ballard, an American journalist for *Vogue* since 1934, when she arrived in Rome from North Africa, where she had served as a Red Cross volunteer.[2] The suffering and hardships of the war had deeply changed this journalist who had once so passionately dedicated herself to the discovery of the latest trends in international fashion. For this reason, she had left the United States and the editorial staff of *Vogue* in search of places and situations to which she could selflessly devote her energies and capabilities. The Red Cross and North Africa provided an answer to her existential crisis. But it had not been easy for her to reduce her wardrobe to the essentials before going overseas, or to don the uniform that she immediately decided to personalize by having it redesigned for her own person, adding a softer touch to its severe lines: a blouse with a shirred-neck collar specially designed by Clare Potter. This feminine addition to the Red Cross uniform signaled her momentary farewell to the world of fashion she had shared and helped build together with so many other women.

Once in Rome, the few outfits she had brought along immediately seemed démodé; they had lost their initial glamour. Yet in 1944, Italy's capital was far from being the fashionable city it would later become when Ballard would return once again as a *Vogue* correspondent to cover the fashion shows inaugurating Italian couture in the early 1950s. The Roman ateliers showed no signs of renewed vitality until 1946. Once freed from the nightmares of the war, the fashion industry still had to overcome a series of obstacles hampering its development. In November 1945, in the first issue of the new series of the high-fashion magazine *Bellezza*, editor-in-chief Elsa Robiola frankly revealed to her readers the difficult conditions faced by the fashion business in the period immediately following the war:

> A great slowness hinders our movements. The enigmatic and grave period we are experiencing, the dearth of means of transport, the horrible threat of a winter without gas or coal, the disappearance of goods needed to make clothes, the shoddy quality of what is available, the lack of electricity which negatively influences the rhythms and output of labor—these are the problems besetting our workshops. Even the most deeply felt enthusiasm would wane in the face of such difficulties; exhaustion and demoralization are more than justified. These same discouraging problems afflict our own work as journalists, slowing us down, and making it harder to reach the goal.[3]

Thus one wonders: judging by what "standards of Roman fashion" did Ballard feel the urgent need to update her wardrobe?[4] It is more likely that, rather than feeling obliged to comply with a fashion regime then dominating the capital, she had sensed Roman women's wish to reappropriate their own city and their own physical appearances—now that they were finally free to reimagine and remake them. Bettina Ballard fully shared this desire, and in keeping with the pioneering spirit expressed by the first Roman collections of the postwar period, she attempted to fulfill it with recourse to do-it-yourself methods rather than high fashion. In her autobiography, she tells the story of how she obtained some parachute silk from a soldier, had it dyed in the bright colors of Italian textiles, and gave it to a dressmaker who made her a dress out of this piece of cast-off war equipment. Nonetheless, it is still difficult to understand fully what Ballard meant by the expression "the standards of Roman fashion." Was it not perhaps her own trained eye as a sophisticated fashion journalist that created this standard, calling it into being the moment she named it? Perhaps she had already secretly imagined it displayed on the pages of *Vogue*. But it was not the ingenious dresses of Roman women that would receive full coverage in the slick pages of the American high-fashion magazine. Instead, they focused on the simple sandals they wore, which elegantly enhanced their charming feet. Ballard once again resumed her former guise as reporter and almost compulsively captured with her camera "the beautiful, small feet of the Princess Galitzine," clad in delicate, graceful sandals. Once they had appeared on the pages of *Vogue,* those sandals instantly became the rage on both sides of the Atlantic.

May we interpret the story of those sandals as a moment of true vision that allowed Bettina Ballard to find her way back to fashion? Or might we say that thanks to the magic of a peripheral accessory, located far below the centrality of the dress and human figure, she rediscovered her former enthusiasm for the world of fashion? In creating this vision, what role was played by the many antique bas-reliefs of sandal-shod marble maids scattered through the city? As if captured in a wide-angle lens, we may glimpse Princess Galitzine, like a new Gradiva, celebrated Pompeian maiden, advancing through the streets of Rome, returning from the past to lead the city's women back to fashion.

> A young archaeologist, Norbert Hanold, had discovered in a museum of antiquities in Rome a relief which had so immensely attracted him that he was greatly pleased at obtaining an excellent plaster cast of it which he could hang in his study in a German university town and gaze at with interest. The sculpture represented a fully-grown girl stepping along, with her flowing dress a little pulled up so as to reveal her sandaled feet. One foot rested squarely on the ground; the other, lifted from the ground in the act of following after, touched it only with the tips of the toes while the sole and the heel rose almost perpendicularly. It was probably the unusual and peculiarly charming gait thus presented which attracted the sculptor's notice and which still, after so many centuries, riveted the eyes of its archaeological admirer.[5]

Thus did Freud describe the image of Gradiva, portrayed in a bas-relief in the Chiaramonti Museum at the Vatican, that in 1903 had inspired a story by German author Wilhelm Jensen, "Gradiva, Pompeian Phantasy." Freud took Jensen's story very seriously, considering it extremely pertinent to psychoanalysis because of the parallel it draws between archaeological research and the psychological investigation of buried memories, which Jensen had masterfully illustrated. Jensen tells the story of a young archaeologist,

Norbert Hanold, who falls under the spell of the image of Gradiva. Through a labyrinth of dreams and delusions, the meaning of which becomes progressively clearer to him, the hero gradually realizes that Gradiva is none other than Zoe Bertang, a childhood play-mate, whose last name is an unconscious translation of "she who steps along brilliantly." Gradiva allows Hanold to discover his buried feelings for Zoe, thereby regaining his zest for life, which had previously been devoted exclusively to studying the ruins of classical antiquity.

Without going further into Freud's psychoanalytical discussion of this story, we may note an analogy between Ballard's experience in Rome and the fictional Norbert Han-old's experience. Both regain interest for worldly forms thanks to a moment of vision. The sandals on the feet of Princess Galitzine, like Gradiva's graceful gait, awaken in the viewer the desire to penetrate their secrets, to violate the wholeness of their perfection, those very qualities inscribed on the marble surface of the antique bas-relief. It is in this

FIGURE 14.1 *Gradiva*, Neo-Attic Roman bas-relief. Vatican Museum.

stance as predator that the mythopoetic attitude of the viewer finds its origin. The object viewed becomes immersed in a narrative flow, fed by the double temporal dimension of past and present and by the disturbing lack of distinction between animate and inanimate.

From the end of the war throughout the following decade, photo essays dedicated to Italian fashion published in *Vogue* and *Harper's Bazaar* used historical and archaeological sites for their settings. Images of models amid ruins and antique draperies scattered through the city constructed for the consumption of American readers a fantasy of a fresh, new style based in myth, intrepidly thrusting itself upon the international garment market while offering a glance at a remote past, by no means irremediably lost, that could be resuscitated through an appeal to the viewer's emotional and affective sphere. Walter Benjamin theorized this temporal shift, representing it through the dialectic image of the tiger's leap:

> History is the subject of a structure whose site is not homogeneous and empty time but time filled by the presence of the now (*Jetztzeit*). Thus, to Robespierre, ancient Rome was a past charged with the time of the now which he blasted out of the continuum of history. The French Revolution viewed itself as Rome reincarnate. It evoked ancient Rome the way fashion evokes costumes of the past. Fashion has a flair for the topical, no matter where it stirs in the thickets of long ago; it is a tiger's leap into the past.[6]

In the last two decades, fashion studies have shown how the dialectic relationship of past and present informs the production and consumption of fashion, as well as its representation in the media. In October 1985, during a conference held at the Victoria and Albert Museum, Gianni Versace, examining the conflation of the notions of past and present, tradition and future, claimed that the creativity of fashion is deeply connected to a double perception of time:

> I believe that the best starting point is the ever-increasing knowledge of and interest in our traditions, as an awareness of the past helps give one the sense of security needed

to face the present and the future. . . . The sense of the past, and awareness of daily life, are elements which, if they are blended and transposed correctly, can result in a fashion style which is suited to and liveable by everybody because it reflects elements which already belong to us and are thus near to us.[7]

The new belongs to us and existed before our past began. Knowing this implies that we are able to inoculate the present in the past.

PAGAN SANDALS

The archaeological site of Pompeii, the place where Norbert Hanold had dreamed his living image of Gradiva and where she had been victim to the eruption of Vesuvius, served once again as the setting for a new scene also inspired by a moment of vision. During a summer trip to Capri in the mid-1930s, Diana Vreeland, fashion editor of *Harper's Bazaar* before becoming editor of *Vogue*, discovered "pagan sandals" that she would launch a few years later in the United States as an extremely popular fashion accessory.[8]

In her autobiography, she recounts how she used to wander around Seventh Avenue, New York's garment district, during the war years, ferreting out fashion news. On such occasions, she usually wore a pair of sandals from Capri, which added a bizarre touch to her look:

I'd walk home those sixty blocks alone all those years. I *loved* the fur district, and that's where I'd walk when I finished working. These are the war years I'm speaking about now. Believe me, there were no cabs: I'd walk these *long, long* blocks. We were practically in a blackout—what they called a brownout—the lights were very dim. I was absolutely *freezing*. There weren't slacks in those days, and there weren't boots—I was in sandals. I had a fur coat on—a fur-lined raincoat—and I'd just shout to myself, "Keep walking! Keep walking!" (108)

Vreeland's self-portrayal radiates eccentricity with a dandy's flair for provocation. Who else could have combined the cozy fur coat, such a heavy second skin, a protective winter barrier between the self and the outer world, with these delicate sandals, comfortable enough but certainly unsuitable for getting about in the cold, on uneven pavement, strewn with obstacles of every sort? Did her unusual choice of outfit express a desire to distinguish herself through a radical elegance that rendered her vulnerable, exposed her to risk, quite in keeping with the drama of the times? Or, more simply, did it express nostalgia for another place and time?

While wandering alone down Seventh Avenue, deserted in the evening or teeming with the workers of the world's most prestigious garment industry in the daytime, Diana Vreeland mused about that lovely summer she had spent in Capri back in 1935.

I never wore clothes from Seventh Avenue myself, you understand. I always kept a totally European view of things. Maybe that's why I was so appreciated there. I was independent. In those days, don't forget, fashion traveled very slowly. When I arrived back in this country after the war started, I couldn't believe what I saw. In the summer, every woman wore diamond clips on crêpe de chine dresses. And they all wore silk stockings —this was before nylons—under these hideous strappy high heels. This is in the summer, you understand—in this *country*. It was *unbelievable*.

For years in Europe I'd been bare-legged and thong-sandaled once the heat came on. I still have some of my original sandals I had made in Capri in 1935 when Reed and I were staying at the Fortino in Marina Grande. The theory of the sandal was that the sandal strap went between the toes. The soles of these sandals were so beautiful. They were built up in layers thinner than my fingernail—layer upon layer. When you walked, it was like walking in satin. In Capri, we used to walk up through the hills, through the vineyards, and all the way out to Tiberius's palace—that's a hell of a walk. I can remember Coco Chanel and Visconti used to do it on donkeys. She'd wear her beret and her pullover and her white duck pants—and her pearls, naturally—and the donkey would carry her uphill over the steep, rocky road. Visconti was infatuated with her, and he'd follow her on his donkey. Capri—pagan and wonderful.

Then the war came, and there was no more communication among any of us. But I had my sandals. (109–10)

Layer by layer, as in a palimpsest, Vreeland's visionary sandals drew their origins from Pompeii, a place where present and past were still entwined:

In Pompeii, everything that can happen in life was captured in the minute and a half a volcanic eruption takes. Women are having babies, dogs scratching their backs . . . *held forever* in eternity. And in the museum I saw a woman having an affair with her slave, who was wearing . . . the slave was wearing, link slave bracelets, which I recognized immediately, because everyone had worn slave bracelets exactly like them in the twenties. But then . . . instead of the very elaborate sandals of a *grand seigneur* or of a warrior, or the sandals of a gentleman of the town or a tradesman, he wore the simplest sandal in the world. It had just one thong which went between the big toe and the one next to it, and one strap around the ankle attached to the heel. You ask why he was making love wearing his sandals? He probably wasn't given the time. She probably jumped him and he didn't have a chance to get those sandals off; and then, of course, Vesuvius knocked them both to the floor. This was the design I took to Capri, where they made the sandals up for me from my description. (110–11)

The war, while confining her free spirit to the other side of the Atlantic, had not deprived her of the comfort of that simple accessory. Those sandals were copied, reproduced, and launched through the pages of the major fashion magazines, delighting thousands of consumers:

And I gave them to a shoemaker from New Jersey called Mr. Maxwell and asked him to copy them. He'd never seen anything like them. So I told him the story of where I'd copied them from—the pornographic museum at Pompeii, which had originally been open only to men. . . . He copied the sandals. But no one could wear them. Apparently, there was something in the health regulations of New York City that said that no one could try on shoes unless she was wearing stockings. Obviously, the thong couldn't go over a stocking and between the toes, and of course that was the *whole point*. Somehow or other, the law changed. Don't ask me how—I've never concerned myself with that sort of thing. But from then on there was a very nice business for Mr. Maxwell.

That was the Birth of the Thonged Sandal. (110–11)

METAPHYSICAL SANDALS

The success that Italian fashion, particularly shoes made in Italy, enjoyed in the postwar years is in part due to the visibility Italian style received in the major international fashion magazines through the work of journalists like Bettina Ballard and Diana Vreeland. Their point of view, like that of many other foreigners working in the emerging fashion sector, chiefly buyers and photographers, was instrumental to the development of a new awareness that allowed native Italian creativity to flourish within the industry.

Anticipating the inaugural show of Italian fashion organized by Giovan Battista Giorgini at his Florentine residence, Villa Torrigiani, on Februrary 12, 1951, *Vogue* journalist Marya Mannes published an article in the United States on Italian style. Titled "Italian Fashion," the article attributes the success of Italian fashion to the excellence of its basic materials, praised for their quality and beauty, and to its inexhaustible resource of skilled and refined labor.[9] However, Mannes did not think that Italy possessed the high degree of creativity vital to innovation in fashion design displayed by Parisian couture. Nonetheless, her article stressed the beauty and stylistic hegemony of Italian shoes. In this regard, it is interesting to note that Mannes did not limit herself to a discussion of the formal qualities of shoes as an accessory. Rather, she captured the reflection of that accessory, its effect on the person wearing and interpreting it. The article celebrated the sophistication of Italian women and idealized their relaxed detachment from the hustle and bustle of the daily grind. This Italian attitude, or perhaps character trait,

FIGURE 14.2 [LEFT]

Riccardo Magni, publicity sketch for the Ferragamo Company, *Bellezza*, December 1945. Courtesy of Salvatore Ferragamo, S.p.A.

FIGURE 14.3 [BELOW]

Brunetta, publicity sketch for the Ferragamo Company, 1926. Courtesy of Salvatore Ferragamo, S.p.A.

found immediate echo in the way Italian women wore their clothes, with grace and an uninhibited freedom of movement. In conclusion, the journalist focused a fetishist's eye on the feet and legs of Italian women, who, she claimed, with their thonged sandals, attained a degree of beauty unparalleled throughout Europe.[10]

Are we dealing here with a sort of culture fetishism? Perhaps, especially if we consider that the growing perception of the Italian woman as elegant and sexy developed simultaneously with the idea of the *belpaese* as the privileged destination of international tourism. The mythopoetic attitude of the media played a key role in creating this image on both sides of the Atlantic. The picturesque, artistic Italian landscape proved to be the ideal setting in which to promote a style that from the outset went together perfectly with the pleasures of a vacation: a dress, a pair of shoes, or a bag made in Italy took on the status of souvenirs. The tradition of the grand tour with its journey through Italy came to an end as the era of mass tourism was born. In those years, a tourist was, by definition, an American. Most certainly this way of looking at Italy has produced effects that have undoubtedly helped the nation conquer the international fashion scene:

Fashion in Italy—it isn't the first and it won't be the last time we say this—is building its base of prestige. And if this foundation is already sufficiently solid, this is also due to other countries' perception of the enormous prestige of our cities. Rome has an evocative appeal with ancient roots, nourished by literature, art, poetry, all over the world; Florence also boasts ancient and recent influences, on which to rely in its effort to lead a major movement in today's fashion; Venice is a magnet, almost bewitching. In the postwar era the cities have also been joined by the islands, famous and less renowned. To use a modern expression in vogue with the latest generations, we might say that it is the stage-like quality of these cities and islands that facilitates the promotion of fashion through photographic media all around the world. That unique touch almost of the director's hand, as in cinema, is what sets the fashion of any one country apart from the others, and we persevere in this so that Italian women can be the first to take advantage, to indulge themselves and in a certain sense, become the players, in all circumstances.[11]

Elsa Robiola's article, published in *Bellezza* in 1954, expresses the maturity attained by Italian fashion journalism at the apex of an awareness that had begun to take shape immediately after the war, and which that very magazine had helped foster. In 1947, Emilia Kuster Rosselli pointed out that in the streets of Florence, fashion had already become a cultural spectacle performed for the benefit of the tourists thronging the city. In her article, "The Origins of Florentine Craftsmanship," she discussed how the secret correspondences between figurative arts and decorative arts and crafts ever-present in Italian art cities had now also become a distinctive cipher of the products of fashion:

Two shops set opposite each other in Via Tornabuoni, each displaying a single pair of shoes. Frattegiani offers a sandal with low-heel decorated with a garland of pale ceramic flowers, with a meshwork of leather enclosing the foot fastened by a bouquet of the same flowers. A Botticellian sandal. Ferragamo instead has placed in his window his haughty creation, an almost invisible sandal, made of strips of nylon. Its solid heel, drawn from the studied elegance of Louis XIV, represents a true stylistic triumph. A metaphysical sandal, a magic sandal, sandals that might have drawn the line between two opposing artistic worlds: Cassandre or Pisanello. But perhaps soon we will see reconciled the two tenor-shoe designers in the pure lines of the sandal worn by the blacksmith Saint now on display at the Academy of Fine Arts. Inadvertently, fashion from Florence spread across the world through its century-old currents of exportation. A fashion determined by the current tastes of the international population living here, but that arises from a local vein of instinctive taste permeated by an instinctive sense of civilization.[12]

And it was indeed to Florence that the photographer Ruth Orkin came, returning from a trip to Israel in 1951. She tells the story of how she met an American student there and chose her as the subject of her photo *An American Girl in Italy*, the title of a portrait appearing in *Cosmopolitan* in 1952. That picture, part of a photo essay titled "Don't Be Afraid to Travel Alone," was taken in the Piazza della Repubblica. It stages a young girl who, ignoring the rude attentions of a group of young Florentine men nearby, advances across the piazza, like a new Gradiva, "she who steps brilliantly."[13] The flowing dress draped at the waist sways slightly with each light yet firm and graceful step. Her sandals aren't made with nylon threads like the ones Ferragamo designed—still they incarnate a metaphysical value.

Certainly this photo with its illuminating visual and visionary itinerary is a touchstone for all that we have discussed here. The figure of the American girl, perhaps beyond the intentions of the photographer, becomes a variation of an inexhaustible theme,

FIGURE 14.4 Ruth Orkin, *An American Girl in Italy,* 1951. Copyright 1952, 1980 Ruth Orkin.

continually reactualized in an unending narrative, surprising us with the effect of the tiger's leap. The narrative pull in Ruth Orkin's photo makes us assimilate it as we would a fashion photograph. Usually, the viewer of fashion photos is compelled to project herself through her own imagination into the action the photo conveys in a suspended dimension. This interior work come to visual fruition produces a form of pleasure similar to the pleasure derived from the consumption of fashion.

Irene Brin, an authority on Italian fashion journalism and Rome editor of *Harper's Bazaar*, dealt with this pleasure in an article, "A Roman Walk," published in *Bellezza* in July 1946. This brief, concise narrative, using a highly visual register, almost like a video clip, succeeds in conveying the creative code informing the act of consumption in daily life:

> On a fierce morning in early August, with white sunlight so dazzling that it almost seemed black (the sky went beyond any limit granted to deep blue, the piazzas were ravaged with light), Vincenza and Valentina went out for a stroll, just as if they were throwing themselves out of the window. Their sunglasses defended them from the glare; their solitude did not defend them from the gloom. They were excessively free, in their already neglected sandals, in their surah dresses, which in May had seemed to them the exact expression of the needs and decencies of summer, and, naturally with no hunger, cheer, or hope, they walked along a Via Condotti as empty as a locust's cast-off shell. The ramp of stairs fascinated them as a novel form of torture, and they labored up, step by step, as far as Via Sistina, dazzling with its hot stones. What could they hope for in a world where their steps led them only to more scorched pavements, to more burning expanses of asphalt? Everything depended on the act of walking: a sandal glimpsed in the window of Frattegiani's, made of slender strips of leather in rainbow shades, made them dream of walking in the cool.[14]

The theme of walking through the city provides the frame in which to portray the characters Vincenza and Valentina. The text quickly records their superficial emotions with which the reader can identify. It belies no trace of psychological depth in the two women;

everything unfolds at surface level. Their figures appear almost weightless, easily reproduced, elaborated through a treatment or montage that captures them only from the outside, in the incandescence of a gesture or a pose. Fast-paced, the narrative tension is
pulled taut until the brief moment when Vincenza's and Valentina's sensation of dissat-
isfaction and emotional depletion is immediately relieved by the sight of a pair of magic
sandals made by the Maestro Frattegiani. They will not buy those sandals, of course, but
the vision concludes with an imaginative pleasure that, according to Colin Campbell, is
at the heart of true consumption, independent of the acquisition or use of the product
consumed.**15** A dematerialized dimension of consumption, but not, for this reason, destined to remain invisible or unexpressed.**16**

NOTES

1. Italo Calvino, "*Still-life* alla maniera di Domenico Gnoli: La scarpa da donna" [Still-life in the
style of Domenico Gnoli: Woman's shoe]," *Franco Maria Ricci* 13 (May 1983), 35 (my translation).

2. Bettina Ballard, *In My Fashion* (New York: David McKay, 1960).

3. Elsa Robiola, "Atto di fede" [Act of faith], *Bellezza* 1 (1945): 4–6 (my translation).

4. Ballard, *In My Fashion,* 187.

5. Sigmund Freud, "Delusions and Dreams in Jensen's Gradiva," in *Standard Edition of the Complete Psychological Works of Sigmund Freud,* ed. and trans. James Strachey (London: Hogarth, 1959),
9:37.

6. Walter Benjamin, "Theses on the Philosophy of History," in *Illuminations,* trans. Harry Zohn
(New York: Schocken, 1969), 261.

7. Gianni Versace, *A Sense of the Future: Gianni Versace at the Victoria and Albert Museum* (Milano: Grafiche Ghezzi, 1985), 6.

8. Diana Vreeland, *DV,* ed. George Plimpton and Cristopher Hemphill (New York: Da Capo
Press, 1997), 108. Further citations in text.

9. Marya Mannes, "Italian Fashion," *Vogue,* January 1947, 119.

10. See Valerie Steele, *Fashion, Italian Style* (New Haven, Conn.: Yale University Press, 2003).

11. Elsa Robiola, "Con la regia di Venezia" [Directed by Venice], *Bellezza* 1 (1954): 22 (my translation).

12. Emilia Kuster Rosselli, "Alle origini dell'artigianato fiorentino" [The origins of Florentine craftsmanship], *Bellezza* 18–19 (1947): 3 (my translation). Emilia Kuster Rosselli's comment on Ferragamo's magic sandal as the potential imaginative expression of both Pisanello, one of the most celebrated Italian artists of the early Renaissance (ca. 1394–1455), and of Adolphe Mouron Cassandre, Ukrainian-French graphic designer and fashion illustrator for *Harper's Bazaar* (1901–68), offers here a palpable example of the protean nature of fashion creations. It also illustrates how fashion is perpetuated by the exotic narrative that fashion writing constructs around it.

13. Freud, "Delusions and Dreams in Jensen's Gradiva," 37.

14. Irene Brin, " Passeggiata a Roma" [A Roman walk], *Bellezza* 7 (1946): 16 (my translation).

15. See Colin Campbell, *The Romantic Ethic and the Spirit of Modern Consumerism* (Oxford: Basil Blackwell, 1987).

16. See Vittoria C. Caratozzolo, *Irene Brin: Italian Style in Fashion* (Venice: Marsilio, Fondazione Pitti Discovery, 2006).

IN CLOSING/CLOSE CLOTHING

Paula Rabinowitz

On December 14, 2008, Muntader al-Zaidi, a twenty-eight-year-old Iraqi journalist in attendance at then president George W. Bush's "farewell" visit to the nation he had invaded five years before, hurled first one then the other of his shoes—black leather oxfords, to be exact—almost hitting his target both times. In stocking feet, he was wrestled to the ground, arrested, and tortured, he claims, for the subsequent year of his imprisonment. His act, a direct refutation of the images broadcast at the war's beginning of Iraqis brandishing their shoes against the downed statue of Saddam Hussein, spurred numerous "shoe demonstrations" since—including thousands of shoes left lying on the street before 10 Downing Street to protest Israel's war in Gaza on January 3, 2009; a Mexican student setting fire to his shoe at a demonstration in front of the United States Embassy in Mexico City protesting Israel's war on January 11, 2009 (this burning shoe packed a double wallop linking Muntader al-Zaidi's act to Richard Reid, the "shoe-bomber"); and another student, Selcuk Ozbek of Anadolu University, flinging his shoe, a Nike sneaker this time, at Dominique Strauss-Kahn, director of the International Monetary Fund at a speech at Bilgi University in Turkey. In the meantime, the Turkish shoe company that claimed to have made Muntader al-Zaidi's shoes saw a worldwide spike in its sales after his act.[1] Thus consumer capitalism rides on the heels of political activism; visibility becomes a marketing tool. This inevitability—from political act to marketing tool—has been at the heart of modern fashion.[2]

That shoes—at once the most fetishized and most useful of accessories, as I argue in my survey, "Barbara Stanwyck's Anklet: The Other Shoe"—have entered political theater speaks to the essence of what many of the essays in this collection on "Accessorizing the Body" intimate: that the body is no-body without its dressings; and so its presence as a political actor requires that the accessories of dress, close clothes, become the means through which the body speaks. Manuela Fraire, in her meditation, "No Frills, No-Body, Nobody," Cristina Giorcelli in "Wearing the Body over the Dress: Sonia Delaunay's Fashionable Clothes," and Paola Colaiacomo in "Fashion's Model Bodies: A Genealogy" explain in various ways—through Lacanian analysis, art and literary history, and semiotics—how the model body/the modern body *is* a clothed body, an accessorized body. Without the adornment of cloth, leather, metal, string, plastic, and everything else draped over, wrapped around, hung upon, tied to, and on and on, the body, its presence is never fully legible. Being seen, the first of any political acts, requires attention to what is on the body—and what gets taken off it.

Sonia Delaunay's patterned dresses, made as potential mass-marketed cutouts, suggest just how strange and ambivalent the modernist body and its accessories are: her bold appliqués, blazoning letters and poems, and iconic names make their way into the tragic and defiant efforts of Hungarian tailors to resist Nazism by decorating the horrible yellow stars. As Zsófia Bán makes clear in "The Yellow Star Accessorized: Ironic Discourse in *Fatelessness* by Imre Kertész," this gesture, remarkably described, harks back to that ur-tale of American resistance, Nathaniel Hawthorne's *The Scarlet Letter,* a novel, as text/ile artist Maria Damon reminds us in her statement accompanying *Terra Divisa/Terra Divina: (T/E/A/R),* in which Hawthorne is reworking the story of his family's own haunting history in the form of his ancestor Judge John Hathorne who presided over the Salem witch trials. Thus the working by hand over a mark of shame (Hester's "A") and murderous humiliation (the canary-yellow Star of David) becomes a means of transvaluation, as pride of workmanship and even beauty insist on an "appeal," as Bán notes, for and of the individual, whose decorated body, whose accessorized body, insists on being seen and being read.

Modernist clothing—as the essays in this first volume of *Habits of Being* show—differs from ideas of dress and its accessories from earlier periods. In the West, premodern clothing, of necessity in colder climates, thickly draped the body: think of the layers of sleeves and aprons and bodices Jan Vermeer carefully painted on his milkmaids and ladies, or the jewels hanging off Queen Elizabeth's already heavily embroidered gowns and cloaks in her many portraits. As clothing minimized and simplified it remade the body itself, and with it its significance. The modernist attention to "model" bodies meant stripping clothes down to essentials—giving the illusion of a body in direct connection with its accessories, its close clothes, so much so that, as Micol Fontana notes in "The Cult of Femininity" and as Coco Chanel made famous, the sleek black dress adorned by a string of pearls or a well-placed button was all any elegant woman would need. A dress itself, as Sonia Delaunay's creations make clear, was a special kind of accessory indicating freedom of expression and movement, a declaration that the body beneath was an essential aspect of its style. As Becky Peterson says of Laura Riding's poem, "The Virgin" "wears her body like a garment." If, as Martha Banta argues in "Coco, Zelda, Sara, Daisy, and Nicole: Accessories for New Ways of Being a Woman," Chanel's little black dress encoded an entire ethos of unspoken feminist sensibility, as the female body became a "sporting" body, one that was identified as the "American Flapper"—in F. Scott Fitzgerald's words, "both 'beautiful' and 'damned'"—and epitomized by Jordan Baker in *The Great Gatsby*, these "clean, hard, limited person[s]" were, as Banta astutely notes, perfect avatars for the ensuing commodity capitalism of the twentieth century. These women thought they were individuals, making up a new form of womanhood, but were in fact responding en masse to fashion's call, even when they were making it up.

Jeffrey C. Stewart reminds us, however, that even slaves to fashion can intervene and redirect the meaning of fashion's accessories. When he quotes Zora Neale Hurston who "'set [her] hat at a reckless angle and walked out'" of a racist doctor's office, Stewart explains she was using this "gesture" to claim her position of authority, despite being black, female, and poor, in the face of Jim Crow. A rakish "Black Hattitude" challenged prevailing notions of African American inferiority and became one of the not-so-secret tactics of black defiance since at least the 1920s. Anyone could buy a hat, it was a democratic symbol—yes, class was marked by fabric, style, ornament, trimmings—but everyone put on a hat to go out in public; yet only a few could *wear* a hat, and wear it with a vengeance. This theme of sartorial rebellion is echoed, according to Bán, in the stylized Stars of David crafted by Hungarian Jewish tailors in response to Nazism. In "The Cinematic Jewel: Fetishizing the Goods," Vito Zagarrio's analysis of Giuseppe De Santis's 1949 *Riso amaro*, the film that made Silvana Mangano into an international star—the Italian Rita Hayworth—he unpacks the multiple ways in which seemingly silly gestures, in this case pawing over a string of (fake) pearls, are precisely how class was expressed in postwar Italy as it recovered from Fascism and war. American popular culture and costume jewelry can be exchanged across geopolitical and economic borders, giving access—the root of the word accessory—to anyone who has the moxie and style to use these new modes for advancement. The results of dabbling in commodity fetishism might have ultimately been disastrous for the *mondine* working the rice fields; still these icons of plenitude beckon and allow momentary escape from the grind of daily labor. After all, Mangano's "boogie-woogie" dance ushered in the hourglass figure of the 1950s; her ripped stockings augur Madonna's 1980s punk-inspired wardrobe.

In her essay, "Enchanted Sandals: Italian Shoes and the Post–World War II International Scene," Vittoria C. Caratozzolo explains how this international exchange between Italy and America, this time reversing the direction and moving from poverty to glamour, worked in the 1950s as she looks at the hidden meaning connecting Pompeii antiquities, Freud's use of archaeology as a metaphor for psychoanalysis, the image of Gradiva and her sandals in Jensen's story, and Diana Vreeland's first pair of leather thong sandals bought in Italy just before the war. This story of cultural interfaces across epochs and continents describes the arc of social mobility connected to fashioning accessories in the immediate postwar years. Poor peasants from Italy pick up on American popular culture; fur-clad free-spirited Americans traipse around New York in their Italian cobbled sandals. By this time, the Fontana sisters, always wearing their strings of real pearls, were styling American movie stars in beautifully crafted Italian handbags and fur collars, bringing touches of elegance into public view through their use of the rich and famous to model their designs, relying on publicity shots in magazines to widely circulate them. Vreeland's description of how she got a New Jersey shoemaker to reproduce her worn-out Capri sandals, so she could walk the streets of New York with the same casual freedom as the transplanted peasant women newly arriving in Rome had, offers one version of "going native," for a profit.

Peterson's discussion of "Precious Objects: Laura Riding, Her Tiara, and the Petrarchan Muse," examines the poems (Riding) Jackson wrote as she donned Spanish clothing and more intimately wore a handmade tiara inscribed with her name. Her acts of dressing and writing detail another form of rebellion: a poet's going native, as she adorns herself with the trappings of her namesake the Petrarchan muse on the one hand, and walks around Mallorca dressed in Spanish mantillas on the other. Like the strands of a pearl necklace or the filigree of an anklet, this gold headpiece encoded her double desire —as poet and as muse. That she chose these residual symbols of tradition just before Franco's war on the Spanish Republic belies the idea that this appropriating gesture might be a radical act. One feature of clothing and especially accessories during the twentieth century is its basic ambivalence. Traditional costume can be used as a form of resistance, as Raymond Williams notes; yet it can also bespeak a regressive desire to return to a mythical past free from the tensions and conflicts inhering in class confrontations and struggles for racial, sexual, and gender civil rights.[3] It is precisely this complicated relationship between individual bodies and social movements that the commodity form and its exchange, so central to any experience of clothing—as a wearer, a (window)shopper, a thief, a collector, an editor, etc.—during the traumatic years of the first half of the twentieth century, made visible.

Laura Riding's appropriation of symbols of social and spiritual transcendence through Spanish dress and regal jewelry, no matter how playful (as when she appears as a Spanish dueña), paradoxically echoed the attentions the Spanish clergy and the Falangists paid to women's attire. Seeking to celebrate pure "Spain" in the face of both French decadence (and its reemerging fashion industry) and American popular culture (with its Hollywood images of abundance) in the immediate postwar years, authorities in the Feminine Section of the Falange instituted a number of regulations to control women's attire and to stress, on the one hand, a proper bourgeois mode of femininity, and on the other, a return to traditional Spanish regalia. They did this through church decrees, school dress codes, and, as Giuliana Di Febo explains in "Spanish Women's Clothing during the Long Post–Civil War Period," primarily through home economics texts and popular women's magazines. Thus Spanish Fascist fashion consisted then of a curious combination of *haute bourgeois* decorum and wild gypsy-like peasant garb, at once restrained and modern, kitschy and retro.

Fascist interest in women's dress took its cues from long-standing restrictions about women's sexualized bodies promulgated by Catholic church doctrine; however, again, the modern body that had to be contained was a clothed one, one whose skirt lengths needed constant monitoring and whose sunbathing required full-length robes. This concept of the reconstruction of the body through regulated clothing had its most outlandish, and prescient, exploration in the various items of dress designed by Futurist artists such as Giacomo Balla in the first few decades of the twentieth century. Art historian Franca Zoccoli traces "Futurist Accessories" through the various extravagant experiments—in sound helmets and metal ties and aerodynamic vests, among others—that resulted from the various manifestos Futurists pronounced on (men's) clothing. Unlike the Fascist repressive emphasis on controlling the female body or the murderous Nazi obsession with marking the Jewish body, Futurists, who celebrated militarism, airplanes, and machinery, saw clothing as a project for redeploying masculinity in the service of modern materials playfully refitted to new and absurd ends. Designing unwearable clothes and especially accessories called attention to the regimentation of everyday life through the "uniform" of the business suit and tie, implying that "free enterprise" was itself authoritarian.

What Mino Delle Site proposed with his metal tie—a kind of quotidian armor—has hauntingly reappeared almost one hundred years later. Photographer Milagros de la Torre exhibited selections from her series of pictures of "protection clothing" at the International Center of Photography's 2009 exhibition, *Dress Codes*. Her portraits of shirts, jackets, and vests, for men and women, which seem to be merely the everyday wear found on citizens of any European, American, or Latin American city, appear unremarkable, isolated as objects lacking much charm. But these are bulletproof clothes designed to be worn as a form of camouflage in the world's dangerous streets. Miguel Caballero, known as the "Armani of Armored Clothing," is doing a booming business among the wealthy elites of his native Columbia and in Mexico, where de la Torre photographed these items for her series *Bulletproof, 2008;* his business is expanding rapidly across the Middle East and Asia.[4] Where the Futurists imagined (and occasionally actually sported) eye-catching designs of industrial materials as clothing in an effort to bring the modern machinery of war into everyday use, Caballero is molding lightweight Kevlar into nondescript jackets and everyday shirts (including the ubiquitous Guyaberas and T-shirts) as protection against current forms of urban class and gang warfare. What is essential is the invisibility of this accessory and its material—a radically antifashion, even antimodern, statement about clothing's meaning: it does not reveal the body but sheathes it, to cloak its class distinctions, to preserve and protect it. The horrors of war turned inside, like lapels shielding against a cold wind.

From shoes, still carrying the sweat and odor of a man's foot, to jackets lined with bulletproof material, contemporary warfare moves in on the modern body, making its clothing and especially its accessories emblems of conflict. Irving Penn, whose fashion photographs, especially of his wife, model Lisa Fonssagrives, set the standard for mid-twentieth-century glamour, published his first photograph for *Vogue's* October 1943 cover in the midst of the horrors of World War II, with massive battlefronts covering the Pacific and Europe. The color image presents a thoroughly placid yet engrossing scene of accessories posed as a modern trompe l'oeil still life—belt coiled as a piece of fruit, handbag positioned as a basket, gloves and scarf draped across a table. In subdued browns and greens, it limns an antidote to the machinery of death, harking back to an aristocratic world of rich leathers and smooth silk. Absenting the human body, it allegorizes the work of accessories—these having their origins in military attire—to carve the contours of modern appropriations and make the body visible as a war machine. It would appear at first glance a far cry from the stark renderings of isolated shirts and jackets displayed without any adornment in Milagros de la Torre's photographs or the anarchy captured in the video of Muntader al-Zaidi's notorious pitch; but the public movements and mobile bodies brought together through these seemingly mundane articles resituate these and other items of modernism's accessories from the naked form to the social sphere. The cliché that clothes represent a second skin must be turned inside out, as the essays in this volume attest: close clothes *are* the skin, or more properly, skin accessorized—the (decorated and decoded) membrane maintaining both social and psychic cohesion as well as disintegration. Identities are constructed in the close clothes accessorizing the modern body.

NOTES

1. Sebnem Arsu, "Another Shoe Flies, This Time in Istanbul at I.M.F. Director," *New York Times,* national ed., October 2, 2009, A4; and Sebnem Arsu, "'Bush Shoes' Gives Firm a Footing in the Market," *New York Times,* December 20, 2008, http://www.nytimes.com/2008/12/21/world/middleeast/21shoe.html. See also Stephen Farrell, "In Step with His Time: Muntader's Legacy," *New York Times,* February 9, 2009, http://atwar.blogs.nytimes.com/2009/02/19/in-step-with-his-time-muntaders-legacy/; Eric Owles, "'Shoedenfreude' and Shame: Reactions from Around Iraq," *New York Times,* "At War" blog, December 15, 2008, http://atwar.blogs.nytimes.com/2008/12/15/iraqis-pick-up-their-shoes-reaction-from-around-the-country/; and Abeer Mohammed and Alissa J. Rubin, "To Make Female Hearts Flutter in Iraq: Throw a Shoe," *New York Times,* March 13, 2009, http://www.nytimes.com/2009/03/14/world/middleeast/14iraq.html?scp=2&sq=&st=nyt.

2. Mohammed Hussein, "Shoe-Hurler Raises Up Iraqis Reputation Abroad," *New York Times,* "At War" blog, December 25, 2008, http://atwar.blogs.nytimes.com/2008/12/25/shoe-hurler-raises-up-iraqs-reputation-abroad/.

3. "A residual cultural element is usually at some distance from the effective dominant culture, but some part of it, some version of it—especially if the residue is from some major area of the past—will in most cases have had to be incorporated if the effective dominant culture is to make sense in these areas. Moreover, at certain points the dominant culture cannot allow too much residual experience and practice outside itself, at least without risk. It is in the incorporation of the actively residual—by reinterpretation, dilution, projection, discriminating inclusion and exclusion— that the work of the selective tradition is especially evident." Raymond Williams, *Marxism and Literature* (Oxford: Oxford University Press, 1977), 123.

4. "Clothing with a Secret: Milagros de la Torre," broadcast by Alex Gallafent for Public Radio International, *The World,* October 5, 2009, http://www.theworld.org/tag/milagros-de-la-torre/. See also the Web site of Miguel Caballero, "High Security Fashion," http://www.miguelcaballero .com/cms/front_content.php. Roberta Smith, "Beyond a Simple Fashion Statement," review of *Dress Codes* at the International Center of Photography, *New York Times,* national ed., October 9, 2009, C23, 25.

Contributors

ZSÓFIA BÁN is a writer, literary historian, and critic. She is associate professor of American studies at Eotvos Lorand University in Budapest, where her areas of study include literature, visual arts, word and image studies, gender studies, the representation of historical traumas, and collective and individual memory. Her most recent books are *Test-Packing,* which received the Palladium Prize in 2009, and *Exposed Memories: Family Pictures in Private and Collective Memory.*

MARTHA BANTA is professor emeritus of English literature at the University of California, Los Angeles. She has written five books and numerous articles on American literature, art, and culture. A former editor of *PMLA: Publications of the Modern Language Association,* she received the J. B. Hubbell Award for Lifetime Achievement from the Modern Language Association and the Carl Bode–Norman Holmes Pearson Prize for Lifetime Achievement and Service from the American Studies Association.

VITTORIA C. CARATOZZOLO teaches fashion cultures at Sapienza, University of Rome. Her principal areas of research are Italian fashion of the 1940s and 1950s and the "dressing design" of the 1970s. With Paola Colaiacomo she coauthored *La Londra dei Beatles* and *Cartamodello: Antologia di scrittori e scritture sulla moda* and coedited *Mercanti di stile: La cultura della moda dagli anni '20 a oggi.* She wrote *Irene Brin: Italian Style in Fashion* for the Marsilio Mode series and is coauthor of *Simonetta: The First Lady of Italian Fashion,* a Fondazione Pitti Discovery project that featured an exhibition in collaboration with Galleria del Costume di Palazzo Pitti.

PAOLA COLAIACOMO was professor of English literature at Sapienza, University of Rome, and at Venice "Ca' Foscari," where she taught the theory and culture of fashion. She has written extensively on a wide variety of topics, from Shakespeare and eighteenth- and nineteenth-century English literature, to styles of contemporary metropolitan life, to swinging London, serial television fiction, and fashion. Her most recent book is on Pier Paolo Pasolini.

MARIA DAMON teaches poetry and poetics at the University of Minnesota. She is author of *The Dark End of the Street: Margins in American Poetry* and *Postliteracy America: From Bagel Shop Jazz to Micropoetries;* coauthor (with mIEKAL aND) of *Literature Nation, pleasureTEXTpossession,* and *Eros/ion;* and coeditor (with Ira Livingston) of *Poetry and Cultural Studies: A Reader.* She is a textile artist and poet.

GIULIANA DI FEBO is professor of Spanish history in the Department of Historical, Geographic, and Anthropological Studies at the University of Rome Three. Her research centers on the Spanish Civil War and the Franco dictatorship, especially gender policies, religion, politics, and Fascism compared to Francoism. Her publications include *L'altra metá della Spagna, La santa de la Raza,* and (with Santos Juliá) *Ritos de guerra y de victoria en la España franquista* and *El franquismo.* She serves on the advisory board of *Cuadernos republicanos, Arenal,* and *Hispania.*

MICOL FONTANA is president of the Fontana Foundation. With her sisters Zoe and Giovanna, she created Sorelle Fontana, which in the 1950s contributed to the prestige of "Made in Italy" throughout the world. The atelier has received national and international recognitions and prizes and has exhibited its models at the Metropolitan Museum, the Guggenheim Museum, the Brooklyn Museum, and the Fashion Institute of Technology in New York, the Hermitage of the Principality of Monaco, the Louvre, and the Musée de la Mode et du Textile in Paris, as well as at important institutions in Italy and abroad. Pope Pius XII donated his skullcap to the Fontana sisters for the fiftieth anniversary of Sorelle Fontana.

MANUELA FRAIRE is a feminist psychoanalyst in Rome. Since 1975, she has practiced *autocoscienza* as an analyst within the feminist movement. She writes about the relationship between mothers and daughters and how this relationship leads to the development of female freedom. Her work has been published in many journals, including *Memoria, Reti, Lapis,* and *Sofia;* she is also editor of *Lessico politico delle donne: Teorie del femminismo.*

CRISTINA GIORCELLI is professor of American literature at the University of Rome Three, where she chairs the Department of Euro-American Studies. Her primary fields of research are nineteenth-century American fiction (particularly Washington Irving, Henry James, Kate Chopin, Stephen Crane, and Edith Wharton) and modernist poetry and prose (Gertrude Stein,

William Carlos Williams, Willa Cather, Louis Zukofsky, Denise Levertov). She is cofounder and codirector of the quarterly journal *Letterature d'America* and editor of the series *Abito e Identità: Ricerche di storia letteraria e culturale*.

BECKY PETERSON received a PhD from the University of Minnesota. Her dissertation studied early twentieth-century women artists (including filmmakers, poets, and craft practitioners) who paid serious theoretical attention to textiles and dress. Her publications have appeared in *Textile: A Journal of Cloth and Culture* and *Arizona Quarterly: A Journal of American Literature, Culture, and Theory*. She teaches film at the University of New Mexico.

PAULA RABINOWITZ is professor of English at the University of Minnesota. A feminist scholar of twentieth-century literature, film, and visual culture, she is author of *Labor and Desire: Women's Revolutionary Fiction in Depression America*, *They Must Be Represented: The Politics of Documentary*, and *Black & White and Noir: America's Pulp Modernism*.

JEFFREY C. STEWART is professor and chair of Black studies at the University of California, Santa Barbara. He has written several books, including *To Color America: Portraits by Winold Reiss*, *Paul Robeson: Artist and Citizen*, and *1001 Things Everyone Should Know about African American History*. In 2003, he was Fulbright lecturer in American intellectual history at the University of Rome Three, and he has been a W. E. B. Du Bois Institute fellow at Harvard University.

VITO ZAGARRIO is professor of cinema and television at the University of Rome Three. He has written and edited several books on American and Italian film, including monographs on Francis Ford Coppola, Frank Capra, and John Waters; collected essays on Ettore Scola, the Taviani brothers, Dario Argento, and the New Italian Cinema; and books on film production and the relationship between film and television. As a filmmaker, he has directed many documentaries, television programs, and three feature films. He is on the board of the Pesaro Film Festival.

FRANCA ZOCCOLI is an art historian and critic. Her research focuses on the period between the two world wars with special attention to women artists. A prolific contributor to national dailies and art magazines, she has published many essays and several books in Italy, the United States, Germany, and France. In 2009, the centenary of Futurism, her books *Le futuriste italiane nelle arti visive* and *Benedetta Cappa Marinetti: L'incantesimo della luce* were published.